New Worlds,
Ancient Texts

Published in Cooperation with
The New York Public Library

New Worlds, Ancient Texts

The Power of Tradition and the Shock of Discovery

Anthony Grafton

with April Shelford and Nancy Siraisi

The Belknap Press of Harvard University Press
Cambridge, Massachusetts, and London, England 1992

This book is printed on acid-free paper, and its binding
materials have been chosen for strength and durability.

Library of Congress Cataloging-in-Publication Data

Grafton, Anthony.
New worlds, ancient texts :
the power of tradition and the shock of discovery /
Anthony Grafton with April Shelford and Nancy Siraisi.
p.   cm.
Includes bibliographical references and index.
ISBN 0-674-61875-0 (acid-free paper)
1. America—Discovery and exploration.
2. Europe—Intellectual life—16th century.
3. Europe—Intellectual life—17th century.
I. Shelford, April.   II. Siraisi, Nancy.   III. Title.
E121.G7   1992
970.01—dc20   92-10692
CIP

Designed by Gwen Frankfeldt

Contents

Foreword

THE commemoration of a historical event often engenders
rhetoric, but it also demands inquiry, scholarship, and careful reflection. This volume marks the culmination of a journey begun four years ago, when The New York Public Library
invited Anthony Grafton, Andrew Mellon Professor of History at
Princeton University and a Renaissance scholar, to explore the collections at The New York Public Library, which contain one of the
most extensive archives in the world on sixteenth- and seventeenth-
century European thought, and to organize an exhibition and write
a book which would trace the transforming effects of the voyages
of exploration upon European scholarship, learning, and culture from
1450 to 1700. The results are fresh insights into the complex and
profound changes set in motion by the infusion of new knowledge
into an established system of thought.

Understanding the dynamics of intellectual change is difficult at
a distance of several centuries. What is dramatic or revolutionary
assumes a prominence that is rapidly reduced to formulas such as
the "Scientific Revolution," formulas that mask the complexity of
change. It is no small achievement that Anthony Grafton has here
revealed this process as a dialectical one. Older and traditional

structures were not swept away immediately by the influx of new and contradictory information, nor were those structures without internal contradiction or usefulness. For example, the traditional biblical view of the dispersion of humanity after the Flood was not immediately supplanted by information coming from the New World, because it provided a much-needed framework in which to locate intellectually peoples the Europeans had not expected to find. The printing press, it is often pointed out, made it possible to disseminate information far more rapidly and widely than ever before; but it also, in combination with the rise of publication in vernacular languages, gave old and new misinformation a second and alarmingly long life. Many of the historical figures discussed in this volume have long been familiar to us; others are less so. What is fresh in Professor Grafton's approach is that he shows us that the new is never as new as we would like to believe. Sebastian Münster's struggles with contradiction and inconsistency as he seeks to encompass within one book all the information a sixteenth-century man or woman might care to know of the world become our own. The stature of a Bartolomé de Las Casas is not diminished by our learning that he formulated his humanitarian views in the context of a traditional scholastic disputation with Juan Ginés de Sepúlveda; rather, we are left with a deeper appreciation of the versatility of an intellectual procedure that had served Europeans well for centuries. The originality of a Hobbes or a Locke is undiminished by a thoughtful reconstruction of their intellectual lineage, a lineage traceable in part to an ancient debate about the nature of humanity's distant past (primal savagery or Golden Age?), a debate given both new relevance by contacts with New World peoples and new political significance as intellectuals struggled with the disorders of their own century. Professor Grafton also places the discoveries in a wider context of intellectual changes already under way in European life—new visions of the universe and the human body, and the rise of humanism, to mention but two. Moreover, and perhaps most important, he reveals to us that our views of the period are just as historically conditioned as those of the men who ventured past the Pillars of Hercules. There is, in all this, something of a cautionary tale. To us the distortions and errors of perception under which explorers, merchants, clerics, and scholars alike labored are obvious, often amusing, and all too often had tragic consequences; but we err if we congratulate ourselves too quickly on our cultural relativism or too naively equate more information with better judgment.

Interpreting great collections is as important as amassing them, and the Library is deeply grateful to Anthony Grafton for the gift of his scholarship, which has enriched every aspect of the Library's participation in the quincentenary commemoration. April Shelford gave valuable help as Research Curator of the exhibition and as a contributor to this volume. Thanks are also due to the advisory committee of eminent scholars who refined the intellectual content of the exhibition: Nancy Siraisi, Hunter College; John Fleming, Princeton University; Werner Gundersheimer, Folger Shakespeare Library; James Hankins, Harvard University; Donald Kelley, Rutgers University; Eugene F. Rice, Columbia University; David Ruderman, Yale University; Noel Swerdlow, University of Chicago; and J. B. Trapp, University of London.

A generous grant from the National Endowment for the Humanities made possible the Library's quincentenary commemoration, which includes three exhibitions at the Central Research Library, educational and public programming, and a traveling panel version of "New Worlds, Ancient Texts," which will visit twenty metropolitan and university libraries in the United States. Additional support has been provided by the John Ben Snow Memorial Trust. The Library is also grateful to the American Library Association for helping to organize the national tour, thereby sharing the scholarly content of the exhibition with a larger audience.

Timothy S. Healy
President
The New York Public Library

New Worlds,
Ancient Texts

Introduction

ETWEEN 1550 AND 1650 Western thinkers ceased to
believe that they could find all important truths in ancient
books. No meeting between text and reader epitomizes that
change more sharply than one that took place—most appropriately—at sea, when the Jesuit José de Acosta, a highly educated
man who wrote one of the most original histories of what he called
the Indies, realized that his own experience of travel contradicted
the views of the greatest of ancient philosophers:

> I will describe what happened to me when I passed to the Indies.
> Having read what poets and philosophers write of the Torrid Zone,
> I persuaded myself that when I came to the Equator, I would not be
> able to endure the violent heat, but it turned out otherwise. For when
> I passed [the Equator], which was when the sun was at its zenith
> there, having entered the zodiacal sign of Aries, in March, I felt so
> cold that I was forced to go into the sun to warm myself. What could
> I do then but laugh at Aristotle's *Meteorology* and his philosophy? For
> in that place and that season, where everything, by his rules, should
> have been scorched by the heat, I and my companions were cold.

Acosta's scene sounds dramatic—even Oedipal. The educated European, trained from childhood to believe what his ancient books

tell him, sees them exposed as fallible. Aristotle's frightening torrid zone turns out to be not only habitable but temperate. The classics dissolve as rapidly under Acosta's laughter as the emperor's clothes in the fairy tale.

The confrontation that Acosta sketches has all the virtues: drama, vividness, a sterling moral. Above all, it provides the climax to a larger, powerful story about ancients and moderns—one that has pleased generations of Americans and won assent from a surprising number of Europeans. This runs more or less as follows: In 1492 all educated Europeans knew where powerful knowledge lay. It was contained in authoritative texts: the Bible; the philosophical, historical, and literary works of the Greeks and Romans; and a few modern works of unusually high authority. These books described the universe, from the unchanging world of the stars down to the excrementary and changeable realm of the elements and man. They traced the operation of God's hand in history and nature. The former they divided into neat ages. The latter they dissected, using tables and taxonomies to lay out its components: the elements, the seasons, the winds that governed the weather, the humors that determined the body's health or illness, the zones of the habitable world, and the development of the races of man. The varied components of the cosmos were theoretically linked by the power of the stars, which governed—or at least revealed how God governed—everything below them; multiple overlapping spiderwebs of reciprocal influences connected all beings and objects, and the conjunctions of the planets governed all great events.

The men who understood these concepts were creatures of the book, trained in the Latinate seclusion of schools and universities. Their mental world was bounded by the knowledge contained on their library shelves: knowledge produced in and largely limited to the ancient Mediterranean and Near East and medieval and modern

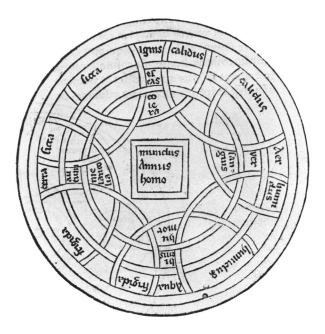

Figure I.1   A diagram of the elements and qualities (outermost circle: dry, hot, wet, and humid), the seasons (middle circle: summer, spring, winter, and autumn), and the humors (innermost circle: choleric, sanguine, phlegmatic, and melancholy) in a 1473 Strasbourg edition of the encyclopedic *Etymologiae* of Isidore of Seville (seventh century). The interlocking circles represent the interconnectedness as well as the hierarchical ordering of the universe, time, and man.

Europe, though occasionally penetrated by a trickle of information from more distant realms to the east or north. Only professionals, licensed by the possession of formal university degrees, could manipulate the texts and master the terms of canonical knowledge.

By the early seventeenth century knowledge had burst the bounds of the library. It now seemed as large and varied as the world itself. It resided in astronomers' reports of telescopic observations, philosophers' reports on their cogitations, mariners' reports of voyages, and physicians' reports of anatomies. Galileo Galilei, Francis Bacon, and René Descartes, who disagreed on a great many other things, agreed that practical men and keen observers were often more reliable, because less prejudiced, than books and book-trained scholars. The thinker who based his work not on the traditional heaps of quotations but on new facts and original ideas deserved more credence than the old-fashioned pedant. After all, the empirical study of the heavens and the human body had revealed large holes in ancient physical science. Even more shockingly, the discovery of the New World peoples had apparently done the same in the biblical narrative of early human history and the classical descriptions of the inhabited parts of the world. Philosophies had proliferated, each challenging the claims of others without fully establishing its own. And as ancient books lost their power and authority, their study became less central to intellectual life. The intellectual of the mid-seventeenth century was as likely to be an independent aristocrat, male or female, as a teacher, as likely to be a crafter of scientific instruments as a professional. Even a professor might well teach at a university equipped not only with books but also with a botanical garden, an anatomical theater, and an observatory—and would certainly agree that knowledge, far from being limited to what the ancients had known, could continue to increase so long as man's capacity to observe and report did not diminish.

Scientists and philosophers lived in an expanding world. They knew that the physical universe was far larger than the ancients had thought and that the inhabited part of the Earth's surface included more than the limited European, Asian, and North African *oikoumene* of Ptolemy. Readers of the Bible had at least entertained the suggestion that the human past might be far longer and more complex than the account in the Old Testament indicated. Historians and political philosophers scrutinized many civilizations when constructing a history of the world or a theory of the origins of the state.

All intellectuals, finally, knew a vital fact that their fifteenth-century predecessors could not have suspected. What men had traditionally revered as Antiquity, the age of perfect knowledge at the beginning of a history of degeneration, was really the youth of mankind, when the greatest philosophers knew far less than an ordinary modern man or woman. *Antiquitas seculi iuventus mundi—*

Francis Bacon's paradox became the motto of many intellectuals who did not share his other views. The age of a system of thought became a sign not of authority but of obsolescence, and many of those who insisted on the aesthetic superiority of classical literature admitted the substantive supremacy of modern science. Novelty became the sign not of an idea's radicalism but of its validity. Modern knowledge, unlike the older, bookish kind, could be communicated to anyone with common sense, in any language—French or Italian as well as Greek or Latin. Accordingly, the new scholars and scientists spoke to women as well as to men, and to artificers as well as to theorists. The world was no longer accessible only through learned books in Latin; it could be known directly.

This new understanding of the world grew from roots planted outside the realm of learning. And it drew much of its sustenance from one of them in particular: the movement, led by practical men rather than scholars, that Europeans called the discovery of the New World. No more tragic event, Thomas Huxley remarked, can be imagined than the collision of a beautiful theory with an inconvenient fact. After the Portuguese began to explore Africa, Western explorers and writers had to deal with lands and societies, customs and religions, men and women whose very existence they had not expected. After 1492 the problems became critical. The encounter between Europe and the Americas juxtaposed a vast number of inconvenient facts with the elegant theories embodied in previously authoritative books. The discoveries gradually stripped the books of their aura of completeness as repositories of information and their appearance of utility as tools for interpretation. The encounter with naked inhabitants of a new world, in short, enabled intellectuals to make naked experience take the place of written authority. No wonder, then, that Acosta lost his faith so suddenly and completely.

In the world of scholarship this account has been questioned and even contradicted. In pioneering, suggestive studies, John Elliott,

Giuliano Gliozzi, and Michael Ryan have argued that in fact the discoveries had very little impact on European thought. They left European notions of history and civilization intact. They did not shake but confirmed European prejudices about the superiority of white Christians to those of other breeds and creeds. The New World proved easy to reconcile with the biblical account of human history and the classical accounts of the physical world, since these were both more complex and more adaptable than the traditional accounts admitted.[1]

This second, revisionist line of argument has much to recommend it. It does justice to the pervasive influence of classical texts and ideas in education, scholarship, and science even after Acosta's primal experience. It allows us to look at texts like Acosta's own with less selectivity—to see that he was delighted not only that his experience contradicted Aristotle, but also that it supported the authority of other, more prescient ancients. Acosta went on to tell his readers that "the most excellent astronomer and cosmographer, Ptolemy, and the worthy philospher and physician, Avicenna, were both of a better opinion, since both believed that there were commodious habitable regions under the tropics."

New Worlds, Ancient Texts tries to enlarge these modern accounts of what the New World meant to the Old, by confronting them with the record of original texts and images—or at least with that rich deposit of both which has been stored up over many decades in the New York Public Library. A revolution in the forms of knowledge and expression took place in early modern Europe. But it resulted as much from contradictions between and tensions within the texts as from their confrontation with external novelties. The ancient texts served as both tools and obstacles for the intellectual exploration of new worlds. These remained vital—and defined authors' representations and explanations of what they found as Europe moved out to West and East—until well into the seventeenth century. This account, then, will hew fairly close to the revisionists', arguing that the actual pace of change was slower and the power of inherited authority more durable and more complex than many historians have acknowledged. Yet it will also concern itself less with strong theses than with the paradoxes and continuities that the sources themselves yield up. Still, we will try to see the new for what it was. Acosta's laughter still rings out more memorably than the qualifications with which he tried to muffle it.

This is a story of Europeans, told from a European point of view. We seek to understand the experiences and visions of European intellectuals and explorers, not to recover the ways in which the peoples they conquered understood the West—much less what sufferings those peoples certainly endured or what benefits they possibly drew from the encounter. Though a limited tale, this one seems eminently worth telling now. Those who follow the arguments and examine the images laid out here will encounter a richer, more complex version of Western culture and its boundaries than the stereotypes that dominate some scholarship and much pedagogy. Instead of one narrative drowning out all others, we will present here a multitude of voices, engaged and argumentative.

It will become clear that Europeans did not see the New World "as it really was," and that most of them did not much like what they thought they saw. Their very name for native Americans, "Indians"—which we will use throughout to stay within period assumptions—proves the grossness of their mistakes and prejudices. But this important point—much emphasized of late—can easily degenerate into triviality, especially when scholars repeat it like a mantra instead of examining individual cases. If the history of contacts between cultures has a moral, it is surely that no one likes anybody else very much. Even al-Biruni, the great eleventh-century ethnographer of central Asia whose account of India remains a model description of a foreign culture, confessed that the Hindus about whom he wrote "differ from us [Muslims] to such a degree as to frighten their children with us, with our dress, and our ways and customs." He and his fellow Muslims felt exactly the same way about the Hindus. But he insisted that these attitudes were only natural—indeed, universal: "we must confess, in order to be just, that a similar depreciation of foreigners not only prevails among us and the Hindus, but is common to all nations towards each other." Al-Biruni set out to make sense of what seemed completely alien assumptions, values, and myths. And any serious reading of his India would surely concentrate not on the general human prejudices that link it with all other ethnographies but on the specifically classical tools and methods that both enriched his analysis and modified his perceptions. Such methods have produced remarkable results in other cases—as in Edward Schafer's *Vermilion Bird*, an exemplary evocation of the multiple failures and remarkable successes of the Chinese imagination as it confronted and tried to depict the wonders of Nam-Viet in the eighth and ninth centuries. Schafer shows how a literary tradition, employed by a wide range of individuals—high officials, unhappy exiles, proud Creoles—shaped a foreign reality both by rich and compelling descriptions and by deliberate and inadvertent exclusions. We hope that readers will be led to look at the European thinkers of the fifteenth through seventeenth centuries with similarly open eyes.[2]

We also hope to stimulate some reflection not only upon the European encounter with a wider world and the history of early modern European culture, but also upon the larger cultural debate that has endowed these long-past developments with a new urgency. Many American intellectuals claim that our country and our culture can be revitalized only if our system of education is rebuilt around a core or canon of supremely vital texts. Others hold that all canonical texts are chosen to support the authority of elites, not to recognize intrinsic literary or intellectual merits (if any exist). Unfortunately, neither side has said anything substantial about how authoritative texts have actually been used in Western culture in the past: how teachers and thinkers actually tried to assemble coherent groups of texts that could satisfy a large and pressing set of cultural needs, and what fates their efforts met. Nor have they usually perceived the many cracks and tensions that inevitably run through the apparent granitic bulk of all sets of supposedly authoritative books.

In the case of relations between the West and the Rest, these polemics have had a powerful tendency to sterilize thought and research. Some have extended backward Edward Said's polemic against Orientalism, arguing that in the Renaissance, too, a monolithic body of thought and imagery imprisoned even the most original thinkers. Few of these accounts have shown Said's sensitivity to the divergent struggles and achievements of the individuals who created and worked within traditions, or to the differences between the modern colonialist world in which Said's Orientalists thought and wrote and the early modern world. And few have given due heed to the point made as powerfully, if less subtly, by Martin Bernal: that the ancient heritage of texts harbored many mutually subversive ways of defining cultural relations between the West and other cultures.[3]

In telling the story sketched here, we hope not to take a side in the debate but to raise its level. We want to show what it really felt like to regard books as the most powerful sources of knowledge and guides to behavior in the world—objects less like the heavy but harmless paperbacks we buy to pass the time at the beach than like bombs, armed, powerful, and ready at any moment to explode. The books that had this high status in their readers' eyes differed radically from one another, and those who wielded them could put them to vastly different uses. It will become clear that the textual canons of the fifteenth century inevitably lost their air of cohesion and completeness and yielded their authority to other cultural forms. But it will also become clear that those canons were more complex, and sometimes contained both far more striking contradictions and far more radical ideas than modern debaters admit.

Any canon of texts formed by a complex society with a long past must contain diverse elements imperfectly mixed. In the particular case of Renaissance Europe, several sets of texts and methods of reading competed for intellectual and institutional authority. Confronted by the New World, none of the available texts proved either too sterile to be useful or so useful as to survive unchanged. Recognition of these historical facts might help to modify both the rages and the enthusiasms of those who now seek to shape our curricula and our public discussion of our past.

Varied in texture and quality, dotted with both the worst and the best of what has been thought and said, authoritative texts provided the Europeans of the Renaissance with the only tools they had for understanding the thoughts and values of alien societies. Like other tools, these often broke in the hands of those who used them, and incompetent and corrupt craftsmen used them badly. But many of them also showed astonishing flexibility and resilience, changing as they were used and often changing those who used them. The task of understanding the full range of problems and possibilities they offered still challenges the historian's learning and imagination.

A Bound World: The Scholar's Cosmos

1

I N 1 5 0 0 many European thinkers saw their world as a narrow, orderly place. Readers and publishers shared a taste for comprehensive books that described the world as a whole, summing up between two covers all intellectual disciplines and their results. Such texts ranged the gamut of scales and densities, from pocket-sized elementary textbooks to vast encyclopedias. But all of them embodied the assumption that a basically complete and accurate body of knowledge already existed. All of them suggested that few surprises could await the explorer of the past or the present, the reader of the Bible, or the student of the cosmos. And all of them heightened their appeal with evocative images of the power of bookish knowledge. Like stages brilliantly illuminated, they frame and highlight many of the powerful and long-lived ideas that would soon be brutally contradicted by experience.

Many of these books had their origins in the center of Europe—in the rich, comfortable, sophisticated free cities of the Holy Roman Empire. In these cities, many readers had a keen appetite for encyclopedic works which summed up between two covers all the intellectual disciplines and their results. Publishers—who, as always, knew and shared the prejudices of their audience—produced useful reference books of every imaginable size and adorned these with powerful, evocative images of the power of books to describe and explain the universe. These purportedly comprehensive books are useful indicators of the general cultural temperature of Europe in the years around 1500.

The German encyclopedias are revealing in a number of ways, which reflect the remarkable communities in and for which they were produced as well as the tastes of their authors. In Strasbourg, Nuremberg, and Augsburg, intellectual life developed with relative freedom, unregulated by university faculties (though occasionally interfered with by town councils). Publishers could produce anything the local patricians thought acceptable, and merchants, lawyers, and craftsmen consumed their books with a confidence enhanced by the robust health of the German economy, the waning of the plagues of the fourteenth century, and the general decline of heretical movements. *Die Gedanken sind frei*, "Thoughts are free"—the words of the old German song perhaps never applied more closely than to the rich cities of Upper Germany in the last decades before the Reformation.

Konrad Peutinger—patrician, official, archaeologist, and correspondent of Erasmus—typifies this cosmopolitan world both socially and intellectually. He came from, and spent most of his life in, Augsburg, the base of the great banking families, the Fugger and the Welser. But his life was anything but confined to the spheres of administration and commerce. He studied the classics and took a law degree in Italy, collected rare books, published the first printed collection of Roman inscriptions; he even possessed and studied a manuscript road map of the Roman empire copied in the twelfth or thirteenth century from a fourth-century original. Peutinger, accordingly, took a broad view of the forms of knowledge most worth having. But he sometimes felt the need for a small-scale reference

Figure 1.1 The title page of Gregor Reisch's *Margarita philosophica* (Freiburg, 1503), iconographically representing the seven liberal arts and philosophy. They are ruled by the imposing woman with three heads, which stand for natural, rational, and moral philosophy. The pagan sages Aristotle and Seneca embody natural and moral philosophy, respectively. The fathers of the Christian church applaud benignly above, pictorially reinforcing the view that theology, here called divine philosophy, has the highest position as crown of the other sciences. This book belonged to the Augsburg humanist Konrad Peutinger.

work, and for that purpose he bought a little book published by a teacher at the university of Freiburg: Gregor Reisch's *Margarita philosophica* (Pearl of Philosophy). The *Margarita* traces the history of the world, beginning from the biblical account of the Creation, and schematically describes the canonical seven liberal arts. It reveals no sense that either the world or knowledge about it has changed dramatically since ancient times. Ancient and later authorities coexist, pulled out of geographical and chronological context to debate in a sort of "philosophical present," rather like the "ethnographic present" in which modern anthropologists have represented their subjects. The woodcut with which the book begins embodies a strikingly static vision of the liberal arts. A personified Grammar brandishes an alphabet in one hand and a key in the other. With this she opens the gate to a castle of knowledge, in which the disciplines and the higher faculty of theology passively await discovery by the student. Everything seems to be in order, neat and tidy. Grammar, the art of reading, gives entry to a world of knowledge entirely bounded by authors, one per subject: Euclid for geometry, Ptolemy for astronomy, Peter Lombard for theology. The traditional arts and sciences appear as finished, perfect entities that invite study rather than improvement. And the body of the text presents, between two covers and in a modest format, everything one could possibly wish to know. Grammar, the arts of argument, the natural sciences, theology, Creation and Damnation jostle here, none treated at very great length. "Sermons in books, stones in the running brooks"—so one might summarize this all-too-simple authoritative message. Yet a well-read and traveled man like Peutinger found it worthwhile to buy this book and adorn it with a signature and a warning not to remove it from his house. Evidently he found its map of knowledge—one as formal, schematic, and devoid of complicating detail as the charts of the London Underground—a useful simplification, basically accurate and helpful.

Figure 1.2 In another illustration from Reisch's *Margarita philosophica* (Freiburg, 1503), Grammar unlocks the door of the castle of the liberal arts.

Peutinger's tastes were not idiosyncratic. A decade earlier, in Augsburg's main rival city, Nuremberg, the most aggressive and successful publisher in Europe, Anton Koberger, brought out his most famous and spectacular book. The *Liber chronicarum*, now known as the *Nuremberg Chronicle*, was written by the humanist Hartmann Schedel and others, printed by Anton Koberger, and magnificently illustrated by the unrivaled woodcut artists of Nuremberg. Dwarfing Reisch's little book in both size and scope, it treats not the structure of the disciplines but the history of man. Vivid—and often fantastic—portraits of biblical and classical heroes and villains and views of ancient cities bring the past to life. The text, more sober but equally comprehensive, describes the Creation, maps the inhabited world, and follows human history step by step through the ages.

Yet in content the *Chronicle* seems as limited as the *Margarita*. It, too, tells a deeply traditional story. Its set-piece illustration of the universe portrays the normal cosmology of the medieval schools: one which confines all change to the world of the four elements at the center of things, earth, water, air, and fire, the realm where human beings live. The planets—the moon, Mercury, Venus, the sun, Mars, Saturn, and Jupiter—move regularly around the Earth, never changing, never suffering harm, embedded in perfect, transparent crystalline spheres. Beyond them appear the fixed stars, also embedded in a globe of crystal; outside that the quiring Cherubim—and eight more orders' worth of angels—sing hymns forever to the Creator. This vision of the universe derived its basic elements from the greatest of Greek philosophers, Plato and Aristotle, and its definitive form from the Neoplatonic philosophers of late antiquity, Plotinus and Porphyry. It was preserved and taught through the Middle Ages by a host of texts, classical and later, big and little, from Dante's *Divine Comedy* to Reisch's *Margarita*. And it seemed fully known, comfortable and familiar.

The *Chronicle*, as its title indicates, was above all a narrative: a history of the world. Like other world histories written in antiquity and the Middle Ages—from which most of its text was drawn, without much editorial intervention—it ranged the millennia from the Creation to the present. It traced the development of human culture and the relations between the holy nation of the Jews and their jealous God. And it folded classical antiquity, the life of Christ, and the later history of the world into its embrace.

For all its cosmopolitan content, however, the *Chronicle* set out to edify rather than stimulate its readers. It arranged all of history into seven ages, not because empirical facts dictated this schema but in order to show that the long-term history of man symbolically corresponds to the seven days of the first week in which God created the universe. The first six ages are described in great detail, and the seventh—in which scarifying images of the arrival of the Antichrist and the Last Judgment precede even more frightening blank pages—shows even more vividly that the end of history will come with a bang, not a whimper, as God's plan fulfills itself with the judgment of the elect and the reprobate. History, evidently, is as logical and orderly as the cosmos itself; and both can be read as the stories of God's will working itself out in physical space and human time. Even the esoteric peoples of the past and present are, for the most part, portrayed in familiar terms. Biblical figures appear in fifteenth-century German costume and hairdo; the ancient cities of Nineveh and Jerusalem appear as modern towns, dominated by Gothic spires and powerful castles and hedged in from the darkness and idiocy of the surrounding countryside by crenellated walls. Both this vast, expensive, widely pirated work of art and Reisch's modest little *Hitchhiker's Guide to the Seven Liberal Arts* portray a past and present, a world and a universe as orderly and meticulously controlled as the guilds of an imperial city. For all their elegance of typography and

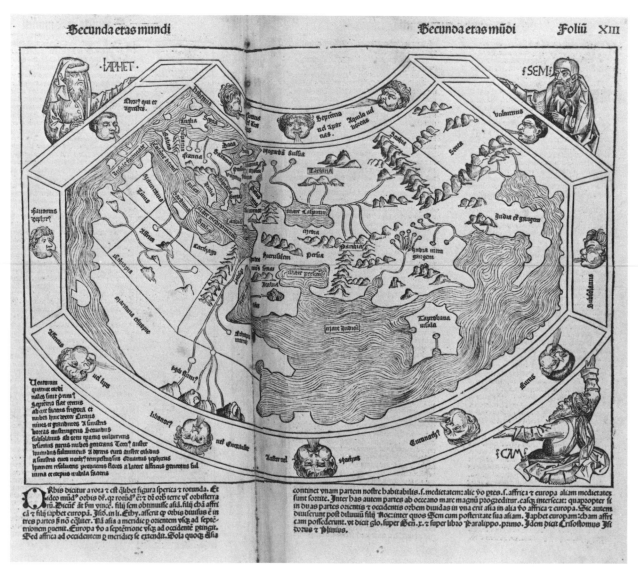

Figure 1.3   An eclectic map of the world from Hartmann Schedel's *Liber chronicarum* (*Nuremberg Chronicle*) (Nuremberg, 1493). The basic layout of the continents derives from Ptolemy's *Geography*, but here the holy city of Jerusalem occupies the center of the world, as it did in medieval schematic T–O maps (Figure 2.3). The map also embeds geography in sacred history by showing the three sons of Noah—Japhet, Shem, and Ham—whose descendants populated the known world.

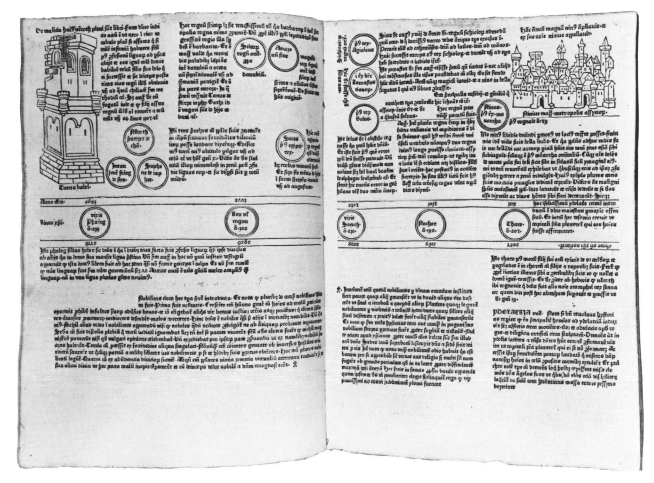

Figure 1.4 The early history of civilization from Werner Rolewinck's *Fasciculus temporum* (Cologne, 1474). The Tower of Babel appears anachronistically as a Gothic structure, Nineveh as a walled medieval city. The central timeline, with its numbers and bubbles, gives the dates of biblical patriarchs both in years counted forward from the creation of the world and in years counted backward from the birth of Christ. The texts above and below identify events in pagan history contemporary with biblical history, such as Zoroaster's invention of magic and Ninus' founding of the kingdom of Assyria.

Figure 1.5 A schematic world map from the Venerable Bede's *Opuscula* (Basel, 1533), representing both the earth's continents and its climatic zones—frigid, temperate, and "burnt." These zones, first laid out in classical antiquity, were widely thought to determine the characters of the peoples who lived in them, though the "burnt" or torrid zone was often described as uninhabited. This map uses Macrobian tradition in representing the Antipodes, an unknown continent, balancing the continents of Asia and Africa.

illustration, these authoritative books are as detailed, as minatory, and as cramping as the regulations that dictated exactly what each craftsperson must produce and exactly how he or she must behave, detail by detail and ritual by ritual. [1]

These images and the texts they accompanied reveal a good deal about the European's cosmos around 1500. They were produced not for individual patrons but for the new, much larger market of buyers of books, who eagerly bought out the 1500 copies of the first edition of the *Nuremberg Chronicle*—not to mention the pirated edition produced within a year at Augsburg, which replicated the text but butchered the illustrations to cram them into a much smaller format. And they can easily be matched by others drawn from other contexts—like the splendid world history of the Carthusian monk Werner Rolewinck. His *Fasciculus temporum* (A Bundle of Histories) innovated by dating the events of ancient history backward from the birth of Christ as well as forward from the Creation, and it ingeniously aligned simultaneous events in outlines and bubbles. But it identified no problems or contradictions in the sources, and it, too, portrayed the history of the Bible and the classical world as taking place in the cities and costumes of late medieval northern Europe.

Many books, prints, and paintings defined learning as reading; many histories and cosmographies presented an unchanging past and a stable image of the cosmos and the earth's surface. For the first century of printing at least, traditional texts and comforting images of the cosmos easily dominated the market—sometimes in surprising places. The first bishop of Mexico took with him to the New World itself a set of treatises by the Venerable Bede which gave a much older but equally coherent account of nature—including a little map which showed the world's land masses as isolated spots on a globe of water.

The Universities: The World Explicated

In the late fifteenth century as now, the currents of intellectual life ran in a number of different circuits. The city halls and printing shops constituted one; another, much larger one was made up of universities. These institutions, which instilled their faculties and graduates with shared methods and convictions, were rapidly growing in both size and number. They varied in many respects, to be sure. Those in the North were generally governed by the masters, those in the South by the students. Northern universities treated theology as the highest of the sciences and envisioned themselves as basically religious institutions; Italian ones had long ago taken the practical studies of medicine and law as their higher faculties, and developed facilities for theological study only toward the end of the Middle Ages.

For all their variations in scope and organization, the universities resembled one another closely in assumptions and methods. All their students had to begin by studying the liberal arts, mastering a sequence of Aristotelian texts that taught them how to construct rigorous chains of argumentation and to refute the arguments of others. All of them concentrated on two forms of instruction, both verbal in form and both dependent on books for their basic material: the lecture, in which a teacher explicated a set text line by line and word by word, and the disputation, in which two scholars argued for and against a proposition in public. In both spheres understanding and the power to convince others required the dextrous manipulation of one set of basic intellectual tools: the formal syllogism, that still-unrivaled method of setting out a chain of arguments, from major term to minor term to conclusion ('Some dogs are red'; 'My dog is red'; 'My dog is some dog').

All university faculties, finally, assumed that the authority of the disciplines they taught resided in a particular set of texts. These canonical works, laid down in antiquity and allowed to mellow in the cask for centuries, had a unique value and function. They furnished the basic body of unchallengeable statements which the specialists manipulated logically to produce usable knowledge. The theologians, for example, knew that they could confidently draw major premises for their syllogisms from the Bible; the lawyers knew that they could do the same with the Roman *Corpus iuris*; the physicians knew that they could do the same with the natural and medical works of Aristotle and Galen. Thus each could happily and efficiently construct whatever structure of doctrine he might need in order to show that the Host could not bleed or that a town could confer citizenship on newcomers—to name only two of the questions to which fourteenth- and fifteenth-century professors provided elaborate answers.

In each discipline, the senior denizens of the university knew that authoritative texts could pose serious problems. The Bible, for example, told many stories that seemed not only unimproving but immoral. In medicine, Aristotle and Galen disagreed about such basic points as the identity of the most important bodily organ. But these apparent flaws posed no danger to the larger structure of instruction and study. For the professors did not take their texts neat. They and their students consumed authoritative books in a form as canonical and closely regulated as the context in which they consumed them.

In the normal university textbook of the time, the authoritative text appears embedded in a modern commentary, which usually surrounds it on the page. The text normally occupies a central position and appears in a larger script or typeface, which provides physical and aesthetic evidence of its supreme authority: the spiky print of the early glossed Bible, for example, physically repels any

Figure 1.6 A Bible published in 1506–1508 in Basel, with an interlinear gloss and the commentary of Nicholas of Lyra. Only the small column with larger type in the center of the page is actual biblical text. The passage considered here is the prophecy of Daniel, often taken to predict the whole later course of human history. The genealogical chart at top left lists the kings who succeeded Alexander the Great in Egypt and Mesopotamia. Providing such neat genealogies was a priority of medieval and Renaissance historians.

suggestion of fallibility. Around it, the official commentary—written or printed in smaller lettering, keyed by symbols to the relevant places in the text—both enhances the authority of the central text and ensures that its message can cause no problems. It does so in the most direct of ways: by using the tools of allegory and inference to show that the text is never inconsistent with its own values or in conflict with other texts of comparable authority. If necessary, whole independent treatises could be devoted to embedding the texts still more firmly in a frame that enhanced their authority. In some cases— like that of the medical *Canon* of Avicenna—the philosophers of medieval Islam, from whom Western scholastics took a great deal, had already produced usable supplementary texts.

Well-trained commentators deftly made the ancient text fit modern needs. They set out to show that it told no stories, taught no ideas, and contained no techniques that were irrelevant or unacceptable to its Christian audience. A theological commentator like Nicholas of Lyra could allegorize away such superficially uncomfortable texts as the Song of Solomon, reading them as veiled statements of higher truths. A medical commentator like Pietro d'Abano could use the tools of logic to reconcile his apparently contradictory authorities, Aristotle and Galen. The former saw the heart, the latter the liver as the central bodily organ. Pietro calmly showed that each was right, in a certain sense—and thus that they did not conflict after all.

Reading—practiced reading—was the master skill, which yielded only useful messages. Thus, when the publisher of Pierre d'Ailly's treatises on astronomy wished to show a master leading a pupil through the mysteries of that complex art, he portrayed them as reading together. Both masters and students, in their thousands— the Holy Roman Empire alone had more than fifteen universities by

1500—were men of the book. The text, imprisoned in its armor of commentary, was forced to yield a single up-to-date sense.[2]

Historians, examining the conditions and results of intellectual life in this period, have often assumed that it was necessarily sterile. They have treated the dark, looming mountain chains of authoritative books that dominated the universities and flooded the bookshops as impassable barriers to intellectual progress. And they have dramatized the intellectual as well as the physical courage of the men of cunning intelligence, the sailors and conquerors, who discovered new worlds in South Africa and the Americas. These men, not the scholars, brought back the vital inconvenient facts that destroyed the authority of venerable theories. As to the scholars—they, like the scholars of Confucian China a century later, preferred reprocessing a single set of authoritative books to noticing the new data that soldiers and sailors had turned up.

This view is not a new one. It was formulated, in the first place, by the intellectuals of the late sixteenth and seventeenth centuries who wrote the fiercest manifestos of the New Philosophy and New Science. Like most polemicists, they wrote less to explain than to undermine the views of their opponents. And their arguments sharply oversimplified the old world of the culture of the book. Its complexities were concealed from the sight of the curious by the smoke poured out by burning straw men.

In fact, no single book or institution can by itself characterize the complex and contentious learned world of the late fifteenth century. The canon of texts that scholars read was less a Gibraltar, a textual pile of unalterable shape and content, than a glacier moving slowly but constantly, composed of the most varied elements, and unstable at many points. The tools and methods that scholars applied to this vast moving target varied as widely as the precious materials they

Figure 1.7 The astronomer teaches the theologian about the stars, using an authoritative text; he indicates the planets, represented by astrological signs, moving about the earth in their crystalline spheres. This illustration appears in a version of the *Concordantia astronomiae cum theologia* (Augsburg, 1490) of Pierre d'Ailly, who wrote numerous compendia on natural philosophy; his many readers included Columbus.

looked for in it. We may find, in both the agitation and the constituent elements of that perpetually moving canon, at least some of the causes for the intellectual revolution of the next 150 years.

Humanism: The War over the Canon

Any panorama of Europe's cultural world around 1500 must include many scenes of battle. For Europe was in the throes of an intellectual revolution well before the discovery of the New World. In Italy from 1350, in northern Europe somewhat later, new men challenged the scholastic system of the universities on every level. They had their own ideas about the texts that should form the core of the curriculum, the form of commentary that should be applied to them, and the identity of those who had the right to explicate them.

The new men (and their enemies) called themselves "humanists": by this they meant not that they were especially moral, or indeed that they were humane, but simply that they defined themselves as experts in the *studia humanitatis*, the humanities. This term encompassed a quite specific range of subjects: grammar, rhetoric, and dialectic, the arts that gave a command of Latin, the language of learning, and oratory, history, poetry, and moral philosophy, the forms of thought and writing that improved the character of the student. Many of these subjects fitted a young man (or woman) to occupy a high place in this world, to make moral choices and give effective commands. After all, so humanists from Petrarch onward claimed, the liberal arts had enabled the Romans both to rule the world and to produce an imperishable heritage of literature and art. Their revival in the fifteenth century had resulted in a new flowering of literature and the fine arts as well, and would, if continued, produce a new elite as cultivated and effective as the Roman one.

The humanists not only argued at length for these ideals; they also denounced the existing universities for failing to live up to them. They criticized the emphasis of the university arts curriculum on formal, logical argumentation; these skills might make men learned, but they would never make them good or equip them to make other men good. They criticized, even more sharply, the university scholars' efforts to embed the classics in commentaries that removed their sting and made them explicitly relevant to modern conditions. The humanists insisted that the classics should be read for what they were. They should be stripped of their medieval armor of commentary; written or printed in a classical-looking, if not a genuinely classical, script; and treated as the products of a society that had not been modern or Christian. In cities and courts from Naples to Nuremberg and Cracow to Canterbury these men founded schools where young men and a few young women could gain access not to the formal, regulated, licensed skills of the university theologians and doctors but to the more general, moral and literary lessons of the ancient Greeks and Romans.

The humanists gradually convinced princes and prelates, city merchants and rural friars, and their new books and schools proliferated alongside the scholastic ones, offering an alternative set of sources and an alternative approach to them. Governments across Europe found that the products of the humanist school were ideally trained to perform a wide range of practical tasks: they could carry out diplomatic missions, write official state histories, compile coherent records, and produce effective propaganda on command. By the late 1490s, Europe had not one but two canons, each of which served a particular set of purposes, gave access to a particular set of occupations, and had its own powerful defenders.[3]

But humanism amounted to more than a second educational system. Both in Italy and in northern Europe, some of the new intellectuals not only offered alternatives to the existing system but also challenged its very right to exist. They argued that the method the scholastics used radically misrepresented the texts on whose authority they relied. The scholastics, in the first place, took Latin translations, not only of Aristotle and Galen but of the Bible itself, as authoritative representations of the originals. They failed to see that the Latin versions were rife with errors—those made by the original translators and those introduced more recently by scribes and typesetters. In the second place, they read these corrupt texts as though they had been written in their own day rather than in a distant society. And they put forth their own conclusions not in the classical prose of the humanists—and the Romans—but in a rebarbative technical jargon that offended classical stylists; such language had all the sensual value of water gurgling down a corroded pipe.

The humanists challenged the traditional scholars even in the domains which were peculiarly their own. Lorenzo Valla pointed out in his mid-fifteenth century *Annotations on the New Testament* that the original text of that supremely important document was Greek, not Latin, and that the Vulgate of his own day misrepresented the Greek at dozens of points. Half a century later Erasmus printed Valla's brilliant polemic, and he and others set to work to take it to its logical conclusions. Under the official sponsorship of Cardinal Ximenes, a group of Spanish and Italian scholars produced a critical text, column by column, of the Hebrew, Greek, and Latin texts of the Old Testament and the Greek and Latin texts of the New. With the less official but more efficient support of a brilliant publisher, Johannes Froben, Erasmus beat Ximenes into print with a Bible that went still further. He retranslated the Vulgate New Testament into a more pleasingly classical—and, he thought, more accurate—Latin of his own. He printed the Greek text beside it, line for line. And in his commentary on the text he showed, again and again, that what had seemed the eternal and authoritative doctrines and prac-

Figure 1.8 The beginning of Genesis from the Polyglot Bible (Alcala, 1514–1517) sponsored by Cardinal Ximenes. The Vulgate or traditional Latin translation appears between Greek (left) and Hebrew (right) versions. Below left is a Targum (Aramaic translation).

tices of the church of his own day rested, in fact, on mistranslations of the Bible. The sacrament of penance which underpinned the whole structure of confession and absolution, the mortifying of the flesh and the buying of indulgences, all found support in the command to "do penance"—*poenitentiam agite*, as the Vulgate had it. But Erasmus showed that the text had actually commanded Christians to "repent"—*metanoeite*—not to carry out external acts to display their contrition but to come back internally to their true senses. The appearance of two such Bibles in one decade fundamentally challenged the authority of the church itself—to say nothing of that of the theological faculties. When a Franciscan or a Dominican preached a traditional sermon, telling of the foundation of the papacy by St. Peter, a young humanist might well wave a Greek New Testament at him and insist that "St. Peter was never in Rome," since the New Testament nowhere described his visit there.[4] Similar developments took place in law and medicine. Even Aristotle, the master of those who know, received a face-lift from the humanists, who set out to renovate the old, overly literal Latin translations of his works by collating them against the original Greek texts.

Both humanists and scholastics, meanwhile, waged their wars outside as well as within the university faculties. The humanists wrote brilliant, biting satires on the ignorance of their adversaries, cheerfully denying that formal philosophy and similar disciplines, with their claim to rigor and their actual deficiencies, deserved financial or political support. We hear the echoes of these sallies in Rabelais's *Gargantua* better than we do those of the replies to them. But the scholastics fought back vigorously. A Dominican theologian, Giovanni Nanni, or Annius, of Viterbo, attacked the humanists for their interest in the pagan histories of Greece and Rome, which he thought both full of factual errors and inappropriate for study by Christians. To replace them he forged alternative histories of Europe, which showed that the Greeks and Romans were late and inferior peoples by comparison with the profoundly learned sages of Babylon, Egypt, and Etruria. As a well-trained systematic theologian, moreover, he provided elaborate formal arguments to buttress the authority of his texts, which he embedded—naturally— in a ring of commentaries.

Annius argued that the new texts deserved credence for several reasons. Their authors were priests, who told the truth *ex officio*, not ordinary men who lied. They derived their facts from archival documents, which could not be falsified, not from ordinary narratives which could say anything. These arguments proved so hard to answer that most humanists accepted the authority of Nanni's fakes (which became best-sellers, more popular than Herodotus and other genuine texts). Reprinted, summarized, sometimes lifted out of their original mass of glosses, the new texts helped to create a humanist fashion: they traced the origins of every race in Europe back, via ancient heroes from Troy and elsewhere, to the three sons of Noah. Not everyone accepted Annius' view that the Lombards (Latin: *Longobardi*) descended from two great founders, Longo and Bardus, and the Franks from a third, Francus; but almost everyone agreed with him that etymology offered a key to history. Genealogies and controversies proliferated. [5]

Other scholastics proved able to find real flaws in such major works of humanist scholarship as Erasmus' *New Testament*. He left out a passage—now considered a late addition—on the Trinity from his new Latin New Testament on the grounds that it occurred in no manuscript of the original Greek. One of his critics had another Greek manuscript drawn up that included the offending words, and Erasmus felt compelled to restore them. Meanwhile many humanists found that they could use their own tools of philology on ancient texts in new fields—like the natural sciences—which had been a scholastic monopoly. Each group, in other words, proved capable of mastering the other's tools when necessary. And the results of such collisions between methods were by no means always conflicts. Marsilio Ficino, the fifteenth-century Florentine scholar who translated all of Plato into Latin, used both humanistic and scholastic methods. He produced a vast and popular range of texts and commentaries designed to serve as an alternative to Aristotle: a new basis for philosophy, at once eloquent and rigorous.[6]

Neither scholastics nor humanists, finally, were harmonious and unified. Scholastics savaged other scholastics, and humanists other humanists, as gleefully as they hurled themselves on members of the other party. Then as now, academic prizes were small and academic politics bitter, and fights raged within every faculty. Scholastics fell into several schools, whose members disagreed fundamentally on the nature of argument and the status of the theories they constructed. In the fourteenth and fifteenth centuries, scholastic natural scientists found themselves challenging the authority of Aristotle, and lawyers that of the *Corpus iuris*, as the need to maintain consistency in argument or to acknowledge new facts required. Humanists debated the identity of the best classics, the nature of the best state, and less edifying matters—like one another's orthodoxy, literacy, and even legitimacy.

In 1517 Martin Luther argued in public that basic teachings and practices of the Western church had no support in the New Testament and must be abandoned. Both scholastics and humanists found themselves pulled into radically new alignments, like two football teams suddenly challenged by a third one appearing on the same field. Protestants insisted that only the Bible deserved absolute credence—but failed to agree on what it said. Catholic scholastics insisted that the whole traditional armament of their profession should be not only staunchly retained but fiercely defended. Even

Erasmus began to see some virtues in the traditional scholastic culture he had mocked; at least it did not threaten complete social and political disorder, as Protestantism seemed to when religious radicals arose in 1520, demanding the abolition of serfdom and even private property, as the Bible seemed to them to command. The most authoritative texts, once the secure foundation of a whole Gothic cathedral of doctrine, had become the source of subversion; and even the revolution split rapidly into sects as its theologians in turn disagreed about the meaning of powerful words and images that no longer had a secure frame of commentary to restrain them.

By the second and third decades of the sixteenth century, in short, the world of the book was not coherent but chaotic, not solid but riven; and the fissures represented not only the quarrels of individuals who disagreed on specific points of detail but also fundamental debates about intellectual standards and knowledge itself. A young intellectual who reached maturity and began to buy and read books in these years might well find it almost impossible to decide which books to read, what sort of reading to carry out, whether to attend a university and seek formal training and licensing or to attend a humanist school and gain access to a new morality and aesthetics.

The West and the Rest

The complexities and contradictions of the canon were nowhere more apparent than in the segment of it which contained models for describing other cultures. The great encyclopedic *Natural History* of the elder Pliny, for example, provided a popular and easily imitated model of how to compile misinformation, especially about remote places. Pliny himself had been deeply curious about the natural world; he died while investigating the eruption of Vesuvius that buried Pompei and Herculaneum. But his book rested more on

Figure 1.9 The monstrous races of Greek ethnographic tradition as described and portrayed in Hartmann Schedel's *Liber chronicarum* (the Latin version of the *Nuremberg Chronicle*, 1493). These images, though medieval, undoubtedly go back to ancient prototypes. The elder Pliny and Solinus, who summarized him, were the richest sources of this brand of anthropological information.

literary sources than empirical investigation, and it made some fantastic claims about the flora, fauna, and sentient inhabitants of distant places. Both Pliny and his eager ancient reader Solinus provided rich information about the monstrous races who inhabited the rim of the world—men with the heads of dogs, men with their heads beneath their shoulders, men with one large foot under whose shade they rested in the desert sun. Generations of readers thrilled, like Desdemona listening to Othello, at these tales of strange creatures, foods, and burial customs—and were no doubt stimulated by them to see the inhabitants of strange lands as literally outlandish, less than civilized or even less than human.[7]

Yet even Pliny did not come close to exhausting the relevant models and materials. He himself inherited and drew on a rich tradition of Greek writing about non-Greek peoples. This tradition had begun in the fifth century B.C. when Greeks lived near, and often within, the large and cosmopolitan empire of the Persians and reported to their countrymen on Persian, Egyptian, and even Indian customs and institutions. It developed further after the conquests of Alexander the Great, as writers followed his armies all the way to the court of Chandragupta in India. The Greeks who wrote these reports did like to describe monsters and marvels: Herodotus told his readers about the gold-digging ants of India, and Ctesias, not much later, wrote about dog-headed men and pygmies. Yet their attitudes were hardly uniform or monolithic.

Herodotus, describing Egypt, sometimes used the simplest of principles for organizing the description of a foreign society: he defined it by opposition to everything Greek. Egypt, he said, was the land where everything was different, where the women urinated standing up and the men crouching. Sometimes, however, he took exactly the opposite tack, arguing that Egyptian civilization was not only far older than Greek, but also the source of Greek ideas and

Herodotus

THE nine books of Herodotus' *History*, completed by 425 B.C., went far beyond chronicling the wars of the Greeks against the Persian empire. They contain a wealth of geographical and ethnographic information, no doubt based in part on Herodotus' own travels, but derived far more from secondhand information that became ever more fantastic as it pertained to peoples and places at the edges of the known world.

In the fifteenth century, Herodotus' *History* became more accessible to Western scholars through a Latin translation by the prominent humanist Lorenzo Valla, and Herodotus' descriptions of the exotic customs of foreign peoples—their marriage and burial rites, religions, and martial skills—became models for Renaissance historians and ethnographers.

In his account of the Scythians, a people living along the northern shore of the Black Sea, Herodotus expresses a keen interest in their origins. After presenting the Scythians' own account, which he himself does not believe, and a second Greek myth of descent from Hercules, he writes:

"There is also another different story, now to be related, in which I am more inclined to put faith than in any other. It is that the wandering Scythians once dwelt in Asia, and there warred with the Massagetae, but with ill success; they therefore quitted their homes, crossed the Araxes, and entered the land of Cimmeria. On their coming, the natives, who heard how numerous the invading army was, held a council. At this meeting opinion was divided and both parties stiffly maintained their own view . . . For the others urged that the best thing to be done was to leave the country, and avoid a contest with so vast a host; but the Royal tribe advised remaining and fighting for the soil to the last . . . Having thus decided, they drew apart in two bodies, the one as numerous as the other, and fought together.

All of the Royal tribe were slain . . . Then the rest of the Cimmerians departed, and the Scythians, on their coming, took possession of a deserted land."

Herodotus' skepticism did not extend to the account of the origin of the Sauromatae. These people claimed to be descendents of Scythians and the Amazons, a legendary race of female warriors who would be eagerly sought in the New World. After marrying, they migrated east. "The women of the Sauromatae have continued from that day to the present to observe their ancient customs, frequently hunting on horseback with their husbands, sometimes even unaccompanied; in war taking the field; and wearing the very same dress as the men."

Source: Herodotus 1862.

practices. Sometimes he dismissed non-Greeks—like the Persian soldiers at Thermopylae—as effeminate, disorderly, "Oriental"; sometimes he looked up to them as profound and learned beyond the ken of any Greek. And sometimes—above all in his account of the Scyths—he used the same contradictory categories to describe a society that lacked firm settlements and other symptoms of what the Greeks took as civilized life. The proliferation of opposites in custom and belief made plain that no civilization could claim universal validity.[8]

Ephorus, Ctesias, and Megasthenes, writing after Herodotus, often attacked or diverged from him on points of detail. But they shared the single great contradiction of his basic attitude, and sometimes showed the warmest interest and respect for the bizarre creatures with which they populated the East. Ephorus argued that Herodotus had described his Scyths too sensationally. Some of them in fact drank milk and showed great humanity in their dealings. Ctesias described the dog-headed men and pygmies not only as human in intelligence, but in fact as "very just"—more so, presumably, than the quarrelsome and difficult Greeks. Although they could not speak, they communicated with and understood the other peoples with whom they traded, and the emperors whom they reportedly served as bodyguards (one wonders if Jonathan Swift had read Ctesias). The Christian writers who took over and passed down the traditional marvels of the East also moralized them, treating the monsters sometimes as morally degenerate pagans, sometimes as signs of divine power and displeasure. But the Renaissance reader encountered classical and Christian texts that treated strange races, dispassionate and disparaging views of them, simultaneously.[9]

Historians like Herodotus and Diodorus Siculus, the geographer Strabo, and other writers on the exotic whose works were translated into Latin by fifteenth-century humanists and sold well in the early years of print were hardly innocent observers or professional anthropologists. But they provided a model for detailed, vivid description of the origins, institutions, and manners of unfamiliar peoples— descriptions by no means confined to cramming disparate data into stereotypical molds.

Other ancients, less specialized in their ethnographic interests, were still deeply influential in their presentation of non-Greco-Roman peoples. They used a palette of many colors, some lurid, some bitterly demeaning, and some potentially flattering, to depict worlds outside their own. Plato, the humanists' favorite philosopher, seemed to state in his *Timaeus* that the Greeks were mere children by comparison with the Egyptians, whose splendid records covered millennia of Athenian history that the Athenians themselves had forgotten—not to mention the tale of a lost continent to the west, Atlantis, where civilization had once bloomed. Aristotle suggested that some barbarians as well as Greeks had had elaborately organized states and that comparisons between Greek and non-Greek polities might reveal a great deal—though he also saw Asians as deficient in that "spirit" that enabled Europeans to preserve constitutional regimes intact.

The Greek medical writers of the fifth and fourth centuries B.C., the Hippocratic school, had argued ingeniously that most human customs and institutions were determined to a large extent by the environments in which the different nations lived. They had accounted for the many different forms of diet, clothing, marriage customs, and military tactics Greeks encountered in Asia Minor and Europe. Following this tradition, Aristotle took different constitutions as adapted to the characteristics of different peoples—a suggestion which would have a spectacular afterlife.

Still others found in cultural difference not only a stimulus to relativistic reflection or to large-scale comparative inquiry, but a powerful provocation—one that could lead them to rethink the nature and merits of civilization itself. Tacitus, the most powerful and problematic of Roman historians, could evoke the spare courage that animated barbarian resistance as well as the corruptions that ensued from Roman power. "They make a desert and they call it peace," perhaps his most Tacitean saying, he attributed to an English partisan who denounced Roman imperialism. And Livy made clear both that the early Romans had looked rather like the barbarians of his time and that the climb to world power had been accompanied by a fall from primitive virtue.

The sophists, the professional rhetoricians of classical Greece, imagined their own forefathers as barbarians. They drew an analogy between the uncivilized peoples of their own day and the primitive ancestors of the Greeks. All peoples, they argued, became civilized over time, thanks to such human inventions as the art of rhetoric; this position implied that even civilized peoples must have started out as primitives. Both the Greek historian Thucydides and the Roman rhetorical theorist Cicero offered powerful versions of this developmental scheme to the Renaissance scholar.[10]

The intellectual who sets out to describe another culture embarks on a task as difficult and elusive as it is fascinating. The would-be ethnographer must make a whole series of strategic and tactical decisions: he or she must adopt an attitude toward both the society to be described and the informants who describe it; select a limited number of topics to cover, since no general description of a society can ever be complete; and choose a literary form to convey the results to a public. In each of these decisions, models matter. Few writers weave whole new tapestries of their own; rather, they make quilts from ready-made ingredients. And the sixteenth-century intellectual who set out to depict the New World could find enough ingredients in the classical heritage to produce a kaleidescopic variety of juxtapositions and compounds.

Tacitus

ACENTRAL enterprise of Renaissance humanist scholarship was the recovery and emendation of the works of Tacitus, the Roman historian (born ca. A.D. 55) who chronicled the corruption of imperial Rome. Historians seeking to emulate Tacitus adopted his essentially moralistic view of the purpose of writing history: "This I regard as history's highest function, to let no worthy action be uncommemorated, and to hold out the reprobation of posterity as a terror to evil words and deeds."

Tacitus' *Germania* and his accounts of the Roman wars with the German tribes had particular significance for German historians attempting to forge and legitimate a history apart from Rome. But the *Germania*, which included descriptions of the customs of the ancient Germans, also shaped European perceptions of non-European peoples in the period of the discoveries. The subtext of the *Germania* is a comparison of the virtues of an allegedly savage people with the corruption of Rome. Tacitus can thus be said to be the intellectual great-grandfather of the concept of the Noble Savage.

Tacitus' description of ancient German mores would also prove useful to scholars laboring in what we today call the field of comparative anthropology. Hugo Grotius, for example, supported his argument that North American peoples were descended from Germans by comparing their customs with those Tacitus describes here (see Chapter 5):

"Thus with their virtue protected they live uncorrupted by the allurements of public shows or the stimulant of feastings. Clandestine correspondence is equally unknown to men and women. Very rare for so numerous a population is adultery, the punishment for which is prompt, and in the husband's power. Having cut off the hair of the adulteress and stripped her naked, he expels her from the house in the presence of her kinsfolk, and then flogs her through the whole village. The loss of chastity meets with no indulgence; neither beauty, youth, nor wealth will procure the culprit a husband. No one in Germany laughs at vice, nor do they call it the fashion to corrupt and to be corrupted . . ."

Source: Tacitus 1942.

Consider *barbarism*, that most loaded of ethnographic terms. It is often said that Renaissance intellectuals had a simple, Aristotelian view of barbarians: they were slaves by nature. In fact, however, "barbarian" had many senses in the Renaissance. Erasmus and other humanists freely applied the term to the scholastics, whom they considered not natural slaves but ignorant free men. Some classical writers had distinguished sharply between Greek and barbarian, assuming a pose of smug superiority to nonwestern noise and disorder, as Herodotus did when he had his Persian king exclaim at Salamis that his women were fighting like men—and his men, unfortunately, like women. Others, however, observed foreign peoples from very different emotional vantage points. Tacitus' *Germania*—a brilliant piece of ethnographic reportage, beloved of German humanists—powerfully praised the virtues of barbarians—by whom he meant noble savages. Knowing the corruptions of civility all too well, he esteemed the purity and courage that could accompany a life lived in huts and outside Roman *civilitas*. This life—so he and others clearly thought—was far closer than the life of modern Romans to that led by such early Roman heroes as Horatius.

The ancient historian of philosophy Diogenes Laertius recorded a popular attitude of a different kind. He used the term *barbarians* to refer to ancient Babylonian, Egyptian, and Persian sages, like Zoroaster, and admitted that many Greeks believed that these barbarians had actually invented the pursuit of wisdom. Diogenes was by no means the only witness to this line of thought: a popular set of dialogues, the religious and theological texts falsely ascribed to the Egyptian sage Hermes Trismegistus, seemed to most humanists to bear out this view, though Diogenes himself rejected it. One of the collaborators on the *Nuremberg Chronicle*, Hieronymus Muenzer, recorded the delight he felt in discovering that Aristotle and Plato had borrowed so much from Hermes and from the "first philosophy [metaphysics] of the Chaldeans."[11]

Ancient poetry, finally, offered powerful images of contact with human, superhuman, and subhuman others. Homer and Virgil evoked in epic the terrors and fascinations of the journey of exploration; Ovid, Lucretius, and Virgil in his pastoral poetry portrayed a primitive age that could be taken as either pure and golden or harsh and frightening. The ancients did not supply a single, coherent attitude toward nonwesterners, which anyone could buy off the rack. Rather they provided the patterns and materials from which each modern intellectual could fashion his own point of view.

Many of these ancient accounts had all the crisp immediacy of new books about them in 1500. The Greek texts, preserved in Byzantium during the Middle Ages, did not become available in the West until humanists translated them; Tacitus, though preserved in the West in Latin, was hardly read until the late fifteenth century. The most up-to-date scholar could envision the inhabitants of the New World with equal classical correctness as the remnants of an ancient civilization, possibly coequal with the Jews, or as the dregs of a normal nonwestern tyranny, neither venerable nor learned. Fresh sources could be cited to either effect.

When the humanist passed from striking a pose to writing a book about distant societies, he was far from being Pliny's helpless prisoner. The ancients offered powerful descriptive models. Herodotus' account of Egypt, with its mixture of natural philosophy and human history, its interest in the names in early records, and its sharp eye for curious ways of eating food and burying the dead, set the most influential pattern, one that lasted for centuries. Herodotean ethnography took the form of a running narrative interrupted by anecdotes and descriptions, supported by the oral testimony of informants, and adorned with wonderful statistics (like the number of onions eaten by the men who built the pyramids).

Other ancients had written romantic ethnography, setting imaginary perfect societies in distant places. Plato's *Critias* provided the definitive model for all such efforts. Still others had written polemical ethnography, works designed to prove the unworthiness of another culture. The *Description of Egypt* by Manetho, the Egyptian priest who wrote in Greek for Ptolemy I, included a vicious attack on the Jews, whom he described as a whole society of lepers, an unclean people. This reached a wide public in the Renaissance because the reliable Jewish historian Josephus quoted it lavishly, in order to refute it, in his own polemical work against the grammarian Apion.

The Romans Cato, Varro, and Macrobius, on the other hand, had written not as narrators or pamphleteers but as scholars in their own right. They had compiled manuals of antiquities, carefully documented collections of the evidence about the ways in which the early Greeks or Romans had worshipped their gods, elected their officials, plowed their fields, and cooked their food. These works were systematic rather than chronological in organization, and their authors felt able to quote primary evidence, describe rituals or buildings, and describe archaeological evidence at length.

Many humanists emulated them, compiling visual as well as textual evidence. Drawings or prints of the statues and inscriptions that lay strewn about the city of Rome and elsewhere could make ancient scenes and customs sharply vivid—and could always be manufactured if they did not exist. A Renaissance ethnographer could, like Fernández de Oviedo, emulate Pliny and fold his anthropological and historical material into an account of the natural world. But he could also tell stories or reconstruct beliefs and institutions without framing them in an encyclopedic description of the natural phenomena that accompanied them—and all without using a single color not available on the palette offered by the ancients. [12]

The careful humanist reader, morever, could hear ancient voices raised in argument about the splendors and miseries of other civilizations not only by collating several texts but often by reading one text carefully. Herodotus, as we have seen, offered portraits in contrast, at once respectful of and demeaning to the nations around Greece. Later writers, less famous now but perhaps more popular, and certainly more trusted, in the Renaissance, taught similar lessons. The great historian Diodorus Siculus, for example, staged a scene of suttee in which two Indian women fought for the right to die on their husband's pyre. His account brought out what seemed to him the underlying—and powerful—logic of the practice, which had been designed to prevent women from marrying in haste and then poisoning their husbands at leisure. He portrayed the women involved as active figures who consciously chose their fate. And he emphasized the confusion that the sight instilled in its foreign witnesses: "Some were filled with pity, others were profuse in their praises, while there were not wanting Greeks who condemned the institution as barbarous and inhuman." Revealingly, even the Greeks, who did not hesitate to call the custom barbarous, treated those who accepted it as reasoning beings; but they also cast themselves as expert judges of others' customs.

The erudite Strabo argued with himself at staggering length about the trustworthiness of the strange tales that he had collected about India and other remote lands. He thought through the problems these posed, giving a clear account of why he believed some writers less likely than others to lie. He ridiculed the earlier Greeks who had brought back from India obviously silly tales about gold-digging ants and men with one foot which they used to shade themselves. And then—many long books later—he repeated the very tales he had ridiculed, with every appearance of interest. Even Ctesias, the first and greatest of Greek travel liars, professed that he had omitted certain marvels in order not to detract from the credibility of those he retained, and criticized other writers for their credulity.

Certain uniformities appear. The Greeks liked to portray themselves as curious about other peoples, as askers of questions. By contrast they represented native informants as blandly incurious, even contemptuous, of the intentional tourists who needed explanations of their monuments. Greek writers liked to imagine bizarre beings in the hinterlands of the inhabited world, and took the ingredients for their strange portraits of strange men from many sources, from Indian epic to Greek humor. No one but the antiquaries clearly understood that non–Greco-Roman societies developed over time, though every rhetorician and historian knew that the city-states of Greece and the Roman state had come into being over the centuries. Most ethnographers envisioned the societies outside their own as living by customs most of which were as solid, fixed, and inalterable as the pyramids themselves: as collections of men and women who often had a chronology but usually did not, in the Western sense, have a history. But these commonalities were only the filmiest and frailest of threads connecting Tacitus with Herodotus, Plato with Pliny.

The mere fact that a scholar turned to the ancients for help in grasping the New World is not enough to enable us to predict the particularities of his project. He might adopt a strategy of wonder ("Goodness, how amazing") as readily as a strategy of superiority ("God, how frightful"); a strategy of alienation ("They turn our customs upside down") as readily as a strategy of assimilation ("Under their skins, they're just like us"). He could insist that other cultures were both similar and different at once—or he could argue that they belonged to a world of their own.

Cartography and the Canon: Ptolemy

No text more clearly reveals the richness, the complexity, or the shiny newness of the implements in the Renaissance ethnographer's toolbox than a work now far more maligned than read—the *Geography* of Claudius Ptolemy (second century A.D.). Ptolemy compiled his work at Alexandria, using both earlier treatises of a technical kind by Hipparchus and Marinus and a wide range of itineraries, route maps, and ethnographies. A great astronomer, he took a deep interest in cartography. Ptolemy explained three different ways of projecting the three-dimensional surface of the spherical earth onto the two dimensions of a map. He collected a vast amount of information about the size of the inhabited world, the locations of and distances between some eight thousand individual places, and the curious creatures who inhabited some distant lands. Among his crisp quantitative data appear references to the magnetic islands, which could tear a ship apart by pulling out all its nails. But for the most part he offered an austere description of distances and places.

In thirteenth-century Byzantium, Greek scholars equipped the *Geography* with splendid maps. These appear to be late reconstructions of the maps Ptolemy might have drawn rather than copies of his actual work. But they collected a vast amount of information in easily readable and physically dramatic form. The *Geography* was translated into Latin early in the fifteenth century by the humanist Jacopo d'Angelo. By the middle of the century it had become a best-seller, as copies newly equipped with colorful maps sailed across the Mediterranean world. Scholars and stationers competed to draw up maps that followed Ptolemy's instructions as precisely as possible, and to complement his work with a second set of maps of the modern world. The *Geography* reached print in 1475, and many editions, as well as many luxurious manuscripts, attest to its popularity thereafter. Unknown in the West in the Middle Ages, it became both a learned authority and a splendid adornment in the libraries of the Renaissance, a huge and brilliantly colored coffee-table book before the advent of coffee, itself one of the most dramatic new products to flood into Europe as a result of the discoveries.

Modern historians of the discoveries and of maps often regret the

Renaissance's interest in Ptolemy. They point out, correctly, that Ptolemy made many mistakes. He made the Mediterranean far too long, Ceylon far too big. He thought the Indian Ocean had no southern opening. And he also perpetuated a few exotic fantasies, lending them his own scientific authority. Especially when encountered in the inaccurate translation by Jacopo d'Angelo, he was more likely to mislead than to inform an explorer or scholar. It seems a pity, then, that deep into the sixteenth century this majestic constellation of attractive errors held unchallenged authority in the realm of geography—even after medieval and modern sailors had revealed so many of its flaws and gaps. Ptolemy's only virtue was a serendipitous one—his curtailed value for the distance to the mysterious East helped to inspire Columbus with the confidence he needed to set sail. Otherwise the tyrannical authority of Ptolemy was a disaster.

This account of Ptolemy's impact is anachronistic and inaccurate. The greatest scientists of the Renaissance, in the first place, had learned the lesson of the humanists. They began work in any field of natural philosophy by returning to the classics of Greek science, in the original texts. They corrected or replaced the medieval translations, many of which had been inaccurate or cryptic, and translated many vital works, like those of Archimedes, for the first time. Regiomontanus, the most original student of the exact sciences in fifteenth-century Europe, went to Italy to learn Greek. He set himself to improve the astronomy of his time by updating and explicating Ptolemy's manual, the *Almagest*. Regiomontanus' *Epitome*, completed in the 1460s, introduced all serious astronomers to Ptolemy's models of planetary motion for a century and more. It was only natural, then, that when he decided to improve geography, he did so in the first instance as a textual critic. He collated Jacopo d'Angelo's translation of the *Geography* with the Greek, identifying many passages in the Latin which neither made sense nor matched the original. And though he died before completing his work, the scientists and scholars of sixteenth-century Nuremberg, Johannes Werner and Willibald Pirckheimer, continued his enterprise, retranslating the *Geography* and printing his notes. The study of the *Geography*, for all its faults, fitted precisely into the most advanced scientific projects of the time.

Ptolemy, moreover, never adopted the persona of an unchallengable authority. He made clear that geography was a cumulative and partly descriptive science, not an exact one. Nations and peoples changed continuously; the good geographer must try to keep up by using only the most recent accounts. But all geographers would err, as Ptolemy's predecessors had. He clearly expected to be superseded over time. The scribes and editors who added new portfolios of modern maps to manuscripts and early editions of the *Geography* worked in Ptolemy's own spirit, as many of them knew. No wonder that Leonardo da Vinci—who usually mocked written authorities and those who depended on them—described his studies of human anatomy as intended to provide "the cosmography of this lesser world [the human body], in the same order as was used by Ptolemy before me." The great student of nature who liked to describe himself polemically as "a man without letters" found himself hooked on the challenge—and the power—of this one old book. [13]

As read in the Renaissance, finally, Ptolemy's book offered a model of a presentation of the facts basically unconditioned by ideology. Every map, it is fashionable now to say, is political; the location of the landmark meridians of longitude, the forms of lettering, the images that designate cities and resources can all express political and cultural claims. Medieval maps had been more political than most others. Schematic rather than strictly representational, they had situated Jerusalem at the center of the world, which they divided into three continents separated by rivers. Their outskirts, naturally, harbored the monstrous races who lived outside civilization.

By contrast Ptolemy's maps—that is, the Renaissance Latin ver-

Figure 1.10   A world map from Willibald Pirckheimer's 1525 Strasbourg edition of Ptolemy's *Geography*, which included the critical notes of the great fifteenth-century scientist Regiomontanus. This updated version opens up the Indian Ocean, although Africa is still portrayed in the traditional Ptolemaic manner.

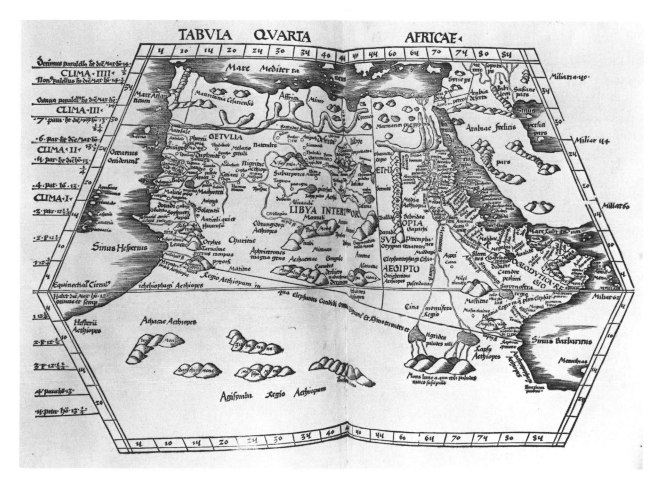

Figure 1.11 The map of Africa from the 1513 Strasbourg edition of Ptolemy's *Geography*. The precise annotation of distances contrasts with random descriptions—for example, that the kingdom of the Ethiopians is where white elephants, rhinoceroses, and tigers are born.

sions of Byzantine Greek ones—located the prime meridian in the Fortunate Isles (the Canaries), a place without evident political significance. They made clear that Asia bulked vastly larger than Europe. And even in their earliest printed versions, they faithfully expressed Ptolemy's sense that his own geography, however coherent and sophisticated, was imperfect. Most of them designated the land with which he closed off the Indian Ocean, for example, not as something known with certainty but as *Terra incognita secundum Ptolemaeum*—"unknown land, by Ptolemy's account." They thus invited exploration and revision.

Both were soon forthcoming. The 1482 Ulm edition of the *Geography* added details to Ptolemy's version of the frozen North; the 1513 Strasbourg edition included, quite in Ptolemy's spirit, a whole second atlas, which included detailed modern maps of Europe and one of the African coast as surveyed by the Portuguese. The Renaissance editions of the *Geography*, in short, were neither a gallery of pretty pictures devoid of use nor a set of images chosen for symbolic content rather than conformity to the known facts. They were the most serious effort that could then be made to comprehend ancient and modern discoveries in one verbal and visual description. Hence the *Geography* provided perhaps the most successful of all ancient models for coping with the flood of new facts from the West.[14]

First Encounters

The fertility of these models is evident. By the second decade of the sixteenth century writers who described the New World or used it as a stimulus for imaginative constructions of their own had already put many of them into play. Peter Martyr, an Italian humanist who worked in Spain, published his spectacular account of the New World in 1516, using the primary evidence of Columbus and much additional evidence, from language to customs. He encouraged those who actually went to the New World, as he did not, to report back systematically. But he also used a vast range of classical authorities to frame his account. He compared New World parrots with those described by Pliny, the life of the islanders on Hispaniola to the Golden Age depicted by Virgil and Hesiod, the elusive cannibals of the Caribbean to the Thracians who went to Lesbos to impregnate the Amazons. Peter admitted that he found the lip-plugs worn by Mexicans repulsive, but insisted that this proved only the parochialism of his own habits of perception: "The Ethiopian considers that black is a more beautiful color than white, while the white man thinks otherwise . . . It is clearly a reaction of the emotions, and not a reasoned conclusion, that leads the human race into such absurdities, and every district is swayed by its own taste." In this combination of attitudes, at once culture-bound and open-eyed, he showed himself the heir of Herodotus.[15]

Thomas More, by contrast, showed himself the heir of Plato, situating his imaginary ideal state in the new realms to the far West; these would long offer a favored site for the perfect societies of Renaissance philosophy. In the same year, Fernández de Oviedo was inspired by his meeting with Peter Martyr to frame yet another comparative account of the New World, this time on Pliny's model rather than a purely ethnographic one, but using others as well. For example, he applied to the destruction wrought by the Spanish in the Caribbean the lapidary phrase of Tacitus' Englishman, Calgacus: "Those who have perpetuated these crimes call the uninhabited places 'peaceful.' I feel they are more than peaceful; they are destroyed."

Even the existence of the New World did not seem altogether threatening. After all, many ancient texts referred in one way or another to unknown lands in the West. Plato had described Atlantis; the Carthaginians had colonized western lands; Seneca had prophe-

Figure 1.12 Thomas More's Utopia was the first of many ideal societies to be located in the realms newly discovered. His *Libellus vere aureus nec minus salutaris quam festivus, Utopia* (Louvain, 1516) is an exercise in European social criticism rather than a depiction of New World realities. A small, densely populated island off a settled continent, Utopia is an ideal form of England where there is no private property.

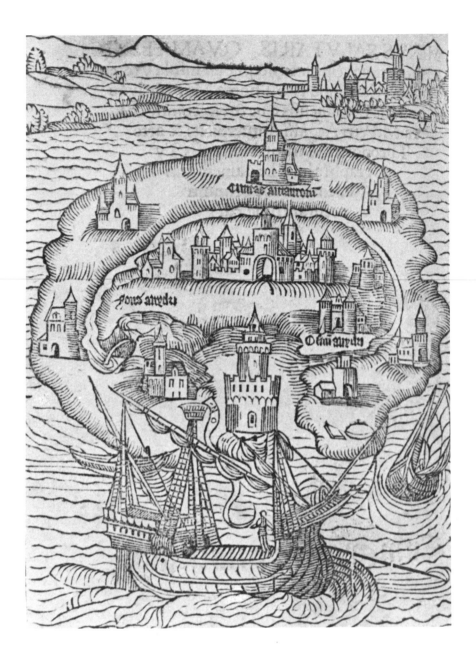

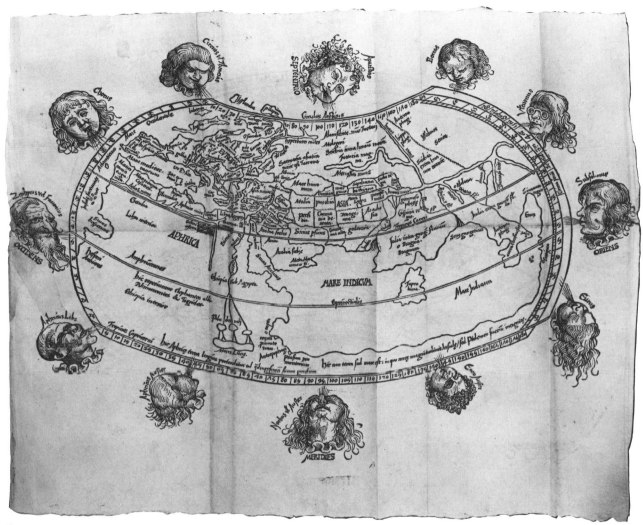

Figure 1.13   Another version of Ptolemy's world map as it appears in the 1503 Freiburg edition of Reisch's *Margarita philosophica*. At bottom right, a legend on the land mass which, for Ptolemy, enclosed the Indian Ocean, states firmly: "Here there is not land, but ocean. In it there are islands of extraordinary size unknown to Ptolemy."

sied the discovery of a new world in his *Medea*. Appropriately, Willibald Pirckheimer—citizen of Nuremberg, scholar and scientist—was only one of many who greeted the news of America by collecting ancient passages that seemed to show that it was not news after all, but another classical revival.

Had a revolution taken place? Did the crust of the canon tear and heave as new facts surged upward? Even the encyclopedias with which we began render this interpretation doubtful. Neither the *Margarita* nor the *Nuremberg Chronicle* was as stable and coherent as it seemed. The *Chronicle*, for example, repeated Pliny's catalogue of monstrous races, framing it between columns of vividly printed images that were probably as old as the imaginary creatures themselves. But it also included a stop-press addendum by Muenzer on the voyages of the Portuguese. Even the humbler little book of Gregor Reisch, which derived its astronomy from the up-to-date work of Regiomontanus, had a revealing fold-out world map. This was antiquated in some respects, to be sure. But it did indicate—only four years after Vasco da Gama's return from India—that Ptolemy had been wrong about the Indian Ocean: "Here there is no land, but ocean with islands of extraordinary size; but they were unknown to Ptolemy." By 1515 a Strasbourg edition had a map that depicted the New World, with a descriptive text on its reverse side. [16]

Reisch, as many modern readers have been willing to point out, knew less than we do; so did Ptolemy. But anyone who has tried to describe a complex set of data in a coherent way may find more cause for admiration than for grumbling in what they achieved. The texts provided European intellectuals not with a single grid that imposed a uniform order on all new information, but with a complex set of overlapping stencils, a rich and delicate set of patterns and contrivances. These produced diverse, provocative, ultimately revolutionary assemblies of new facts and images.

Navigators and Conquerors: The Universe of the Practical Man

2

A Merchant's Culture

On 1 January 1404 the Florentine merchant Goro Dati made a set of vows. He promised himself that he would not go to his shop or do business on church holidays; that he would keep Friday ("with Friday I include the following night," he added, with a merchant's precision) as a day of chastity; and that—if at all possible—he would pray or give alms every day. Dati knew that he would probably fail to keep his vows; so he supplemented them with a codicil, promising to give alms to the poor every time he slipped. The combination of calculation and piety, understanding of the basics of Christian doctrine and commitment to the life of profitmaking and the flesh, is typical of a second world of Europeans to which we now turn: the world of sailors, soldiers, and salesmen, the men who sailed past the Pillars of Hercules while the humanists argued about the canon and destroyed empires while historians dreamed of a Golden Age in the West.

It has been usual to describe this world as contrasting in all respects to the learned world or worlds we have just surveyed. After all, the world of craft and trade, not that of books, produced the forces that really revolutionized the European and then the entire world. Unknown sailors, not scholars, learned to navigate by the compass and

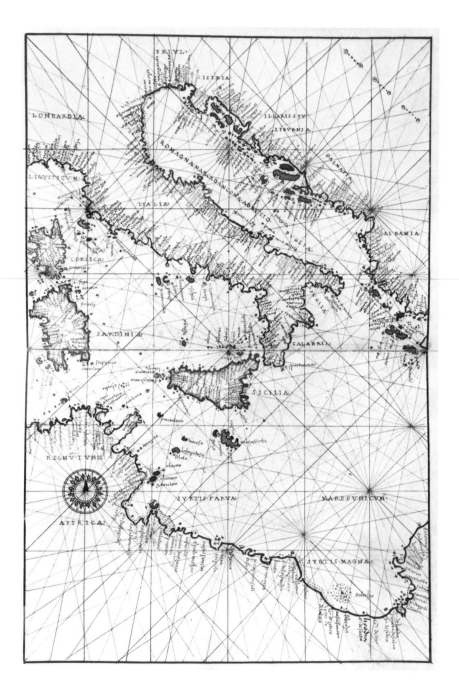

Figure 2.1 This *portolan* chart of the central Mediterranean, made by Battista Agnese around 1552, is characteristic in its detailed portrayal of the coastline.

the stars. They developed the large three-masted sailing ship that could manage voyages of many months and survive out of sight of shore. And they recorded the new coastlines they found on their own new maps, the *portolans*—sophisticated, practical aids to navigation which indicated direct routes between ports and taught no symbolic or theoretical lessons.

Soldiers and military engineers, not scientists, developed the military uses of gunpowder and devised portable cannon and muskets, the weapons that gave Western soldiers vast advantages over all nonwestern opponents. Craftsmen developed that most characteristic new technology of the fifteenth and sixteenth centuries, the printing press, which ensured that news of all the frenetic activity of travel and conquest would spread throughout Europe, and thus be forced on the attention of even the most traditional thinkers.

By the middle of the sixteenth century even men of the book celebrated these three inventions as something that gave their age a special character. All of them unknown to the ancients, all of them developed outside the world of learning, they had transformed the powers of the race and opened up the world. Ever since, we have tended to accept these assessments and embroider on them. In the nineteenth century, for example, that age of mechanical progress and sound business sense, it became normal to insist that Columbus, too, had been one of the practical men, unconstrained by the limits of book learning. The scholars had believed that one could not sail to the West because one would fall off the end of the Earth. Hence Columbus had to convince Ferdinand and Isabella that the world was round before he could gain support for his first expedition. Amerigo Vespucci and Hernando Cortés too came to be celebrated as heroes who had done what no intellectual could imagine.

These views derived less from scholarly research (good nineteenth-century scholars knew better) than from notions about the

Figure 2.2 By the seventeenth century, when this engraving was made, Columbus had already been transformed from the equivocal figure that his own writing reveals him to be—deeply traditional yet willing to take tremendous risks—into the prototypical hero-explorer celebrated here. He wears the armor and carries the banner of a chivalric crusader, but he is serenaded and attended by classical Nereids and Tritons and the pagan deities Diana and Neptune. From Johannes Galle's *Speculum diversarum imaginum speculativarum* (Antwerp, 1638).

nature of progress—the same ones that found embodiment in the Columbian Exposition of a century ago. They are contradicted, as we have seen, by even a brief exposure to the real world of Renaissance learning, which clearly took the world as spherical and entertained the possibility that exploration might open new parts of it. But they are also contradicted by even a brief exploration of the world of the explorers. They, too, had a culture of the book, connected to that of the scholars though not identical with it. They, too, found in ancient wisdom the stimulus to explore and exploit and the tools for understanding what they met when they did so.

Dati was a characteristic figure of the real world of trade and exploration. A merchant who rose to riches in the rag trade, he led a cosmopolitan and dangerous life. He did business across the Mediterranean, living for years in Valencia. He suffered shocking losses when the king of Castile died before paying off debts to his firm, when a lawsuit went against him in Barcelona, and when he fell prisoner to pirates. Yet he survived everything, remaining active in business, holding public office, and diversifying his investments.

A prolific writer as well as a busy investor, Dati left an ample paper trail that yields many glimpses of his ideas and values. His strong sense of honor made him fight off bankruptcy whenever it threatened. A powerful sense of calculation also ruled his life, however. Not only did he compute appropriate sums to give to the poor when he had sex on a Friday; he also computed, far more ambitiously, the resources that Giangaleazzo Visconti, the tyrant of Milan, would have needed to defeat the Florentines when he went to war against them early in the fifteenth century, and concluded that Visconti would necessarily have lost even if he had not died suddenly in 1402. At the same time, Dati respected and feared the power of chance. "Fortune," the impersonal power that he repeatedly invoked in his diary and his history of Florence, could sweep aside the strongest preparations and destroy the richest merchant.

Dati wrote a treatise called *The Sphere*, in Italian verse, which circulated widely in the fifteenth century in both manuscript and, later, printed form. The book describes and celebrates the Mediterranean culture of maritime adventure. One copy begins with a magnificent full-page image of the new ship of the fifteenth century, its sails spread. Dati's own verse portrays with naive vividness the life of the navigator, dependent on technical skill and constantly vulnerable to fortune:

> With maps that lay out like a frieze
> The winds, the ports, the seven seas,
> Pirates and merchants sail the main,
> Hunting for plunder or for gain.
> A single day, from dawn to dusk,
> Can bring them either book or bust:
> No other trade, no other way
> Of life thus makes men fortune's prey.

No life could seem more alien to the schemes and traditions of the university or the eloquence of the humanist school than this dangerous search for stable riches in a constantly changing environment. Dati's text, moreover, emphasizes the range of practical skills and technical data that the adventurer needs. The fourth section of *The Sphere* lays out travel routes in the Near East and in North Africa, offering precise directions and distances from city to city. Some texts contain what amount to *portolan* maps, the navigator's vade mecum, showing these coastlines in great detail and indicating possible routes between ports with a spiderweb of straight lines.

Yet the book also sets the navigator's enterprise into a very large context. It starts in fact with the universe as a whole, describing the whole array of spheres that hold the stars and move the planets. Dati describes the astrological properties of the twelve signs of the

Zodiac and seven planets, apostrophizes the sun ("O light that shines on men both near and far, / more noble art thou than any other star"), and describes in detail the traditional system of the four elements. He accepts the notion that every star exercises a particular influence on the earth, though he shows skepticism about human efforts to base predictions on these. And he analyzes in detail the weather, the season, and the human temperaments, all neatly laid out in exactly the same taxonomic grids that a university textbook of the time would have deployed, and illustrated by colorful but traditional schematic diagrams that might as well adorn the *Margarita*. Throughout Dati takes pains to show that God has planned the entire world, and that man must use it in ways acceptable to Him, not striving too hard for temporal goods, since "these are only lent us to be used."

Even Dati's descriptions of maps and of the Mediterranean world draw heavily on traditions embodied in texts. The map he portrays in verse, at length and in detail, is not the practical man's *portolan* but the schematic, symbolic geography of the schools:

> A T within an O shows vividly
> How all the world is cut up into three

The accompanying map, laid out in the normal way, with the East on top and the North to the right, shows Asia above the arm of the T, formed by the great rivers of the world, Europe and Africa to left and right of its vertical, and Ocean surrounding all the landmasses, like an O. And the Middle Eastern landscape Dati describes is marked by—and apparently still littered with the results of—biblical history, from the landing of the Ark to the construction of the Tower of Babel.

For all his bourgeois mentality, Dati lived in a world defined as neatly as those of the scholars by the events of the Bible and the

Figure 2.3 A T–O map from a 1473 Strasbourg edition of Isidore of Seville's *Etymologiae*. In this very popular scheme, illustrating not geographical reality but rather a theological vision, Jerusalem is, literally, the center of the world. Asia and the East appear at the top of the map, Europe at bottom left, and Africa at bottom right, separated from one another by the Nile, the Don, and the Mediterranean Sea. The entire habitable world is surrounded by the ocean sea. The map also identifies the son of Noah whose progeny populated each continent.

cosmos of Aristotelian philosophy. His summary of these matters—presumably aimed at the young boys who prepared for practical life in the vernacular-language "abacus schools" of Florence—taught practical and symbolic geography, useful information and Christian precepts, at all once. To be sure, Dati may only have translated and adapted a Latin work on the sphere by his brother Lionardo, General of the Dominican order (and, obviously, an educated man). But the connection between merchant and mendicant culture only reinforces the general point. Merchants and navigators on the one hand, scholars and philosophers on the other inhabited much the same cosmos, imagined much the same history, and saw no necessary conflict between the lessons of experience and those of books. This should hardly surprise us. In Florence, Dati's city, merchants and scholars attended with equal pleasure and assiduity the public lectures on a far grander presentation than Dati's of the Aristotelian cosmos, Dante's *Divine Comedy*.[1]

Techniques and Traditions

Like the learned culture, the culture of practical men was neither simple nor unified. It included a range of practical techniques that scholars usually did not master. Men like Dati, as his text suggests, learned business arithmetic, the whole range of rules for computing interest, exchange rates, weights, and measures that commerce required one to know—especially in a world where standards of weight, length, and currency changed not from nation to nation but from city to city. They learned how to judge quality in the work of craft, stitch by stitch. They mastered a range of new navigational facts and methods—how to use and extend a *portolan*, for example—to which few scholars had access. In their centers of exploration—above all Prince John the Navigator's settlement on its windswept Portuguese peninsula—traditions were swept aside by irresistible tides of new fact about the coasts of Africa and, eventually, the ocean route to the Far East.[2] But they also had access to their own versions of the tools and skills of Latin learning, and these, too, often shaped their experience.

In navigation, for example, Dati was by no means the only one who tried to graft the systematic maps of high scholarship to the practical ones of real seamen. The Latin versions of Ptolemy's *Geography* made available to sailors as well as scholars a coherent vision of the surface of the Earth—something the *portolan* tradition did not provide. If the long, technical, often obsolete textual matter of the *Geography* baffled some readers, enterprising craftsmen and entrepreneurs adapted it in more accessible forms. Metal globes, a fifteenth-century novelty, could present Ptolemy's version of the continents more vividly than any two-dimensional map. Translation and summary could make his main conclusions available to a public who could not necessarily cope with the Latin original. A German adaptation of the *Geography* appeared in Nuremberg, sometime between

1486 and 1493, in the form of a booklet accompanied by a fold-out map. Reference numbers in the German text made clear which sections referred to which areas. This map—though basically Ptolemaic—contained, like the maps in the big Latin versions of the *Geography*, ample evidence that his theories were not complete and perfect. The land mass that closes off the Indian Ocean, for example, bears the normal legend "unknown land, according to Ptolemy"— not a record of Portuguese expeditions to the East, but hardly a dogmatic assertion of their impossibility either. It did not take a learned man, in short, to learn such basic principles of ancient cosmology and geography as the sphericity of the Earth and the unknown character of parts of its dry surface. These facts were ready to hand in broadsides and pamphlets that anyone literate in the vernacular could read and buy.[3]

Like the learned, those who lived in a vernacular world were both curious and alarmed about the lands at the extremes of the habitable world. They, too, had an ample literature to read and marvel at—a literature which often stimulated reflection of all sorts. The travel account of Marco Polo, the most exciting of all documents of the high medieval age of safe travel overland from Europe to the far East, portrayed a China possessed of vast wealth, ruled with great justice, and even accessible to Christian preaching. The novel of Sir John Mandeville—compiled in the fourteenth century by an unknown hand, mainly from learned works in Latin, and then endlessly translated and adapted, illustrated, and reprinted—offered a still wider and more stimulating panorama of the extremities of the world.

Mandeville described the magnificent realms—the kingdom of the Christian emperor Prester John, the earthly paradise itself—that invited brave explorers. He populated the distant regions of the world with kingdoms rich and strange, of whose customs and institutions, alphabets and diet he gave vivid reports. And in doing so he drew, indirectly but unmistakably, on the rich current of reportage about the exotic East that began with the Greeks. Like Ctesias and Megasthenes, he conjured up a world of dog-headed men and pigmies, at once terrifying in appearance and wise and just in conduct. Mandeville told of ritual cannibalism on the island of "Dondun." But like Diodorus describing suttee, he treated this apparently monstrous custom as a rational set of actions carried out with care and dignity. On the island, when someone became ill, an idol would be consulted. If it identified the disease as mortal, the patient would be executed humanely by suffocation and then eaten by his nearest and dearest, who thought that by doing so "they freed him from pain and suffering." Cannibalism could be a sign of civility, not its reverse.[4]

Like the Greeks, Mandeville insisted that the pigmies were skillful craftsmen and brave warriors; unlike them, he also pointed out that normal men were as monstrous to them as they to normal men: "They . . . despise [men of large stature] just as we would despise the Pigmies if they lived among us." Mandeville more than anyone else helped to create a sort of vernacular ethnography, one that suggestively transformed the far reaches of the world into a sort of explorer's Club Med, where mild climates, strange but colorful customs, and only the occasional attack of indigestion—in this case, to be sure, caused by the traveler as a dragon ate him—awaited the intrepid tourist. A more aggressive attitude toward distant cultures

Figure 2.4 A carnivorous monster, naked and shameless "Indians," an islander on Thama adoring an idol (others there adore the sun, fire, or the first thing they encounter in the morning), and a legendary blemmye from Mandeville's *Reysen und Wanderschafften durch das Gelobte Land* (Strasbourg, 1483) and *Monteuille compose par Messire Jehan de Monteuille* (Lyons, 1508).

John Mandeville

THE fabulous fourteenth-century travels of the fictitious knight John Mandeville proved far more popular than Marco Polo's more authentic account of a journey to the East, written in the 1290s. Repeatedly copied, abridged, illustrated, and translated in manuscript form, Mandeville's *Travels* lost none of its popularity in the age of print. Sir Walter Raleigh's approving citations of it in *The discoverie of the large, rich and Bewtiful empyre of Guiana* attest to Mandeville's longevity and continued credibility (see Chapter 5).

In Mandeville's account, Christian miracle-working monks coexist with Pliny's monstrous races—the anthropophagi, Amazons, one-eyed men, *blemmyes* and dogheads, one-legged men whose feet were so large they could be used as parasols against the blistering sun. And the farther Mandeville strays from Europe, the more marvelous the account becomes. In Sumatra, he claims, he encountered a people who simultaneously invert, live out, and transgress Christian custom in a peculiar combination of Utopian ideal and savagery:

"In that land is full great heat. And the custom there is such that men and women go all naked, and they scorn when they see any strange folk going clothed. And they say that God made Adam and Eve all naked, and that no man should shame him to show him such as God made him, for nothing is foul that is of kindly nature . . . And they wed there no wives, for all the women there be common and they forsake no man. And they say they sin if they refuse any man. And so God commanded Adam and Eve and to all that come of him when He said, *Crescite et multiplicamini et replete terram* . . . And also all the land is common . . . And every man there taketh what he will without any contradiction, and as rich is one man there as is another . . . But in that country there is a cursed custom, for they eat more gladly man's flesh than any other flesh . . . Thither go merchants and bring with them children to sell to them of the country, and they buy them . . . And they say that it is the best flesh and the sweetest of all the world."

Mandeville also popularized the theory of the circumnavigability of the earth. His evidence is both "scientific" and anecdotal: he writes of sightings with astrolabes and observations of the heavens; he also tells a tale of circumnavigation accomplished well before Magellan's time, though by an easterly route:

"And therefore hath it befallen many times of one thing that I have heard counted when I was young, how a worthy man departed sometime from our countries for to go search the world. And so he passed Ind [India] and the isles beyond Ind where be more than five thousand isles. And so long he went by sea and land and so environed the world by many seasons, that he found an isle where he heard men speak his own language, calling on oxen in the plough such words as men speak to beasts in his own country; whereof he had great marvel, for he knew not how it might be. But I say that he had gone so long by land and by sea that he had environed all the earth, that he was come again environing (that is to say, going about) unto his own marches. And if he would have passed forth, he had found his country and his own knowledge. But he turned again from thence whence he was come from, and so he lost much painful labour, as he himself said a great while after he was come home . . ."

Source: Mandeville 1968.

Figure 2.5 Cannibals, paradoxically in European dress, from Mandeville's *Reysen und Wanderschafften* (Strasbourg, 1483).

inspired a more modern genre, the chivalric romances, which took the Crusades as a favored setting and treated the majestic East as mysterious and alluring, but also as dangerous and corrupt—a haunt of evil that brave Christian knights must conquer if they hoped to earn merit.[5]

The past, finally, also had a clear embodiment and outline in vernacular culture—above all that of the European aristocracies, with their passion for creating vastly extended family trees. Columbus was only one of hundreds who traced their families back to a Roman forebear. Vernacular as well as Latin histories of the world began with the Creation. They, too, laid out the incestuous, enclosed dramas of early human history, as portrayed in the Bible, in firm genealogies and short bursts of prose. They also traced the origins of the modern European nations—preferably, though not exclusively, back to the heroic Trojans who had fled westward after the fall of the city, and whose spread represented a dramatic secular equivalent to the settling of the world by the descendants of Noah. The practical man's vision of the past was thus defined, limited in length by the Bible and in extent by the need to fill in every branch of family trees. But like the pasts of the learned and the Far Easts of the travel writers, it also offered a site where the imagination could play. The ancient heroes did not have to be set back into context, as the humanists did; they could also be portrayed as fifteenth-century knights in armor and ladies in tall hats, immediate models for conduct in the here and now.

Dati's case and the others we have looked at so far are suggestive, in at least three ways. They reveal that men and women without formal education often had access to, and could express in their own way, the same sorts of concepts and images that put order into the universe, the past, and the diversities of the human race for scholars. They reveal also that the images were rich and pliable, and that the concepts were often shot through with fruitful contradictions—especially when confronted by the real world of profit and power. Dati knew perfectly well that he entertained contradictory desires when he tried to seek profit and serve God in one career and lifetime.

Finally, they reveal that mercantile and learned cultures were not separated by an impermeable membrane. They met at many points. Vernacular writers often drew their matter, and sometimes their manner, from learned Latin texts. Latin, moreover, was not a parochial dead language but a universal living one, which many could read and understand even if they could not speak and write it fluently and grammatically. The medium of every church service, every university lecture, every science, and even some tourist guides, it prevailed as English does in the modern world. Many who did not fully belong to the learned milieus could nevertheless draw on scholarly books as easily as young Poles, Russians, and Chinese today draw costumes and concepts from American music and movies

The Discovery Reported: Columbus and Vespucci

Two of the first Europeans to reach the New World were also two of the most articulate observers ever to touch ship there. The deracinated Genoese Christopher Columbus and the Florentine Amerigo Vespucci, a lesser navigator but a more skillful writer, both observed with open eyes and recorded what they saw with active pens. Both, however, were also active readers, and peered through tightly woven filters of expectation and assumption from the past. The pamphlets which carried versions of both men's visions to a wide world of readers and the detailed logbooks in which Columbus preserved his thoughts and reactions show a most intricate interaction of tradition and the new, weighty books and the weight of fact.

The American legend of Columbus more or less inverts the facts

Sye figur anzaigt vns das volck vnd insel die gefunden ist durch den christenlichen künig zů Portigal oder von seinen vnderthonen. Die leüt sind also nacket hübsch, braun wolgestalt von leib, ir heübter, halß, arm, scham, füß, frawen vnd mann an wenig mit federn bedeckt. Auch haben die mann in iren angesichten vnd brust vid edel gestain. Es hat auch nyemantz nichts sünder sind alle ding gemain. Vnd die mann habande weyber welche in gefallen, es sey mütter, schwester oder freünde, darjnn haben sy kain vnderschayd. Sy streyten auch mit einander. Sy essen auch ainander selbs die erschlagen werden, vnd henckeen das selbig fleisch in den rauch. Sy werden alt hundert vnd fünftzig iar. Vnd haben kain regiment.

Figure 2.6 A 1505 depiction of Indians. Froschauer's caption describes these newly discovered peoples in terms long familiar to a culture weaned on Pliny and Mandeville. After describing their physical characteristics, it notes that "no one has anything of his own, but all things are common. And the men who have wives that please them make no distinction whether it is their mother or sister or friend. They fight with each other. They also eat one another and they hang and smoke the flesh of those killed. They live to 150 and have no government." Caption and picture together formed a broadside—a single-leaf publication, aimed at ordinary readers—printed at Augsburg in 1505. Johann Froschauer entitled his work *Dise Figur anzaigt uns das Folck und Insel die gefunden ist durch den christenlichen Kunig zu Portigal oder von seinen Underthonen.*

of his life and thought. The historian of the Indies Bartolomé de Las Casas saw Columbus as one of the great heroes of history—though he deplored his hero's willingness to make slaves of innocent natives. Most unexpectedly, he also saw Columbus as a great reader, if one of a peculiar kind. He showed in detail, using the primary sources, that Columbus had read and annotated a number of books—the geographical *Commentaries* of Pope Pius II, the *Geography* of Ptolemy, the *Imago mundi* of the fifteenth-century French cardinal Pierre d'Ailly, which quoted and summarized a vast range of authorities. He decorated these books with elaborate notes, written in a handsome script (so Las Casas thought) but in imperfect Latin, which often seem to point toward his great enterprise: "every ocean can be navigated," he wrote in his Ptolemy. He read the texts, moreover, actively and urgently, not passively, and sometimes showed a humanist's eye for the sources of the text before him. What stimulated him most in Ptolemy, for example, was his attack on the earlier geographer Marinus, whose own work was lost. Marinus had offered a still smaller value than Ptolemy's for the circumference of the earth—a natural inducement to one who hoped to sail west to China. Columbus was delighted when his voyages proved Marinus trustworthy, as he thought. He also looked for expert help wherever he could find it. An encouraging letter from the Florentine astronomer and mathematician Paolo Toscanelli, for example, corroborated his hope that a short westward voyage would bring him face to face with a Great Cham of China ready and waiting to be converted to Christianity.

As Columbus observed and reported on the New World, he naturally turned to his reading—and extended it—as he looked for a framework in which to insert what he saw. Sometimes the confrontation between eye and text refuted the books; he found none of the monstrosities, he announced in his first letter, that many had

Figure 2.7   This seventeenth-century engraving by Theodor Galle after
Johannes Stradanus, titled *Lapis polaris, magnes,* shows an obviously learned
man comparing the empirically derived results of navigation with texts. The
collection of objects—measuring devices, the ship's model, and large floating
compass—juxtaposed with the pile of big books at far left nicely represent
the interaction of learned and practical traditions.

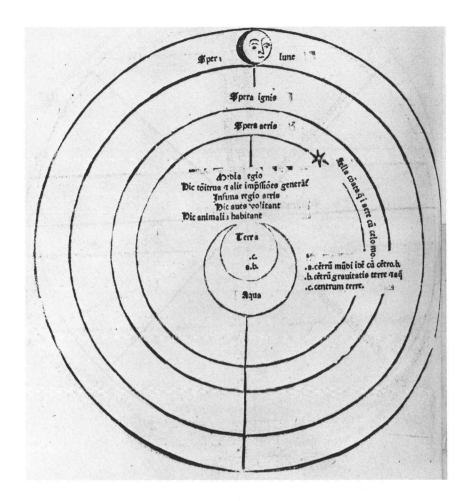

Within the diagram:

Spera lune

Spera ignis

Spera aeris

Orbis egio
Dic toitrua ⁊ alie impſſioes generat
Infima regio aeris
Dic aues volitant
Dic animalia habitant

Stella coaca ꝙ aere cũ celo mo...

Terra
.c.
a.b.

.a. cētrũ mũdi ioē cũ cētro. b.
.b. cētrũ grauitatis terre ꝗaꝗ
.c. centrum terre.

Aqua

Figure 2.8   At the center of this diagram from Pierre d'Ailly's *Imago mundi* (Louvain, 1483), the earth is represented as a sphere of land floating like a cork in a sphere of water. The next circle is the realm of generation in which birds fly and animals live; the airy and fiery realms are represented by the second and third circles respectively. Columbus apparently studied his copy of d'Ailly assiduously, making hundreds of notes. There he read that "Seneca writes in his five books of natural history that the sea may be navigated in a few days if the wind is fair."

expected to exist in the far places of the world. Sometimes, too, the books simply offered no applicable words. Columbus' detailed log of his observations swarms with efforts to describe a world that seems simply new, inaccessible to European analogies. The most eloquent of these take the form of simple confessions that he cannot describe what he sees—the now-ancient strategy of marvel.

On the whole, however, the closet full of received ideas that

Figure 2.9   The image of a ship dramatically introduces the Latin translation of Columbus' letter to the secretary of King Ferdinand announcing his discoveries. In the letter Columbus describes the newly discovered land as islands in the Indian Ocean. The letter was widely distributed as a printed pamphlet in many languages; this edition of *Epistula de insulis nuper inventis* was published at Basel in 1493.

Columbus brought to the New World shaped his presentation of what he saw in more precise ways. His enterprise as a whole, in the first place, always remained what it had been at first: an effort to find the vast wealth and many potential converts of China, the journey that Toscanelli had encouraged him to make. Again and again his conversations with natives confirmed his belief that he could locate his exact position on a world map. "I wished today," he wrote on 23 October 1492, "to set out for the island of Cuba, which I believe must be Cipangu, according to the indications which these people give me concerning its size and riches." His motives also remained inextricably mixed. Like Goro Dati, he wanted profit, and emphasized again and again the potential riches that stretched before explorers of the New World, the possibilities for founding cities and harbors, the fragrant spices, precious herbs, and tantalizing hints of gold. But like Dati, too, he wanted to serve God, and always saw his mission as part of a Crusade.

As Columbus' own condition and his relations with the Spanish crown deteriorated in later years, his sense of the urgency of his task sharply increased. Texts helped him cope with disaster as they had with triumph. With the help of a friar he calculated the length of human history to date; from Revelations and more recent millenialist works he inferred that the end must come within a rather short time. The unification of the world by travel seemed—not for the last time—to herald the approaching end of history itself. This would be preceded, if Columbus could only find attentive hearers, by a conversion of the Chinese and a massed two-pronged crusade against the Muslims. A traditional schema for world history thus made sense of Columbus' great assault on traditional geographies.

Columbus' portraits of natives were as riven with contradictions as his motives. As he sometimes admitted, he could not really communicate with them, and his efforts to follow their directions constantly revealed gross errors in his comprehension. But he did not hesitate to interpret what they said; and the terms in which he did so clearly came from books. The natives were poor, naked, generous, willing to exchange treasures for trinkets—a portrait evidently drawn from memories of life in the Golden Age the poets had described, before *meum* and *tuum* entered the world. But the natives were also greedy, crude, "bestial." Columbus heard that one island, "Quaris," was "inhabited by a people who are regarded in all the islands as very fierce and who eat human flesh." Evidently monsters lurked in the fringes of the world after all—even if they bore human shapes. Comely native women attracted Columbus; Peter Martyr, his still more literary reader, was reminded of classical nymphs. But cannibals also lurked nearby. Columbus' letters owed much of their vividness, many of their most prominent traits, to the traditional strains of vernacular ethnography.

Latin scholarship came with him too. Analyzing the vast streams of water flowing outward, in fact from the Orinoco, Columbus decided that they indicated the presence of another great land mass too far south to be Asia. But this new presence on his charts failed to dismay him. After all, both Aristotle and the medieval authority Petrus Comestor had asserted that the land mass of the world was very large, the waters small; Pierre d'Ailly agreed with them. The Bible too—at least the book of Esdras, in the Apocrypha—said that land covered six-sevenths of the earth's surface, and "This authority is confirmed by saints" (Augustine and Ambrose). Columbus went on to say that "experience" had shown the land mass to be far greater "than the vulgar believe" and commented, "This is no wonder, for the farther one goes, the more one learns." Columbus did not mean to assert the superiority of the naked eye to the clothed book; rather, he meant to express his pleasure in the fact that experience in the field confirmed the texts that he had preferred to believe.[6]

Even more than Columbus, Vespucci proved to be a man of the book. His own achievements as a sailor did nothing to merit the naming of the Americas after him. But the brilliant pamphlets that circulated about his adventures in the West made him the reputation that his voyaging could not. Even more vividly than Columbus, the texts attributed to Vespucci reveal the weight and impact of traditions. His description of the naked savages of the Caribbean took the form of a fantastic ethnography. He, too, populated the new world with happy, naked savages and evil, threatening cannibals. Like Mandeville, he felt deep ambivalence about the edges of the world, and emphasized both the barbarism and the decency of those he found there. The natives in his original account showed their lack of civilization by their lack of set mealtimes and their shamelessness in urination, but proved their virtue by their cleanliness and their modesty in defecation. Their long lives proved the excellence of their environment; but the women's shamelessness and lustfulness, the latter no doubt transferred from observer to observed, proved the degeneracy of the inhabitants.

Vespucci's hints, moreover, were soon amplified into powerful statements by those who rewrote his accounts for publishers across Europe. His own plain account was decked out with still more startling details that would have done credit to a Mandeville: the cannibal whom the original Vespucci met, who confessed to having eaten more than two hundred bodies, ate three hundred in the rewriting. Vespucci himself was made to say that he had seen pieces of salted human flesh hanging like pork in a European butcher's shop. The printers' correctors who amplified Vespucci's account also grounded it still more firmly in the literary tradition than the author had done—though he had left them plenty of hints. The natives in Vespucci's original account "have neither any law nor any faith, and live by nature"; those in the rewriting "live by nature, and can be called Epicureans rather than Stoics." Vespucci's Indians, living in a vague Golden Age, could thus be assimilated to the worst of the pagans, who had shared their lack of shame without having a lack of civilization to excuse it.

Yet Vespucci's literary toolbox enabled him to perform one vital task. Columbus used his texts to make the new familiar, to locate it. Vespucci—like Herodotus and Mandeville—did the reverse. He emphasized that those he met were "so barbarous," their customs "so varied and diverse and different from our affairs and methods," that familiar terms could not apply. He framed his whole account, in other words, as something new. At the outset of his account of the voyage of 1497, for example, he made clear that he had come on something completely different: "This voyage lasted eighteen months, during which we discovered many lands and almost count-less islands (inhabited as a general rule), of which our forefathers make absolutely no mention. I conclude from this that the ancients had no knowledge of their existence." And he drew deftly on the grandest text in the vernacular canon to prove that the new world was noncanonical: "I may be mistaken; but I remember reading somewhere that the [ancients] believed the sea to be free and un-inhabited. Our poet Dante himself was of this opinion."

Vespucci's *Mundus novus*, similarly, took the New World's physical wonders as evidence that ancient physical science fell short. The many trees of the New World, all of them fragrant and emitting useful gums and saps, proved that "Pliny did not touch upon a thousandth part of the species of parrots and other birds and the animals, too, which exist in those same regions." The new stars of the Southern Cross inspired Vespucci to think that he himself should produce "a book of geography or cosmography, that my memory may live with posterity"—the start of a new canon based on new observation of a genuinely New World. The learned redactors who translated him into Latin picked up these hints as well, emphasizing that Vespucci's account required a massive revision to traditional cosmography, which had divided the world into three parts only.

Vespucci's insistence on absolute difference was as literary as Columbus' insistence on familiarity. He no doubt drew from Mandeville and other texts his sense that the outskirts of the world should present the alert traveler with a real shock of unfamiliarity, and his redactors no doubt found in the same sources many of the vivid imaginary details with which they filled out his sketchy descriptions. Yet the tools did serve their purpose. Within less than a decade after the New World was discovered, it received a name and a location of its own. We would be deluded to think that modern travelers are more alert—or less prone to impose on what they find the values and visions they bring with them—than the self-consciously alert Vespucci. At least he made one thing clear beyond doubt: a journey to the West could never, for a European, cross a familiar landscape—even one familiar from texts.[7]

Power and Inquiry

In the four decades that followed Columbus' landfall, explorers would find parts of the American mainland and settlers would occupy the Caribbean islands and conquer the mainland empires. A regime of forced labor and contact with new diseases would destroy the first populations Europeans encountered. Even more would die than had died in Europe when the new diseases from Asia known as the Black Death struck a population already weakened by famine in the fourteenth century. As slaughter took place in America, models for discussion and description, both of the cultures that had been and of their destruction, would multiply in the New World and the Old.

Two sorts of practical men did much of the initial writing—men

Hernando Cortes

THE New World career of Hernando Cortes will always spark controversy. Living in a brutal age, he could without apology be methodically brutal toward New World peoples as he proceeded into the heart of the Aztec empire. His relentless assault on Tenochtitlán, its bustling, rich capital, destroyed not only the city but also the civilization that had built it. Cortes had help, of course—notably from the European diseases that preceded him, diseases that struck native American populations with devastating results. Human allies also played a vital role. It is doubtful that Cortes and his band of four hundred men would have been so successful in conquering Mexico had not enemies of the Aztecs such as the Tlaxcalans become his willing allies, allies whose brutality towards the Aztecs shocked even him.

Whatever judgment we make of Cortes' character, however, his letters to the Emperor Charles V make compelling reading. A son of the Réconquista, Cortes never questioned either his right to claim for Spain the territories through which he passed or the absolute necessity of converting the native populations to Christianity. Yet, as the following description of a Tlaxcalan city makes clear, he was impressed by New World cities. His comparisons with Granada, the last Moorish city to fall to the Spanish reconquest in 1492, are particularly telling:

"The city is indeed so great and marvellous that though I abstain from describing many things about it, yet the little that I shall recount is, I think, almost incredible. It is much larger than Granada and much better fortified. Its houses are as fine and its inhabitants far more numerous than those of Granada when that city was captured. Its provisions and food are likewise very superior—including such things as bread, fowl, game, fish and other excellent vegetables and produce which they eat. There is a market in this city in which more than thirty thousand people daily are occupied in buying and selling, and this in addition to other similar shops which there are in all parts of the city. Nothing is lacking in this market of what they are wont to use, whether utensils, garments, footwear, or the like. There are gold, silver, and precious stones, and jewellers' shops selling other ornaments made of feathers, as well arranged as in any market in the world. There is earthenware of many kinds and excellent quality, as fine as any in Spain. Wood, charcoal, medicinal and sweet smelling herbs are sold in large quantities. There are booths for washing your hair and barbers to shave you; there are also public baths. Finally, good order and an efficient police system are maintained among them, and they behave as people of sense and reason; the foremost city of Africa cannot rival them . . . The order of government so far observed among the people resembles very much the republics of Venice, Genoa and Pisa for there is no supreme overlord . . ."

After waxing eloquent on the marvels of Tenochtitlán, he writes: "Finally, to avoid prolixity in telling all the wonders of this city, I will simply say that the manner of living among the people is very similar to that in Spain, and considering that this is a barbarous nation shut off from a knowledge of the true God or communication with enlightened nations, one may well marvel at the orderliness and good government which is everywhere maintained."

Sources: Cortes n.d.; Crosby 1972; Clendinnen 1991.

Figure 2.10　This illustration is taken from a French translation, published in Paris in 1544, of the continuing adventures of Amadis of Gaul, a chivalric hero particularly popular among Spanish conquistadors: *Le cinquiesme livre de Amadis de Gaule*. Bernal Diáz, who accompanied Cortes on his expedition in what was to become New Spain, evoked Amadis when he first sighted Tenochitlán, and "California" possibly derives from Californie, the queen of the Amazons. The Amazons were eagerly sought by many European explorers.

who reflected in the split between their origins and aims the contradictory motives that a single man like Columbus had entertained. Conquerors and their associates produced exciting, apologetic narratives to justify their disobedience of royal commands, their destruction of rich cities, and their killing of native princes. At the same time priests— above all mendicant friars—produced systematic memoranda on the beliefs and customs of the natives and the actions of the Europeans.

Both sorts of writer sometimes forced the most refractory facts into familiar packages. Cortes described the fall of the Aztecs in brilliant, vivid letters that crossed Europe in many languages. His artfully artless prose transformed the brittle, recent coalition headed by the Aztecs into a great empire; the strange great city of Tenochtitlán into a Muslim *souk* lined with fascinating shops; and Moctezuma, the haunted ruler on a tottering throne, into an obedient vassal of Charles V murdered by rebellious subjects. His own brilliant improvisations, his massacres and compromises, took on a subtle, artificial logic as he bent them to fit the rules of Spanish feudal law, and the nightmare struggle with warriors fighting by a completely alien set of rules, which ended in the destructions of a world, became the heroic single combat of romance.

Cortes could shock as well as soothe. The remarkable image of Tenochtitlán that accompanied his second letter into print, for all the European qualities of the houses it portrayed, did represent an urban world centered on an alien sacred space, the place of temples where men were sacrificed to pagan gods. This vision of a hierarchical urban order seemed both strange and alluring to so gifted an observer as Albrecht Dürer, who deeply admired New World artistry as well.[8] Practical men did send home facts and objects as well as images.

The first priests in the New World saw only savagery around them. Some of their reports substituted for the warm earth tones of

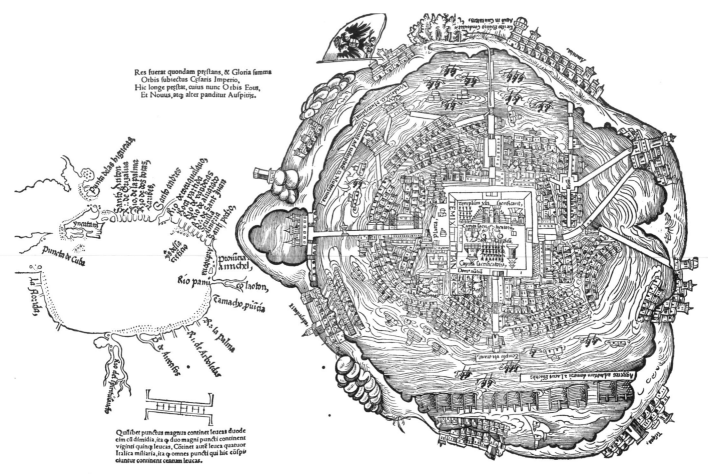

Figure 2.11   A map of Tenochtitlán, supposedly drawn at Cortes' own direction and published in Nuremberg in 1524 with the Latin translation of his report to the Emperor Charles V of his expedition into Mexico and claiming of Aztec lands for New Spain: *Praeclara Ferdinandi Cortesii de nova maris oceani Hispania narratio.*

La conquista del Peru.

Figure 2.12 An early representation from *La conquista del Peru* (Seville, 1534) of the Spanish conquest of Peru. This encounter between a Spanish priest and soldiers and the litter-borne Incan emperor Atahualpa would have a long pictorial life. Although the Spanish generally considered the conquest an enhancement of their and the church's glory, other European nations would increasingly perceive it as a signal example of Spanish treachery and hypocrisy. Years later, Michel de Montaigne would close his essay "On Coaches" with a powerful evocation of the steadfastness of the emperor's litter-bearers.

Old World and New World Demons

BELIEF in witches and witchcraft was shared by Catholics and Protestants alike throughout Europe, and the largely unquestioned assumption that demons and Satan were at work everywhere in the known world no doubt enhanced the sense of danger and threat as Europeans ventured into the unknown. It was an unhappy coincidence for New World peoples that the period of exploration coincided with that of the sixteenth-century religious wars, always cast as battles between orthodoxy and heresy, and the particularly virulent eruption of witch-hunting in the seventeenth century. The notion that Indian peoples were under Satan's sway was widely held. When European visitors encountered ceremonial or doctrinal aspects of Indian religion uncomfortably similar to Christianity, many argued that Satan had broadcast these perversions of the true religion to ensure the hapless natives' perdition.

The widespread belief in sorcery and witches led New World visitors to interpret as the work of the devil what we might respect as religion. Here André Thevet describes the susceptibility of native Americans to visions:

"It is a wondrous thing, that these poor people, though they may be rational, are subject to many fantastic illusions and persecutions by the evil spirit because they are deprived of true reason and knowledge of God. We've said that a similar situation existed prior to the coming of our Savior, for the evil spirit endeavors only to seduce and debauch the creature who is outside the knowledge of God. Thus these poor Americans often see an evil spirit, sometimes in one form, sometimes in another, whom they call Agnan in their language and who persecutes them very often night and day. [It persecutes] not only their spirits, but also their bodies, which it beats and outrages exceedingly [and] in such a manner that sometimes you hear them make a hideous cry, saying in their language if there is a Christian nearby, 'Look, don't you see Agnan beating me, defend me, if you desire me to serve you and chop your wood.' [A]nd thus sometimes one can put them to work cultivating brazil wood in return for little."

Sources: Kramer and Sprenger 1971; MacCormack 1991; Thevet 1557.

Vespucci a litany of abuse worthy of Conrad's Mr Kurtz: [nakedness, sodomy, cannibalism,] the triad of inhuman customs that proved the Indians worthy only to be conquered. Others allowed Columbus and his ilk to delude them in the opposite way, shared the expectations that great changes would soon occur, and assumed that innocent naked Indians, free from property and corruption, could be transformed at once into Christians more faithful than Europeans.

Friars were trained to do more than denounce and predict. They also knew how to observe and investigate. The tools of the Inquisition, especially in its Spanish form, the methods of inquiry by which they had sought out witches and Jewish recidivists in Europe, provided them with a set of questions to ask about beliefs and rituals in the Americas. Many of these clerics assumed that most Europeans were not Christians in a sophisticated sense—that is, equipped with real knowledge of theology or guided in their conduct by Christian morality. They could see and cry for action against the horrors of Conquest; they could also report in detail on what the natives of the New World actually did and thought in their temples.

As reports proliferated, so did interpretations, and traditions of learning and new experiences intersected. The canon underwent new stresses and performed new services as scholars in Europe and elsewhere tried to fit masses of difficult data to the inherited shapes of learning.

All Coherence Gone

3

Sebastian Münster: A Cartographer in a Quandary

I n 1550 the Basel professor Sebastian Münster published a spectacular book. His *Cosmographia* surveyed the lands and peoples of the world, ancient and modern, European and American, Eastern and Western, on a scale so grand that the book itself would become a legend. The tidal wave of erudition is accompanied by a carnival funhouse's store of curious illustrations. More than a thousand closely-printed pages describe everything from the dynasties of royal houses to the monsters that inhabit northern and eastern lands and waters. Like the *Nuremberg Chronicle*, the *Cosmographia* awoke eager interest among readers, was translated and reprinted, pirated and plagiarized. Like the *Chronicle*, it would eventually be transformed from a monument of erudition for scholars to a source of delight for collectors: a copy of it provides the detective interest in a story by Dorothy Sayers. Like the *Chronicle*, finally, the *Cosmographia* constitutes a wonderful diagnostic tool for cultural analysis.

Münster's title page emblematically reveals the wonders to come and many of the intellectual problems they pose. At the top, the close-packed authoritative figures of the European states represent power, authority, and the tight-knit settlement patterns of the civilized. Flanking the long Latin title in the center of the page appear

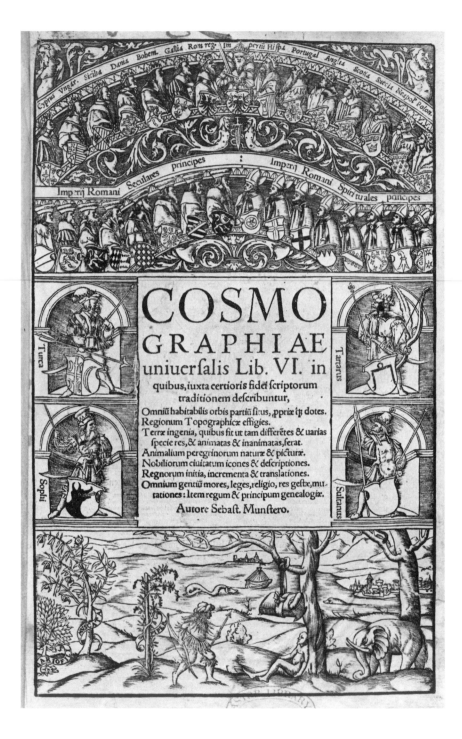

the ancient barbarians whom Europeans had long both feared and admired, figures at once cultured and frightening. At the bottom of the page, in the spaces of the worlds newly laid open, natural resources invite exploration. These include pepper and elephants, traditionally the products of Ceylon in Ptolemaic cartography. But the same space is also inhabited by archetypal New World figures: a prowling, clothed hunter with a bow and a naked mother, her child suspended from a tree. Cities loom in the background; these could either represent the spread of European settlement or reveal the existence of high cultures before white men arrived. From the start, evidently, Münster claims the authority of encyclopedic coverage and graphic vividness; from the start, too, he mingles a clear-eyed effort to sort facts from fables with a credulous openness that puzzles and delights.

Münster surveyed the peoples of the world very systematically, giving genealogies and then describing customs and resources. But his method was as random as his coverage was uniform. Like many compilers of Renaissance encyclopedias, he reared his structure on textual foundations laid by someone else: the comparative survey of the customs of peoples published by Ioannes Boemus some thirty years before.

Boemus, a widely read though not a deeply reflective scholar, produced a small-scale, wide-ranging survey of customs and manners. He explicitly stated that he followed Herodotus, whom he called the father of history and cited first in his list of authorities. His short, comparative book was one of several popular surveys of customs, beliefs, and material culture which the scholars and publishers of the early sixteenth century churned out in profusion. Another work, by Polydore Virgil, revived a Hellenistic genre and catalogued the inventors of everything from writing to music with similar brevity and breadth. Others compiled specialized treatises on the worlds and beliefs of single ancient peoples—notably the ancient Germans.

Boemus, like his competitors, noted many diversities across space but showed little sense of change over time. He told his readers, mixing his metaphors with abandon, that he offered them a "bundle of customs, ancient and modern, bad and good, so that they could see as in a mirror all the examples" that might help them organize their own lives. But like Herodotus, Boemus taught few clear moral lessons. In fact he tried to weave together several largely inconsistent plots. One was a narrowly focused account, derived from the Bible and the fakes of Annius of Viterbo, of the descent of all men from the patriarchs. The other comprised a much wilder series of speculations, derived from Diodorus Siculus, about how the sun had generated men and animals from the primeval ooze. On the one hand Boemus told the story of how the human race had moved from the Golden Age of its earliest history, in which people lived under trees and had no desire for possessions, to modern civilization. On the other, he praised the great legislators of the East, the Brahmans and Magi and Gymnosophists and Egyptian priests, who had taught civilization to eager if primitive travelers from the West. Two of his plots were progressive, the other two static or episodic. Each made data from well-known sources fit molds of equally high classical authority.

Münster often copied Boemus, moving topic by topic in the same order. Sometimes he mixed up his notes and gave the same material for two different nations. But he also extended Boemus' framework and updated his material. Boemus and Polydore Virgil had written ethnographic world almanacs that could fit comfortably in a rucksack; Münster produced a monstrous encyclopedia that only a desk could hold. Boemus, though clearly inspired by the discoveries, had largely stuck to the areas covered by ancient writers; Münster tried to cover the New World too. But where the data squirmed and writhed, Münster proved no better than Boemus at making them behave. He not only inherited contradictions from his source, but added to them. His survey, at once shapeless and vivid, reproduces not the orderly cosmos of the *Chronicle* but the kaleidescopic variety of facts and images that danced tauntingly around a learned European, like succubi around Faust, when he tried to survey the world in 1550.

Some of Münster's visions, to be sure, took reassuringly solid and objective shapes. He drew up a new map of the world in which the continents had attained sharp definition and recognizable shapes, as though a microscope had suddenly focused on a previously blurry field. Africa appears in the form laid out by Portuguese explorers; North and South America, though roughly outlined, are neither mere islands nor appendages to Asia. Ceylon has shrunk and India has grown. Many of the illustrations—like those of the *Nuremberg Chronicle*—vividly depict real cities in a decipherable perspective, constructing a local geography (or chorography) as modern and empirical as his geography. As the geographers and artists of an earlier generation had created an imaginary Germany on paper out of the social and political chaos of the Holy Roman Empire, so Münster created an imaginary universe on paper, the outlines of which, at least, were not fanciful.

In many cases, however, the shades of old images hovered and gibbered between Münster and the world he wished to describe. Like Schedel and his collaborators, like Boemus, he produced a text riven with contradictions in substance and method. As a cartographer, he fully recognized the independent existence of the Americas: a new continent in the West, not part of the East. As a narrator, he denied it, and perpetuated the original confusion of Columbus and others about the identity of the Americas with the Indies. His descriptions of the explorations did not follow a clear chronological or geographical order (Magellan comes before Vespucci). But they inserted the story of the New Indies within that of the old ones. Like the ancient geographer Strabo, Münster denounced the tellers of tall tales about the monstrous races, Megasthenes and Ctesias; like Strabo, he then repeated their stories at length. Unlike Strabo, however, he illustrated them with fine versions of the traditional images, which would seem perfectly in place in a printed copy of Mandeville, and filled the seas with monstrous species of fish. Sometimes Münster showed himself vividly aware that all cultures and societies, even "primitive" and non-European ones, change over time; sometimes he quoted classical authorities as if, for example, the intricate and stable Indian castes they described had been preserved in amber from the Hellenistic world to his own time, eighteen hundred years later. The book merges a compendium of rigorous and up-to-date information with a panoply of fabulous stories and popular errors. One could produce a similar effect by interleaving the nineteenth-century Baedeker's guides to Europe with a copy of *The Innocents Abroad.*

Münster's whole life had prepared him to survey the known world, place by place and people by people. He had mastered scientific and scholarly techniques and devised his own improvements on them. Both his successes and his disasters reveal something immensely valuable. His book is less a miniature of the idiosyncrasies of a single scholar than a panorama of the night sky of the European mind of his day, populated with a zodiac's worth of fantastic monsters as well as neat constellations accurately plotted and recorded.

As a student at Tübingen early in the sixteenth century Münster confronted the world that the encyclopedias portrayed, with all its contradictions and suggestions. His teacher, Konrad Pellikan, lectured on Gregor Reisch's *Margarita philosophica,* secreting new layers of facts and concepts over the many strata that already made up that tight little pearl of a book. Münster soon began to explore a wider range of texts. Becoming interested in the science and scholarship of the Jews, he learned Hebrew and became one of the great Judaic scholars of the day. As a young scholar at Heidelberg he published what soon became the standard work on the Jewish calendar. He also translated on iconoclastic work by the Jewish scholar Elias Levita, which revealed that the vowel points and punctuation of the Hebrew Bible were not established until long after the text itself was written.

Even more assiduously, however, Münster studied the Earth's surface and man's past. He not only read Ptolemy but painstakingly made his own copies of the maps in the printed editions of 1486 and 1513. He worked with printers, learning how to reproduce drawings with what he considered absolute precision. He corresponded with scholars, begging them for their own new maps and comments on ancient texts. And he himself explored the wild world that still stretched around the urban islands of light and noise in large tracts of western Europe, sometimes wandering for days with nothing but his compass to keep him on the path. He knew the difficulties and delights of geography and history at first hand.

Münster's edition of Ptolemy's *Geography* appeared in 1542. It summed up the work of two generations of scholars, above all in Germany. These men had continued to edit and comment on the text. But they had also added substantially to it in their commentaries; Willibald Pirckheimer, for example, had suggested in his edition of 1525 that one ought to add to Ptolemy's three methods of map projection a fourth that reproduced more closely the effects of stretching a three-dimensional sphere on a two-dimensional surface—a crude version of the projection that Gerhardus Mercator would devise and become famous for fifty years later. Michael Serv-

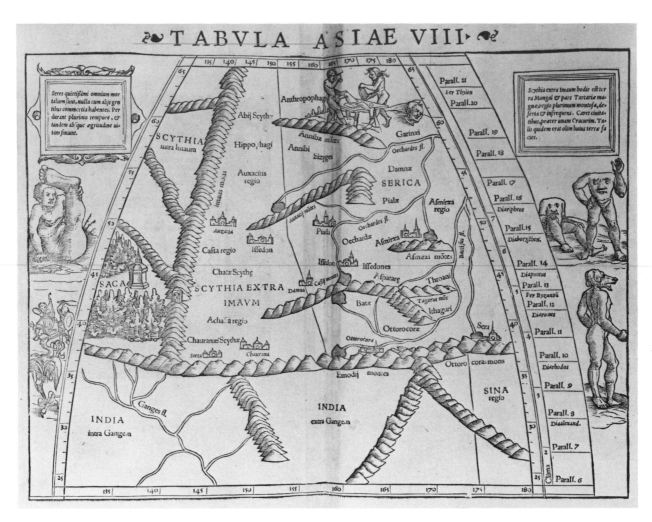

Figure 3.2 A map of Asia from Münster's 1542 Basel edition of Ptolemy's *Geography*. The monstrous races occupy the map's edges; cannibals, who had always according to legend inhabited Scythia, are shown top center.

etus, who would die at the stake as a convicted heretic, showed even more independence in his edition of the text, sometimes a little arbitrarily—as when he turned Columbus from a tall man, the traditional description, to a short one. The second atlas of modern maps that always accompanied editions of Ptolemy grew larger, and its contents more accurate, edition by edition.

Münster warmly acknowledged the work of others—then as now an unusual act of graciousness in a scholar. But he did more. In his preface to this classical text, he insisted that he and his contemporaries had lived through a mental revolution. "In our time and that of our ancestors," he wrote, "everyone believed" that no island could appear in the mass of waters that surrounded the land mass of Europe, Asia, and Africa. Now, "those who try to furrow unexplored oceans" had found islands swarming with inhabitants and riches in the East. Reasonably, then, Münster added more new details and modern maps to the original text than anyone else had. He juxtaposed his version of Ptolemy's world map with a version of the modern map, New World and all, that would start off his *Cosmography* some years later.

For all that Münster added to Ptolemy, however, he continued to take his prime intellectual tools from the *Geography* itself. He knew that Ptolemy's description of the surface of the world was less accurate than his description of the heavens. After all, Ptolemy had stayed in one place, Alexandria; from there he could observe the whole sky, but hardly the whole land mass. But Münster did not simply criticize Ptolemy for his failings. After all, Ptolemy himself had admitted, in the first book of the *Geography*, that the scientist would find it hard to keep up with changes in borders and place-names and newer, more accurate reports of foreign lands. Münster composed elaborate variations on this simple piece of advice, embroidering in good Renaissance style on the mutability of all things:

"Though the earth always remains the same and preserves the same form and layout, and some kingdoms and territories remain as they were, still in the course of time great changes take place in kingdoms, lands, peoples and cities. Kingdoms are destroyed or conquered, new ones rise, many nations can become one, or one nation be cut up into many; deserts become habitable and habitable places are reduced to deserts. Great forests are cut down and become human habitations; great cities are destroyed and others rise." In making use of this insight to emend and supplement Ptolemy's text, Münster saw himself as continuing, not contradicting, his ancient authority.

As he worked on his own *Cosmographia*, Münster's ambitions grew. He collected information systematically, sending what amounted to questionnaires to scholars all over Europe and reworking the results into the grand final structure of his book. One of these survives; addressed to a Swedish scholar, it asks him to list the rulers of Sweden, define its boundaries, assess the royal revenues, and describe the local monsters—of whom, Münster had heard, there were quite a few. As this sample of his method suggests, Münster simply went on working in a classical mode. His text, for all its new detail, grew along the lines that Herodotus and Strabo had laid down long before. He himself labored with undiluted zeal to tie more nations to the family trees that the Bible and Annius of Viterbo had laid out.

New information did not modify or cancel the old, but piled up alongside it like fresh coal beside clinkers. New facts about the world—such as the existence of western continents—did not modify the old structure, which put the wild things Columbus had found where they had always been, in the East. And clear evidence that the world had changed radically with time did not modify the timeless analytic structure of most of what Münster had to say about unfamiliar peoples. They hung suspended in a world without devel-

Figure 3.3   In Münster's *Cosmographia* (Basel, 1550), clothed and armored Europeans make contact with the comely classically modeled naked savages of the New World. A conventional image rather than a realistic depiction, this illustration appeared in other texts in other contexts—for example, as representing the African *ichthyophagi* in Conrad Lycosthenes' providential world history (1557).

opment, even if occasionally one of them took land from another, or moved from timeless primitivism to civil order founded by a great king.

The classical templates, in short, served Münster fairly well. They enabled him to create a coherent survey of the world (even if his concentration on Germany led the French historian Jean Bodin to complain that he had written a *Germanographia* rather than a *Cosmographia*). They empowered him to describe the world visually in a surprisingly objective way. Like Ptolemy's map of the world, on which it was based, Münster's made no effort to assert European superiority or power by its ordering of the data. The center of the map lay not in Christian territory but near Mecca; Europe still appeared as a spit of land to the west of Asia, and was how dwarfed by Africa as well. But the conventions also imprisoned him. He could portray the inhabitants of the New World only as naked

Cannibalism

EUROPEANS had always known that cannibals and other monstrous races inhabited the fringes of the known and *ipso facto* civilized world. Pliny had written of them in his authoritative *Historia naturalis*, and Sebastian Münster and other cartographers obliged their contemporaries' curiosity by indicating exactly where they might be found—Scythia, Ethiopia, or the New World. European publishers, illustrators, writers of firsthand accounts, and compilers of compendiums made cannibalistic images virtually emblematic of America. Three widely translated and reprinted accounts were enormously influential in shaping Europeans' perceptions of a cannibalistic New World, and all three record encounters with one South American tribe, the Tupinambas.

Hans Staden's *True History of His Captivity* was first published in German in 1557. The account contains much ethnographic detail, including a complete and horrifying account of the cannibalistic acts he witnessed. But Staden's primary goal is to tell a traditional Christian moralizing tale both to edify and to inspire devotion.

The illustrations in Staden's account are as important as its text. When Theodore de Bry prepared the engravings for his republication of Staden's and Jean de Léry's accounts, he used the same crude woodblock prints that appeared in Staden's first edition as a starting point for his much more elaborate versions. Bry's masterly reworking of these materials heightens the horrors of scenes in which Staden himself appears, often in an attitude of prayer, and Bry merely repeated the appropriate Staden engraving when de Léry wrote of similar occurrences.

Jean de Léry was no less devout than Staden. Indeed, he came to America to join the ill-starred colony that its leader Nicholas de Villegagnon, a knight of Malta, envisioned as a sort of New World Geneva. But Léry was better educated, as his many references to classical authors testify; and, though he was no less horrified by the Tupinambas' cannibalistic rites and deplored their godless state, he clearly liked them as people. (Significantly, his account lacks chilling illustrations of cannibalism.) The Tupinambas' liberality and general benignity (when not eating enemies) offered a marked contrast to the contentious doctrinal disputes within the colony and to Villegagnon's increasingly cruel and arbitrary behavior.

The third account, *Les singularités de la France antarctique*, was by André Thevet. His account of the Brazilian cannibals is only one part of a work that covers many areas of the New World, the whole of which would be reprinted in his later influential compendium *La cosmographie*. In one terrifying illustration a cannibal appears wielding an Old World implement, the hatchet, to accomplish his gruesome butchery.

Some Europeans could look beyond the horror in order to explain, if not sanction, the custom. The essayist Michel de Montaigne, much influenced by New World literature, writes in "On Cannibals" that he finds much admirable in these so-called primitive societies that live according to natural rather than European law. His conclusions could sting, as when he writes after his résumé of a cannibal feast:

"I am not sorry that we notice the barbarous horror of such acts, but I am heartily sorry that, judging their faults rightly, we should be so blind to our own. I think there is more barbarity in eating a man alive than in eating him dead [through the practice of usury]; and in tearing by tortures and the rack a body still full of feeling, in roasting a man bit by bit, in having him bitten and mangled by dogs and swine (as we have not only read but seen within fresh memory, not among ancient enemies, but among neighbors and fellow citizens, and what is worse, on the pretext of piety and religion), than in roasting and eating him after he is dead."

Sources: Staden 1557b; Léry 1927; Montaigne 1943; Las Casas 1974; Scaglione 1976; White 1976; Arens 1979; Friedman 1981; Bry 1987.

Figure 3.4 The title page of volumes 3 and 4 of Theodore de Bry's *America* (1592) demonstrates that cannibalism had become virtually emblematic of the New World.

Figure 3.5 These two versions of alleged cannibals taunting their victim give insight into how Theodore de Bry (*America*, 1592) reworked the original crude woodblocks of Hans Staden's *True History of His Captivity* among the cannibals into highly polished and powerful images in accordance with European aesthetic standards. The smaller image is taken from Staden's *Wahrhaftig Historia und Beschreibung eyner Landtschafft der Wilden Nacketen Grimmigen Menschenfresser Leuthen in der Newenwelt America gelegen* (Marburg, 1557).

Europeans, their naughty bits aesthetically concealed by draped cloths, or as cannibals energetically sawing another human into loin chops. He could imagine strange races only in terms of the ancient oppositions between gentleness, nudity, and the Golden Age and savagery, monstrosity, and murder. Münster could neither create a sound new vessel nor dam the stream of information that threatened to overwhelm him. Instead he varnished the surface of the old one, energetically plugged its leaks, and ignored the water that still poured in. [1]

Ancient Authorities and Modern Questions

Münster's predicament—however quaint it now appears—was not unusual. In fact he shared the mental space he inhabited with figures who now bulk far larger in our imaginary maps of the sixteenth century: for example, Nicolaus Copernicus and Andreas Vesalius. In 1543, between the appearance of Münster's edition of Ptolemy (1542) and the first German-language edition of his *Cosmographia* (1544), these men published the two most famous and influential scientific works of the sixteenth century: *De revolutionibus orbium coelestium* (On the Revolutions of the Celestial Spheres) and *De humani corporis fabrica* (On the Structure of the Human Body). Each book implicitly challenged basic tenets of the old, tight world picture.

Copernicus moved the sun to the former position of the Earth, in the center of the universe; he made the Earth itself both rotate on its axis every day and revolve about the sun once a year; and he reduced what had always been the unique abode of man, the habitation of change, history, the elements, sin, and grace, to one celestial object among many. The astrology and cosmology of Ptolemy and the physics of Aristotle would have to be rebuilt from their foundations if he was right.

Vesalius retraced the anatomical investigations that the greatest of ancient medical authorities, Galen, claimed to have carried out. He dissected human bodies systematically instead of checking the texts randomly against occasional empirical evidence, as most earlier anatomists had. He drew on the work of artists—who had pioneered in dissection—using pictures as well as words to record his finds so vividly that no one could refute them, though some tried. And he admitted that his work had revealed many problems in Galen's individual statements and his system as a whole. For example, he found himself unable to discover, however hard he probed, the pores

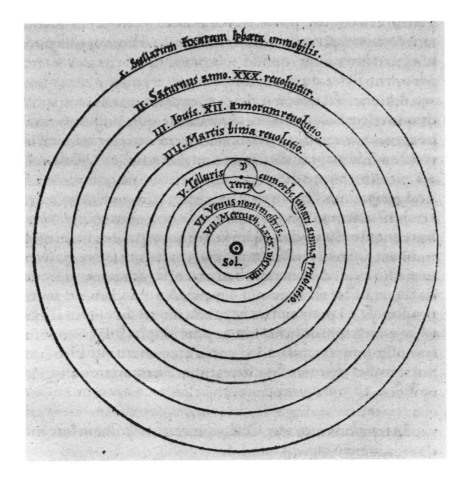

Figure 3.6   In *De revolutionibus orbium coelestium* (Nuremberg, 1543), Copernicus combines tradition and innovation. The sun, not the Earth, stands at the center of his model of the solar system; but the remaining planets, including the Earth, still ride on transparent crystalline spheres as in the ancient Aristotelian model.

in the septum or thick central membrane of the heart that, according to Galen, allowed blood to pass from auricles to ventricles. Vesalius insisted in his first edition that they must exist, because he felt unable to make mere empirical evidence refute his prime authority on so central a point (though he criticized him sharply enough on many others). Eventually he came to admit that Galen was simply wrong.

Figure 3.7   In this representation of a new ideal of scientific inquiry on the title page of *De humani corporis fabrica libri vii* (Basel, 1555) Andreas Vesalius poses beside the gaping body cavity of a cadaver as a fascinated crowd looks on. Vesalius' discoveries lent credibility to the belief that continual and systematic dissection should be the foundation of medical science, rather than texts only sporadically confirmed by empirical observation. Scythe-bearing death is proof, however, that belief in the morally edifying function of all scientific endeavor remained.

This simultaneous attack on great authorities seems exciting, even radical, and historians used to portray it in that light. After thirteen hundred years of tyrannical power, the great statues tumbled to lie in ruins like that of Ozymandias, in monitory fragments indicating that time destroyed intellectual as well as political power. In fact, however, Copernicus and Vesalius were no intellectual radicals, any more than Münster. Both used classical precedents as well as modern evidence to support their iconoclastic enterprises. Copernicus knew of Hicetas and Heraclides of Pontus, who had already believed the universe to be heliocentric. Vesalius saw himself not as attacking but as reviving true Galenic medicine, based on dissection, in place of what he saw as the false Galenic medicine of the schools, based only on corrupt texts.

More important still, both Copernicus and Vesalius used classical concepts and models throughout their work. Copernicus still imagined the planets as embedded in the rims of solid crystalline spheres that carried them through the heavens. His model of the planetary system was as conservative in this respect as it was radical in its placement of the sun. Moreover, his tables and their underlying geometrical models reproduced Ptolemy's, detail for detail; so did the larger structure of his book. Vesalius, too, committed himself as ardently to traditional concepts as to new empirical data. Like his ancient predecessor, he understood the shapes of human bones and organs teleologically, assuming that each one was formed to carry out unique functions which could be inferred from its design and constitution. Both Copernicus and Vesalius expected that their innovations could coexist with—and even rest on—the very structures we now see them as attacking.

Many readers agreed. George Agricola, scholar and engineer, spoke for much of the learned public when he expressed his surprise in 1543 that Vesalius could have found something new to say about anatomy, after Galen had worked so hard in the field. He hoped that Vesalius was not trying "to sell the discoveries of others as his own." But he also hoped that Vesalius' claims would prove justified. For, as he explained, "I would really like men to exist in our time who can add something to the discoveries of the ancients." Tradition and innovation, modernity and reverence for the antique seemed compatible.

Münster's revision of geography, with its combination of tradition and iconoclasm, its necessary reliance on intellectual traditions and zealous but intermittent efforts to come to terms with problematic data, fits naturally into the scientific world of the first half of the sixteenth century. Throughout Europe, in fact, the same pattern of partial challenge and partly conscious traditionalism appears. The iconoclastic physician Theophrastus Paracelsus denounced the medical authorities of his day, men and texts alike; he actually burned the *Canon* of Avicenna, the standard medical textbook of the universities. But he tried to replace it with a recognizably Neoplatonic vision of the cosmos, one derived from ancient ideas about the influences that ran through the physical world, connecting beings and objects that resembled one another. The prominent and theatrical astrologer Girolamo Cardano, who embarrassingly predicted a long life for Edward VI of England and did important work in algebra, tried to revise traditional cosmology. He insisted that the moon and planets must have qualities of heat and warmth, dryness and wetness, like the Earth, and held that comets moved not in the atmosphere, where Aristotle had put them, in the realm of change, but in the supposedly changeless heavens. But he also maintained the whole panoply of traditional practices that made up horoscopic astrology, used the movements of the heavens to explain the great events of human history, and believed in a vast range of ancient stories of omens, prophetic dreams, and magical recipes. Even the botanists who began to revolutionize their science in this same decade by inserting multiple illustrations of plants drawn from life into their texts, replacing the conventional illustrations of the manuscript herbal, sometimes complained that their publishers had gone overboard, substituting fancy pictures for learned quotations from the classics. Meanwhile less original—but more representative—scientists, the professors in university faculties of arts and medicine, often introduced isolated but genuinely new ideas into their comments on standby texts like Avicenna's *Canon*. A raft of cosmographers like Münster—for example, the brilliant and prolific Frenchman André Thevet—described a new world in which traditional myths about gods and men constantly interfered and interacted with observations.[2]

Ancient science, though evidently unstable, remained fruitful. It still offered the only moorings to which one could affix new facts and ideas; it still provided the only structures of argument and inference that seemed valid; yet it was obviously, as Münster had said of Ptolemy, the work of fallible men. How was one to proceed? Should one retrofit traditional systems of ideas to match the new facts about the world? or bend the New World to the old systems? or try to devise radically new patterns of thought and expectation? At the midcentury no one could be sure.

Many intellectuals tried desperately to impose any form of control on the blizzard of paper that flew at them, rather like the cards that fell on Alice at the end of her adventures in Wonderland. Consider a characteristic reading device of the mid-sixteenth century—the book wheel. This massive and splendid construction enabled its owner to sit still while moving within his library. The reader could spin from text to text, compare authority with authority, seek rapidly for truth in the bedlam of competing voices, while still remaining in the calm posture appropriate to scholarly contemplation. A won-

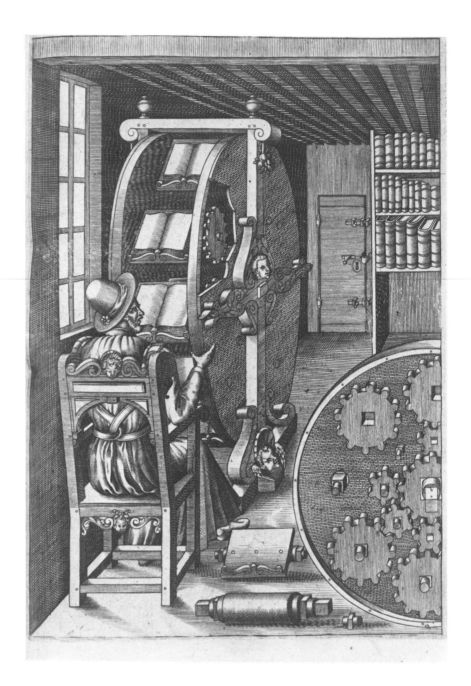

Figure 3.8 The book wheel, from Agustino Ramelli's *Le diverse et artificiose machine* (Paris, 1558).

derful machine for rapid information retrieval, the book wheel facilitated comparison and contrast, collation and note-taking. Some readers accelerated the process, adding a barber's chair to the wheel so they could whirl from book to desk or shelf and back again. Others tried to facilitate mastery of the world of letters with indexes and other written tools—like the vast bibliography produced by Conrad Gesner and abridged by Josias Simler, which ranked all authors, ancient and modern, in one alphabetical series, listing and ordering their works. But naturally none of these devices, the physical or the literary, could do more than open an entrance into the maze of history and mystery, myth and science. The reader had no Ariadne thread to bring him out at the other end, and was likely to find that his library and his reference guides did not enable him to achieve clarity and order. Rather, they enabled him only to pile up—as Gesner himself did in his spectacularly learned work on natural history—still more inchoate heaps of contradictory experiences and quotations, texts and testimonies. The books could be whirled about; but no amount of physical or mental force seemed sufficient to establish them in stable, permanent new orbits.

Perhaps the most rational response would have been withdrawal. In the 1560s two ancient schools of thought that had had relatively few expositors in the earlier Renaissance, Skepticism and Stoicism, became more and more prominent. Their ancient sources found printed editions, translations, commentaries; their tenets gained adherents. The Skeptics knew what to make of contradiction: it proved the partial or entire fallibility of human knowledge (depending on which school of Skepticism one adhered to) and licensed the wise man to stay home and cultivate his garden. The Stoics, by contrast, knew that in a complex and confusing world, an underlying providential order guaranteed a good outcome. Before that happy moment came, the truly wise man must remain calm and do good. Both schools seemed to many intellectuals to offer codes of conduct at once more sensible and more humane than either the rigid philosophies of the schools or the absolutist theologies of the religious denominations. The great essayist Michel de Montaigne tried on both of them for size and found rewards in each. Yet neither—as he also found—could possibly give guidance through the whole range of aporias that confronted a literate and thoughtful man in his time; and neither was completely reconcilable with Christianity. Europe's intellectual life seemed to spin into confusion and decay.[3]

The Crisis and Its Causes

Yet even while Montaigne struggled in provincial seclusion with these questions, other European intellectuals found powerful new answers. The centers of innovation ranged from Tycho Brahe's observatory in Denmark to the cartographers' shops of Antwerp and the university of Padua. But nowhere did intellectuals argue more heatedly or change their fashions of thought more rapidly than in France, where religious strife made the devising of new theories a matter of more than theoretical importance. From the early 1550s, Huguenots and Catholics confronted one another throughout the kingdom, more and more belligerently. The death of Henri II in 1559 left the throne in the hands of his immature and not very competent sons. Their mother, Catherine de Médicis, had neither the power nor the influence to make peace, and great Catholic and Protestant nobles gathered their retainers into private armies, while mobs clashed in the cities. Efforts to make peace collapsed, and in the 1560s religious war of unheard-of brutality broke out. As often happens, severe political crisis spawned intellectual activity of great depth and import.

French intellectuals, then as now alert, dogmatic, and attuned to social and political change, tried to find remedies for what seemed a threat of the total dissolution of the French state. They hoped that history—and above all the history of the laws of all European and non-European states and societies—could provide the knowledge they needed. France required a constitution suited to its historical tradition, its people, its place in the universe. But France had no single constitution; its legal system was a double one: some areas accepted the written *Corpus iuris*, the law of ancient Rome taught in the legal faculties; others used local customary laws, codified (if at all) in the vernacular. Some of the basic laws of the realm, moreover—like those that defined the rules of succession, excluding women from the throne—had no stable written form. Everyone who hoped to restore the realm to unity and peace had to become something of an ethnographer. And as the cosmographies and histories multiplied, the number of possibly relevant cases expanded exponentially. Perhaps the Incas or the Chinese—who might not be Christians, but certainly ruled their citizens with less difficulty than the Christian French—might have something that the West could borrow. In the 1560s, French jurists like François Baudouin and Jean Bodin published manifestos that codified, not solutions to the French crisis, but historical and comparative methods for seeking such solutions.

Baudouin and Bodin agreed that all humankind was one, and that the experience of any age and any people might offer an example usable in any circumstances. They also agreed that the student of laws and institutions must be a universal historian as well as a jurist— a new sort of scholar, one who combined the humanist's interest in history and context with the Roman lawyer's desire to draw up universally valid codes. He must study the histories of all nations, times, and places. He must use critical methods to determine which accounts deserved credence. And he must then sift the accounts he accepted for useful information. Elaborate, systematic notebooks would contain vital extracts from the sources, with marginal notes assessing their value. Careful comparative study would determine which examples might be relevant in which nations. For, Bodin held, each nation had a basic character, determined by its original geographical location; Asians were intelligent but also irremediably prone to despotism, while northerners were violent and the men of middle areas were prudent—and thus adept at governance. Etymology—the careful study of the roots of each nation's language—could identify the place of origin, and once the lawyer-historian had established this he could readily explain why a given people had come to have the institutions it did—and determine whether these were relevant to his own society.

Bodin's etymologies often came from dubious sources. When he explained that Janus, who settled Italy, was named as he was in Hebrew because he was "full of wine" (Hebrew *yayin*), he drew on the omnipresent forger Annius. When he connected the characters of each nation to their original habitats and climates, he drew on a traditional taxonomy of stereotypes elaborated by the Hippocratic doctors and astrologers of the ancient world and the Middle Ages. Both he and his many, many imitators tended less to derive new insights about foreign races than to confirm with the apparent authority of a new historical science the traditional canards that Englishmen overate, Irishmen lied, and Frenchmen bragged. Old wine like this could hardly inspire its consumers to build a new Europe.

For all its traditional components, however, Bodin's *Method* and the works that accompanied and were inspired by it did advance some powerful and influential theses, less about the particular problems of the French state than about the nature of history itself. Bodin, in the course of his research, found himself compelled to confront the vast array of data he commanded with the traditional schemes that put order into world history. He examined the theory—inherited from the book of Daniel—that four empires, Assyrian, Persian, Greek, and Roman, would rule the world in succession until the end came. Daniel had embodied this schema in the powerful form of a vision: a statue with a head of gold, a breast of silver, a belly of brass, legs of iron, and feet of clay represented the monarchies, and a great stone that smashed it played the part of the End. In the frightening time of the Reformation, when all ground seemed to shift, this impressive image had naturally captured the imaginations of historians. Bodin also scrutinized the vision—inherited from Greek and Roman poets—that early man had lived in a Golden Age without property and violence, and that the goddess of justice, Astraea, had not left the world until the arrival of civilization and all its discontents. And he found that neither scheme could possibly do justice to the facts.

Anyone with Bodin's comprehensive knowledge of the world could identify many empires larger than the four mentioned by Daniel and his readers. The vast empire of the medieval Arabs found no clear position in Daniel's statue. The Turkish empire of his own time, also ignored by Daniel, covered far from territory than the Roman empire of the Germans—if indeed that was still the original Roman empire, which Bodin heartily doubted. Anyone who looked systematically at the earliest times could see that these had been not a Golden but an Iron Age. Nimrod, the founder of the first monarchy, was a robber. So were those impious rebels against God whose true story, that of the Tower of Babel, appeared in the Bible, while a mythical retelling of it made up the Greek myth of the revolt of the Titans. So, finally, was that lustful pirate Hercules. Bodin replaced the poets' dreamy vision of peaceful shepherds piping in the fields with a capriccio worthy of Goya: "These were the golden and the silver ages, in which men were scattered like beasts in the fields and the woods and had as much as they could keep by means of force and crime."

Careful study of ancient society revealed how primitive the supposed sages had really been, Bodin reflected. They had treated theft, for example, as a mere civil crime instead of punishing it with death as the more sophisticated moderns did. Careful reading of modern history and travel literature proved that the moderns had far outdone the ancients in material and scientific culture alike. The discovery of the compass had enabled Europeans to break out of their isolation. Whereas the ancients had lived within the Mediterranean basin, the moderns "traverse the whole earth every year in frequent voyages," and by doing so they had both revolutionized the scientific study of geography and transformed the human race itself into a single vast city-state linked by commercial relations. Even those—like Louis Le Roy—who considered the ancient world far more powerful and idyllic than Bodin did agreed with him about the superior knowledge and prowess of modern scientists and explorers.[4]

These views soon found echoes outside France. In Antwerp, for example, Mercator bluntly declared that Ptolemy was out of date. Editing his *Geography* was still worthwhile, but it was a historical, not a scientific, task, and required the scholar not to add to the substance of the book in the light of modern discoveries but to correct its text in the light of what Ptolemy himself could have known in the second century. The presentation of modern knowledge about the lands and peoples of the world must be left to new works in a new form—like the atlases in which Mercator and his friend Ortelius departed from all classical precedent to lay out a panorama of modern discoveries, area by area. Mercator's projection—which combined the mathematically derived projections of

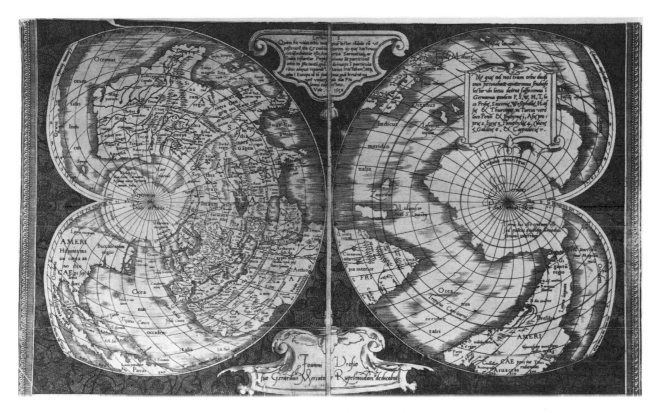

Figure 3.9 Gerhardus Mercator's cordiform map of the world, the *Orbis imago* (Louvain, 1538), applies a new method of projection. Mercator explicitly describes the map both as "later and more correct than the ones previously in circulation" and as an effort intended to supersede rather than amend the Ptolemaic world map. He makes the Americas separate continents but, like the makers of Ptolemaic maps, explicitly labels areas such as the northwest coast of North America and Antarctica "terra incognita."

Ptolemy with the precise directions for straight sailing routes of the *portolans*—outdid the greatest ancient authority at his greatest skill. By the 1570s some learned men saw themselves as living in a genuinely new world—one in which old certainties had vanished, old areas of ignorance had been replaced with knowledge, and the disappearance of all the old fixed schemes licensed a certain confidence in the possibility of progress.

In the realms of history and cosmography, then, not that of science, ancient wisdom first came to seem outmoded. The discovery of the non-European world and the discovery that the ancients were not wiser than the moderns seem indissolubly linked. Only the brute fact of the discoveries inspired Bodin and his contemporaries with their confidence in modern achievement and their condescension toward ancient ignorance. It seems only reasonable to infer, as many scholars have, that the content, as well as the format, of Bodin's new vision of the past also derived from the confrontation with new worlds outside the Mediterranean. Surely the discovery of real savages in a real wilderness inspired the drama and pathos of his vision of ancient Europeans living a savage life—a vision soon to be given concrete embodiment by the artist John White, who would use images of Virginia Indians as the models for his depiction of the ancient Picts and Britons.[5]

In fact Bodin was reticent about the New World. Although his own ten-page effort to put order into the literature of historical study lists Francisco López de Gómara and Vespucci, Francisco Alvarez and Alvise da Ca da Mosto, he says little about the Indian kingdoms in the body of his work and draws few inferences from New World data. Did Bodin's reading of new texts about new races reshape his vision of old Europe as well? In a larger sense, how far did the effort to describe and explain new realities contribute to the overthrow of classical authority?

Figure 3.10   Ortelius' map of the Americas in his *Theatrum orbis terrarum* (Antwerp, 1570) shows them clearly as separate and only partially explored continents.

Theodore de Bry

THEODORE DE BRY, a Protestant refugee from Liège who settled in Strasbourg, began publishing his *America*, a multivolume compilation of previously published New World accounts, in 1590. After his death in 1598 his sons published volumes seven through twelve; and Mattieu Merian, his son-in-law, published the thirteenth and final volume in 1634. From the beginning, the work was aimed at an international readership: the first volume was printed in four languages, the others in German and Latin, still the lingua franca as the vernacular languages slowly came of literary age.

The *America* is famous for the artistry of de Bry's engravings. They are also a superb melding of text and image that, for many European readers, no doubt came to define the New World. Yet de Bry himself never set foot in the New World; like other illustrators, he reworked or recombined older illustrative materials. Second, his choice of the accounts illustrated was guided by a clear editorial program. That program was shaped by the struggles between Catholic and Protestant that plunged Germany, then France into brutal wars, touched off the Dutch Revolt (which prompted Bry's own flight), and lit the fires that consumed heretics in small German towns and Marian England alike.

When de Bry looked at the New World, he projected onto it his theology and his politics. The engravings of Adam and Eve in the first volume and of Noah and the Ark in the second are integral to his vision of a New World whose peoples, however admirable, were irredeemably lost because they lived outside Christianity. Given de Bry's point of view, it is no surprise that idolatry and cannibalism figure so prominently on his title pages.

His political agenda pitted the Protestant nations of Europe against the sixteenth-century superpower and defender of Catholic orthodoxy, Spain. One modern scholar has called the de Bry illustrations a *machine de guerre* in the confessional struggles dividing Europe. True, he did not create the Black Legend, according to which the Spanish were hypocrites, acting out of avarice rather than religious zeal. Accounts such as that of Bartholomé de Las Casas, widely translated, abridged, and gruesomely if primitively illustrated, had come before. His illustrations for Girolamo Benzoni's account of Spanish actions in the New World linger over scenes of brutality and duplicity, scenes that must have resonated especially powerfully in the minds of European Protestants keenly aware of Spanish atrocities in the Netherlands. Thus when de Bry exalts the Genoese Columbus in his introduction to Benzoni's work, he does so at the expense of the Spaniards who followed him.

Although he was motivated by contemporary political and religious concerns, de Bry also gives evidence of a growing intellectual trend when he appends several portraits of the Picts, inhabitants of ancient Britain, to the account of the settlement of Virginia. Universal decline, whether dated in the classical world from a Golden Age or in the Christian from the fall of Adam and the expulsion from Paradise, had been the leitmotif of Western visions of history. The tendency of Europeans to equate the alleged barbarism of the American populations they encountered with the cultural life of their own ancestors would eventually lead some people to believe that human societies, rather than inevitably deteriorating, progressed through increasingly sophisticated stages of civilization.

Sources: Bucket 1977; Bry 1987.

Figure 3.11 Theodore de Bry's depiction of a female warrior of the ancient Picts in the first volume of his *America* (Frankfurt, 1590) attests the growing interest in comparative study of cultures. In his introduction, de Bry writes that he was directed to append these illustrations based on "a certain old English history" to those of the Virginians "to demonstrate that the inhabitants of Britain had been no less forest dwellers than these Virginians."

Figure 3.12　In his republication of Thomas Hariot's account of the English colony of Virginia in the first volume of *America* (Frankfurt, 1590), Theodore de Bry based his illustrations on the watercolors of John White. This example cleverly combines ethnographic detail about the native Virginians' way of life with details of New World flora and fauna, and attempts to provide detailed and accurate images of non-European life.

Fielding the New World

The intellectuals of the Hispanic world were of course the first ones to confront the necessity of describing and explaining new societies, flora, and fauna. But their problem was not simply an intellectual one. In the first fifty years of the discoveries, the Spanish conquered the two great empires of the Aztecs and the Incas. They overthrew the great temples, prohibiting the public exercise of the traditional religions and, above all, the Aztecs' massive human sacrifices. And they carried out a massive human sacrifice of their own, deliberately killing and subjugating native peoples and inadvertently using the microbes they carried to depopulate the new lands. Thousands of native Americans suffered and died laboring for the Spanish colonists—and some native lords—on the *encomiendas* that grew up in the Caribbean and New Spain.

From the first, church and government worried about the vast human cost of the new system and tried to regulate it. The *encomenderos* were equally intent on maintaining it. The government of Charles V repeatedly sought to control and modify the colonial system, both to ensure that the native peoples had an opportunity for conversion and in order to maintain an orderly flow of tax monies. The Roman church insisted on the humanity of the Indians, and large numbers of missionaries—especially idealistic mendicant friars bent on bringing what they saw as the simple, incorrupt peoples of the New World to Christ—arrived. They built churches and religious communities. At Tlatelolco they founded a college for the education of a native clergy, where young Aztecs learned to write Latin letters apologizing for the barbarity of their script and syntax. The mendicants for their part learned Nahuatl and other native languages and translated into them both the basic documents of the Catholic faith and manuals for hearing confession. Confrontations—between

Figure 3.13 This illustration from André Thevet's *Les singularitez de la France Antartique* (Paris, 1557) shows how easily legendary races could go on living beside the New World peoples that the Europeans actually encountered. In his text Thevet dismissed the notion that the Spaniards did not find a land inhabited by Amazons; the illustration shows them tormenting two captives.

Figure 3.14 This scene of a New World battle from the influential *Cosmographie universelle d'André Thevet* (Paris, 1575) illustrates a chapter in which Thevet writes, conflating all native peoples, that Americans have particularly bellicose natures. Unlike "other nations, even . . . the most cruel or barbarous, such as the Turks, Moors, and Arabs," they never make peace.

colonial rulers and European authorities, between colonists and missionaries, between mendicant orders, between missionaries and Indians—were inevitable. In this unpredicted situation, books still provided guidance to all parties to an astonishing extent.

Bartolomé de Las Casas, for example, is rightly remembered as a heroic defender of the Indians against a level of violence to which, perhaps, no population in history had previously been exposed. His vivid pamphlets argued from what he himself had seen that "Satan could not have invented any more effective pestilence with which to destroy the whole new world" than the system of *encomiendas*. He thus created the view that Spanish rule had brought destruction, not religion, to the New World. A pious Catholic, Las Casas gave Prot-

Figure 3.15 This illustration of a New World atrocity committed by the Spanish is from Bartolomé de Las Casas' *Narratio regionum indicarum* (Oppenheim, 1614), which, translated into many European languages, did much to create the Spanish Black Legend.

estant propagandists ample armament to create the sixteenth-century Black Legend of Spanish cruelty.

It is less well known that, as Antony Pagden has shown, both Las Casas and his opponents were above all men of the book. Like Luther—who drew his new theology and personal vocation from a single verse of Romans—Las Casas became the advocate of the Indians as a result of reading the Bible to prepare an Easter sermon. A text in Ecclesiasticus, "The bread of the needy is their life. He that defraudeth him thereof is a man of blood," transformed him from *encomiendero* to interpreter and opponent of the *encomienda* system. And the conclusions he drew struck many of his contemporaries as so powerful that they required a response.[6]

Las Casas' objections to colonial practices prompted the university-trained intellectuals in the Spanish government to convoke in Valladolid a formal debate on the colonial enterprise. The colonists chose a professional scholar as an advocate for ther position: Juan Ginés de Sepúlveda, a humanist who had studied and worked in Italy and counted among his friends the most brilliant scholars of High Renaissance Rome. A student of Aristotle, Sepúlveda found in the *Politics*—as interpreted by the Paris scholastic John Major—exactly the text the colonists needed: a declaration that some races were barbarous, as their feeble minds, inadequate bodies, and primitive culture showed. Aristotle explained that war against such men, "who, having been born to obey, reject servitude," is "just by nature." Divine law ("It is written in the book of Proverbs that he who is a fool should serve the wise") and human philosophy concurred: Indians should be slaves to Spanish Christians.

Las Casas cast his reply in the same classical key but in a profoundly different tradition. He drew both on the scholastic culture that flourished in the Spanish universities and on the wide range of Greek texts that had recently been translated into Latin by the humanists. Admittedly, Aristotle was "the philosopher," and he had classified some men as barbarians. But as the great Aristotelian Francisco Vitoria had shown, all barbarians were not the same: the wild and stateless men that Aristotle condemned to natural slavery were not barbarians in the same sense as those who lacked Christianity, but clearly possessed governments, cities, roads, and the other appurtenances of civil life. "Not all barbarians," then, "are either lacking in reason or slaves by nature." Moreover, the very Greek writers who have invented the term *barbarian* showed that its application was broader—and its legal implications less powerful—than a reader of Aristotle might suspect. Strabo admitted that the term originally referred to foreigners who mispronounced Greek, making noises like "bar, bar"; in that sense, Las Casas pointed out, "there is no nation which is not considered barbarian by some other . . . Just as we consider those peoples of the Indies barbarians, so they, since they do not understand us, also consider us barbarians and strangers." The facts of colonial rule, finally, suggested something even worse: that the Spanish, in their brutality, might be the real barbarians, especially when compared with the rational, charitable, sophisticated Aztec and Inca rulers whom they had murdered and whose splendid societies they had destroyed.

Classicist and mendicant, professor and preacher often reached for the same bits of evidence. To Sepúlveda, the extreme simplicity and centralization of the Indian states, the absolute power of their rulers, proved that their inhabitants had been not rational men but animals. Their cities resembled beehives, the creations of natural instinct, rather than states consciously designed in the Western way. Las Casas drew opposing morals from the same stories: the Indians' rulers had been more rational and efficient, their subjects more docile and humane, than any Europeans. Classical and medieval templates, deftly wielded, shaped the same facts about foreigners into opposed statements—into the most profound debate waged in modern times within a conquering power about the justice of its own actions.[7]

The elaborate histories of the New World that reached print in the 1550s and afterward also used ancient tools to impose coherence on the splendid horrors of the conquests. When Cortes' associate Gómara needed a literary form for his account of the conquest of New Spain, Herodotus provided exactly what he needed. Like Herodotus, Gómara insisted on the dazzling greatness of the deeds he would record: the great king overthrown, the idols hurled down, the human sacrifices ended. Like Herodotus, he made his account as entertaining as it was dramatic. Fast-moving action scenes and matched, eloquent speeches told a dramatic story of high political actors in crisis. Omens played the part that the oracles of Delphi had in Herodotus: they simultaneously explained the course of events and weakened the resolve of the side that ultimately lost. Detailed accounts of Indian customs, from calendars and divination to harems and human sacrifices, revealed the age, the wealth, the sophistication, and the brutality of Aztec culture, much as they did Herodotus' Egypt. That the analogy was in Gómara's mind is clear from the analogy he drew between Aztec pictorial codices and the Egyptian hieroglyphs which he, like so many Renaissance scholars, saw as the code that embodied a profound, primeval wisdom. The Aztecs were not only "barbarous" because they sacrificed human beings to their gods; they were also kin to the learned barbarians of the ancient Near East. Taken together, narrative and description proved the same double lesson that Herodotus had taught so long ago about Greeks and Persians. The Indians were at once so barbarous as to deserve conquest and so splendid as to endow their Spanish conquerors with unimaginable glory. No wonder that Gómara's brilliant book won the compliments of translation into other languages, plagiarism, and even inversion, as French Huguenots turned his story of Catholic courage and chivalry into one of Spanish barbarism against innocent, if hardly noble, savages.

Even those who thought themselves most deeply committed to an accurate portrayal of the Indians and their discoverers shaped their data to the authoritative lasts they found in print. The identity and effects of these models, indeed, come as some of the greatest surprises in the constantly surprising history of Renaissance culture. Consider Las Casas' greatest enterprise, unpublished in his day and almost unreadable in ours: the sprawling *History of the Indies*, in which he told the story of the first three decades of discoveries in grinding detail, sometimes day by day, stopping for excursuses of the most dizzyingly varied natures and subjects. In preparing this vast book Las Casas did exacting and exhaustive archival work. He followed Columbus through the margins of the books the explorer had read in order to root the discoveries in the traditions of ancient science that his hero had known. He followed the voyages day by day through Columbus' log books, which he copied out; his imperfect transcript, preserved in Spain, remains in fact our earliest, sometimes problematic source for the admiral's thoughts and actions during his first voyage. Las Casas incorporated slabs of these primary materials in his book. Most Renaissance historians contented themselves, as Gómara did, with a less exhaustive account of the facts, and carefully transmuted most raw documents into smooth artistic prose. Following the precepts of rhetoric, which treated history as a work of oratory and eloquence, they concentrated on imposing a unified style and structure on their story. Las Casas, by contrast, often let the documents speak for themselves, extracting them at length even though doing so entailed inelegant variations in tone, style, and pace.

Las Casas chose this idiosyncratic presentation deliberately. In his long preface he pointed out that Greek historians, though eloquent and entertaining, had often mingled myths with true stories. Others, fortunately, had rejected their falsehoods. Metasthenes the Persian had gravely pointed out that historians must not simply follow their idiosyncratic opinions, as the Greeks did. Cato the Roman and Josephus the Jew had said much the same. Berosus the Chaldean had argued that "one should not accept all" historians, but only priests, whose annals had a "public and approved authority." Las Casas himself made clear that the honorable, priestly historian could best avoid the Greeks' errors by reserving credence for stories preserved "in the public archives of kings or kingdoms or cities, and by publicly appointed persons." Las Casas, in short, presented himself as a superior sort of historian: not a mere writer of appealing stories but a doer of archival research, whose probity was guaranteed both by his own religious status and by the primary, documentary evidence of his sources. The source of this vision of the historian's craft is not in doubt. Metasthenes, Berosus, and Cato were not real ancient writers but the fakes created by Annius of Viterbo. Annius, as we saw, based his own attack on the authority of the Greek writers on the priestly honesty and archival research of the Near Eastern and Western intellectuals whose texts he wrote and glossed. It seems somehow appropriate—though certainly ironic as well—that modern scholars have sometimes wrongly accused Las Casas of forging parts of his Columbian materials. He did in fact learn from a forger to master and manipulate historical evidence; his most powerful and idiosyncratic ancient models were only fifty years old when he wrote.

Some mendicants, to be sure, plunged much deeper than Las Casas into native customs and beliefs, and produced work still harder to compress within an obviously traditional carapace. Motolinía (Toribio de Benavente), Diego Durán, and Bernardino de Sahagún learned Indian languages, worked for long periods with native informants, and sometimes developed a sneaking sympathy for Indian ethics based on far more evidence than Las Casas had possessed. Like the Inquisitors of the Old World confronted by magicians or *conversos*, they took the Indians as the adherents of a coherent system of beliefs—probably one inspired by the devil, or just possibly one inherited in corrupt form from the ancient Jews. They interrogated those suspected of backsliding from Christianity to paganism. They cursed their own predecessors, who had burned the native codices they could not understand, and hunted for surviving documents in outlying villages. Above all, they used systematic questionnaires, repeated interviews, and other practices proleptically reminiscent of modern fieldwork to understand the society and religion that the conquistadors had torn apart. They came to understand Meso-American religions in a rigorous and technical way; Durán, for example, knew that the Indians of New Spain celebrated certain church feasts with special enthusiasm because these happened to correspond with feasts in their own secretly preserved calendar. He reviled the priests who did not understand such basic facts about the old calendar, though he also despaired of eliminating such survivals. Once he described himself as wearily picking up a feathered staff of his own and marching with the Indians whose Christianity he felt to be so radically different from his own or that of any Spaniard.

These mendicants tried to fill the great intellectual lacuna, to make Indians and Westerners see one another for what they were. So they produced exhaustive compilations—in Sahagún's case codices written in both Spanish and Nahuatl, in other cases texts in Spanish only. These systematic studies, clarified by glosses and illustrations, explained the calendars, the divinatory rituals, the gods and the customs, the rhetoric and the morality of this strange new world. In their density of observation, their firsthand portrayal of a world that seems extraordinarily fresh and alien, their counterpoint of strange images and strange stories, these books seem a far more

St. Thomas: An Apostle in America

"THE men have a bare space on the head with a circle of hair round it like a monk. I asked them frequently from what they took this fashion, and they told me that their forefathers had seen it on a man called Meire Humane, who had worked many miracles among them, and this man is supposed to have been a prophet or one of the Apostles."

The apostle to whom Hans Staden refers in the account of his captivity among the cannibals is St. Thomas. Very early on, visitors to the New World accounted for potentially discomfiting similarities between Christian and Indian religious rites and symbolism by assuming that, in addition to proselytizing in India, St. Thomas had made his way to America. St. Thomas' legendary mission to farflung locales, even to China, had been continuously recounted in the letters of Prester John, Mandeville's *Travels*, and Marco Polo's account, among others. Crosses or sculptures which, so the explorers thought, resembled Christ, the Virgin, or the Trinity were the saint's equivalent of "Kilroy was here." The Spanish even believed they had discovered a statue of the evangelist in Peru.

Yet perhaps no one argued for a pre-Columbian mission to the New World in such a thoroughgoing fashion as the Dominican monk Diego Durán.

Durán was hardly a disinterested observer of Aztec rituals and beliefs; he described them only so that they could be more readily extirpated. He based his belief in the ancient proselytization of America on scriptural authority and on similarities between Aztec and Christian religious customs and sacraments such as the Eucharist, penitence, and the training of monks and nuns. He stopped short of wholly identifying the Aztec Topiltzin with St. Thomas, but his suspicions are obvious:

"The great deeds and wondrous acts of Topiltzin, his heroic acts, are famed among the Indians. These deeds are of such renown and remind one of so much of miracles that I dare not make any statement or write of them. In all I subject myself to the correction of the Holy Catholic Church. But even though I wish to adhere to the Holy Gospel of Saint Mark, who states that God sent the Holy Apostles to all parts of the world to preach the gospel to His creatures, promising eternal life to all baptized believers, I would not dare affirm that Topiltzin was one of the blessed Apostles. Nevertheless, the story of his life has impressed me greatly and has led me and others to believe that, since the natives were also God's creatures, rational and capable of salvation, He cannot have left them without a preacher of the Gospel. And if this is true, that preacher was Topiltzin, who came to this land. According to the story, he was a sculptor who carved admirable images in stone. We read that the glorious apostle Saint Thomas was a master craftsman in the same art. We also know that this apostle was a preacher to the Indians but that, having become discouraged there, he asked Christ (when the Lord appeared to him at a fair) to send him wherever He wished except to the Indians. I am not surprised that the Holy Apostles were reluctant to deal with these natives—rude, inconsistent, rough, and slow in understanding the things of their salvation. They are fickle and inclined to believe in the most fabulous omens without any true basis or facts."

Of course, Durán did not equate Christian with Aztec customs. He makes clear in the chapter on human sacrifice that its rituals are degraded and corrupt vestiges of the true religion. Rather than securing salvation, they ensure only perdition. Yet the similarities also impressed him:

"Let the reader note how cleverly this diabolical rite imitates that of our Holy Church, which orders us to receive the True Body and Blood of our Lord Jesus Christ, True God and True Man, at Eastertide. Furthermore, another thing is remarkable: this first fell on the tenth of April, that is, around Easter, which usually comes at this time . . . either (as I have stated) our Holy Christian Religion is known in this land or the devil, our cursed adversary, forced the Indians to imitate the ceremonies of the Catholic Church religion in his own service and cult, being thus adored and served."

Sources: Durán 1971; Vigneras 1977; Friedman 1981; MacCormack 1984; Staden 1557b.

Figure 3.16 This illustration from Perè Yves d'Evreux, *Suitte de l'histoire des choses plus memorables advenues en Maragnan, és années 1613–1614* (Paris, 1615), purports to represent a trio of Tupinamba dancers in characteristic costume and poses. According to the caption, they were brought to France in 1613 to be baptized and presented to the king of France.

Portraict au naturel des barbares amenez en france du pais de Topinambous . par le S.r de Razilly pour estre baptizez. et conuertiz. a la foy de Jesus Christ et presentez a sa Ma.té en lannee presente 1613 .

P. Firens sculp.

polished mirror of Indian ways than the more formal literary works that actually reached the sixteenth-century public (and that usually drew from the mendicants' manuscripts their most precise details about New World beliefs and customs). Sahagún's vast codices, for example, accumulate and translate vast series of native texts without explicit commentary. They offer a panoramic and apparently direct view of religion and education, thought and feeling in a nonwestern, non-Christian world.

Yet even Sahagún and his fellows were men of the European book, as well as of the dusty, sun-stricken plazas where they sat and discussed the ancient gods with Aztec sages. When Sahagún collected samples of Aztec oratory, he packaged their words in Western shapes and colors. They represented, he explained, the "rhetoric and moral philosophy and theology of the Mexican people"—three concepts which, of course, had no place at all among the assumptions of those whose eloquent and powerful metaphors he recorded (though he sometimes muted them in translation). When Sahagún came across a particularly heinous heresy in an Aztec aphorism, he identified its source or analogue in Western thought without hesitation. "What was done in very old times," the Aztec sages said, "is no longer done, but once again it will be done . . . Those who live now will live, will exist once again." No well-trained Western theologian could fail to recognize under the Meso-American belief in cyclical recurrence Origen's heretical belief in the transmigration of souls, or the dangerous pagan doctrines that lurked behind that: "This proposition," Sahagún allowed himself to comment, "is from Plato, and the devil teaches it, because it is wrong, it is most false, it is against the faith . . . it is most false and most heretical."

Sahagún's enterprise as a whole imposed the Western form of an encyclopedic, canonical text on a culture that had had no such texts and could never have conceived of such an enterprise. The Aztecs had had pictorial codices that recorded their beliefs about the gods, the past, and the future. They had also had schools in which young priests and nobles learned to interpret the codices orally, expounding them at length. This oral tradition of exegesis changed constantly, with the larger society and culture that it served, even if the style and iconography of the images remained more constant.

Sahagún by contrast set out to provide the Aztecs with something analogous to the Western Bible—and not the plain Gideon Bible of our hotel rooms, without commentary, but the traditional Bible of the later Middle Ages and Renaissance, embedded in a structure that explained it. He himself made his intention clear in the preface to his *History of New Spain*, where he explained that his informants had provided him with paintings, an explanation of them which they wrote down, and a *postilla*—that is, a biblical commentary, like Nicholas of Lyra's authoritative *postillae* on the Bible, which he and other mendicants knew intimately. As his research expanded, so did his ambitions, and he superimposed on his subject matter the hierarchical organization of abstract topics characteristic of the late antique and medieval encyclopedias.[8]

Sahagún insisted that his glosses and cosmologies came in the *ipsissima verba* of the trilingual Indian scholars of Tlatelolco; but the very permanence of his record transformed its content. He freeze-dried the multiple, protean ingredients of their cultural tradition, producing a solid and immobile text and commentary, unchanging if readily accessible in form, and as divergent in character from its oral sources as its illustrations—which reflected Western techniques of construction and drawing—differed from those of pre-Conquest codices. The Indian wise man, a creature of the spoken word, was to be transformed into a reader of the single written Word. It was perhaps predictable that this rich and appealing Creole version of Meso-American culture did not long survive the suspicions of Christian authorities and the indifference of native students. The college at Tlatelolco collapsed, the plague struck New Spain, and the authorities found much to deplore in the great mendicant compilations. These were stowed away in libraries, to reach print only in later centuries. The mixed vision of native culture they presented, like Plato's legendary Atlantis, hung mistily between the continents, belonging to neither, and eventually sank from sight. The culture that eventually took shape in New Spain and to its south was a uniquely New World amalgam of native American and European beliefs, customs, and images—one that Durán and Sahagún would have deplored.

It would be as wrong as it is easy to deplore or regret the fact that heroes like Las Casas and Sahagún needed to attach their vast firsthand knowledge to an existing literary framework. From the standpoint of the modern historian of the Great Encounter or Meso-American culture, of course, pure accounts—straight transcripts of Columbian logs and Indian speeches—would be far more valuable than the mediated knowledge their texts offer. But no such texts could in fact have been produced in the early modern world (if indeed they could be produced now). If Las Casas and Sahagún had had no models, they would also—as Las Casas made clear—have had no vocations to carry out, no questions to ask. They trained themselves to see and look and record because they had a vision of the final, orderly, basically traditional texts they hoped to write. Without that goal, they could never have carried out the unique efforts of sifting and preserving for which we are still in their debt.[9]

Back in Europe, naturally, models bulked even larger and alien realities seemed both smaller and more adjustable than they could in a Mexican village square. As political interests intertwined or collided and scholars sought to show that history supported the interests of their competing sponsors, accounts of the origins and nature of the New World changed kaleidoscopically in manifest content. But they always drew their structure and methods of presentation from the pullulating world of textual sources spinning before writers' eyes. English writers under Elizabeth I, for example, proved as adept as Spanish ones at grafting their colonial enterprise into an existing literary tradition. The English myth of empire was connected with the Middle Ages, when peoples had wandered, King Arthur had briefly built a powerful overseas empire, and later kings—or so the legend said—had built great navies. Arthurian literature provided the scripts for the festivals and tournaments with which the Elizabethan court celebrated Accession Day. John Dee and other Elizabethan intellectuals went not to ancient but to medieval sources for their justifications of English empire abroad. Some rooted their support for the justice of the English colonial enterprise in the success of Arthur's overseas campaigns. They even found support for the right of the English to establish colonies in the New World in the decent of the Indians—whom they traced back not to the lost tribes of Jews but to the Welsh, who had stepped westward in the time of Madoc, and whose descendants now peopled the wilderness across the seas.[10]

Paradox rears its attractive head. By the middle of the century many European intellectuals knew they could not provide the sort of authoritative guidance to the past and present that Reisch or Schedel had been able to offer two generations before. They knew that they lacked conceptual schemes, neat histories, ways of tying empires and events to the stages of God's realization of his plan on earth. They knew, moreover, that they confronted not only a confusing past but a terrifying present—a unified human and natural world that the ancients had almost certainly not known as a whole, and certainly had not traveled as they did. Yet the actual writings that described the new realities did not confront the old conceptual schemes with the new facts; rather, they accommodated the one to the other, shaving off or tamping down unattractive verities when they did not fit a template dictated by political pressures, individual perceptions, and—above all—literary traditions. How, then, did the encounter with a New World affect—if at all—the growing perception that men lived in new times? Or was some other encounter more important?

Ancient Solutions and Their Virtues

Individual ancient texts and theories proved surprisingly resilient, yielding solutions to agonizing historical, ethical, and religious problems. The discovery of human beings in the Americas, after all, posed a hard question to scholars who believed that the world had a seamless and coherent history: where did they come from? Neither the Greeks, the Romans, nor the Jews had known of their existence. How, then, could Greco-Roman and Hebrew texts be complete and authoritative?

All too easily. The Bible provided ample opportunity to slot the Jews into the coherent story of the families of Noah's descendants. The Indians could have descended from Ham, or from his descendants, the Canaanites, or—if one felt more sympathy for them— from the Israelites lost in the Babylonian exile. If solutions differed, methods did not; etymology, above all, resolved the mystery of New World origins with brilliant—if spurious—clarity. Benito Arias Montano, an influential Spanish theologian who worked on the great multivolume Polyglot Bible published at Antwerp in 1572, insisted that one could easily find New Spain in his old text. The origins of New World settlement he tied to Joctan, son of Eber, of the family of Shem. He had given his name, after all, to that "very old city IVKTAN" which lay in the midst of the Andean mountains. Even the later history of Peru was touched on in the Bible; after all, when Solomon's ships fetched their wealth from Peruaim, they were clearly paying a visit on the gold-rich land still called Peru. Montano's theory, made vivid by a neat map which included the New World in the world's ancient past, found critics; but it also found imitators and modifiers across all confessions and countries. In 1614 Sir Walter Raleigh's magnificent *History of the World* still dealt at length with exactly the same enterprise, that of tying the Indians to the biblical history of man.

Physical questions also confronted scholars: if the ancients had lacked compasses and large sailing ships, how could they have reached the New World at all? Here the Bible was silent but the pagans spoke informatively. In his *Timaeus* and *Critias*, Plato's char-

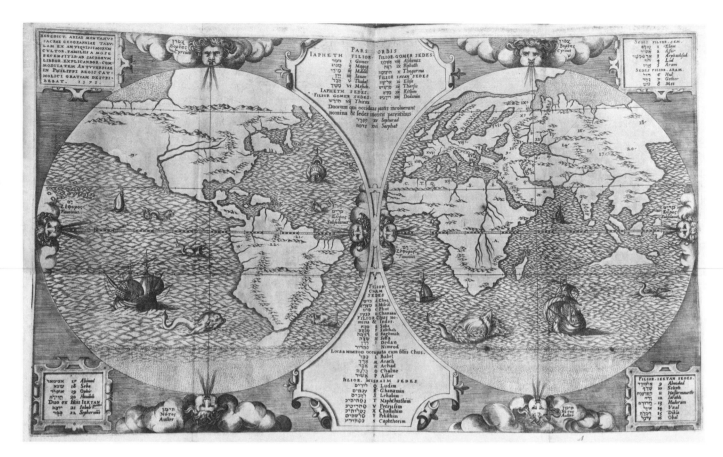

Figure 3.17   This map in Benito Arias Montano's *Antiquitatum iudaicarum libri ix* (Leiden, 1593) traces the migrations of Noah's sons to North and South America. Peru is identified as the site of the biblical Ophir.

acters described the great island kingdom of Atlantis, which had once existed in the ocean outside the Pillars of Hercules, and which the Greeks, in their habitual ignorance of the past, had forgotten. Some writers—like Gómara—made Atlantis into America, cheerfully pointing to the presence of the phrase _atl_ in the original language of the Aztecs. Others—like Agustin de Zárate—took Plato's story more literally, and saw Atlantis as the sunken land bridge that had enabled the Indians, whoever they were, to pass from the original continent of mankind to what became their isolated habitat. True, Plato's story had problems of its own; his Egyptian priest claimed to have records of nine thousand years of history, which made his society start long before the Creation. But Plato's own disciple Eudoxus had explained this problem away: the Egyptians had meant by "years" not one revolution of the sun about the earth but one revolution of the moon—a mere lunar month. Nine thousand months, of course, posed no challenge to biblical authority. This handy solution, preserved in the ancient commentary on the _Timaeus_ by Proclus and neatly repackaged by the great fifteenth-century Neoplatonist Marsilio Ficino, enabled Las Casas, Zárate, and many others to proclaim, as Ficino did, that Plato offered not allegory but real and vital history.[11]

Even the new conceptual schemes that overthrew the old grew in part from classical roots. When Bodin argued for the technical inferiority of ancient times, he drew explicitly on Thucydides' history of the Peloponnesian Wars. Thucydides began his book with a long demonstration that the war he meant to record was far greater than any previous one, the Trojan War included. He proved his point by demonstrating "that a little before his time such was the barbarity and ferocity of men in Greece itself that by land and sea piracy was openly practiced." And he showed in detail that the great armies, navies, and fortifications of his day were innovations, far larger in

Figure 3.18 Jean de Léry's account of his New World Voyage, *Historia navigationis in Brasiliam, quae et America dicitur* (Geneva, 1586), contains this illustration of a native American family. It suggests the difficulties European artists had when called upon to portray peoples whom they had never seen. Here the subjects' proportions are those of classical heroes, and their facial expressions suggest the Holy Family, admittedly stripped of clothes and placed in an exotic landscape characterized by a hammock, pineapples, and mangoes.

scale than anything the Homeric kinglets could have mustered. In short, a great Greek writer provided Bodin with one of his strongest arguments for rejecting the intellectual authority of the Greeks. An ancient text, not the modern encounter with naked Indians, enabled Bodin to envision ancient Europeans, too, as savages, not sages.

Yet the very resilience and variety of the ancient texts also proved their undoing. On the one hand, they themselves supported innovative and open-ended as well as tightly packaged and stereotypical views of history; they handed their readers the very tools that could be used to dismantle them. On the other hand, they also competed with one another, each claiming to explain a great deal but none of them fully reconcilable with the rest. If the Bible gave adequate guidance to the past, what need of Plato? If Plato's Atlantis had really existed, how could the Bible have omitted so dramatic an event as the passage of the Jews through a lost continent that sank? This set of concerns—the uneasy feeling that no single ancient text gave complete guidance to the past—emerges clearly in Bodin. He believed that the Old Testament was the basis of all true history. He traced all major races back to the three sons of Noah, in a good traditional fashion. But he made no effort to fit the New World races into his human family tree, and he excused its lacunae in words that reveal the misgivings he felt. The Bible, he explained, gave "only the origins of that people whom God alone chose . . . not of the others." The New World appeared in his system only when the Spanish sent colonists there. The same sense of unease emerges also in Louis Le Roy. In his great treastise on the vicissitudes of all things he praised, like Bodin, the amplitude of modern travel and knowledge, comparing those who insisted on the superiority of the ancients to old men insisting on the superiority of the world of their youth. But he also had no system that could accommodate everything he knew. Le Roy lined up incompatible theories about the origins and duration of human history, ancient and modern, Near Eastern and Greek, pagan and biblical, and made no determined attempt to sort them out.

To be sure, few intellectuals went so far as to reject all ancient accounts of human history as partial and inaccurate. One who did, Giordano Bruno, ridiculed the notion that the years of Egyptian and Aztec history had been months and insisted on the separate origin of the New World peoples. He paid for his views on the Campo de' Fiori, where he was burnt in 1600, insisting that Adam and Eve were the parents of the Jews alone, not of the entire human race.

Traditions clung to the New World like ivy to brick. Even the half-Inca Garcilaso de la Vega, who loved the past of both his peoples, found in Herodotus the model for a history that could do justice to two civilizations in conflict, preserving the great deeds of Westerners and Indians alike from oblivion. And when he set out to rebut the notion that Peru had been known to the ancients, he used standard tools. Etymology still had authority. But the true etymology of *Peru* proved that the name was not a key to the early wanderings of man but a typical Western mistake. Spaniards, asking an Indian in a river where they were, had received the answer "Beru"—"In the river." They had simply mistaken this for the name of the country— an argument as humanistic in its methods as it was radical in its conclusions, and one that Garcilaso owed more to his intimate knowledge of humanistic philology, as practiced in Spain, than to his oral knowledge of Indian traditions, gained while he was very young.

Before Bruno died for his lack of faith in the canon, however, others were already testing more modest—and perhaps more influential—forms of criticism on all ancient authority. Montaigne began his great essay "On Cannibals," first published in 1580, with a glance at Plato's story of Atlantis. But he rejected that and all other ancient

Garcilaso de la Vega: The Inca Humanist

"WHILE these peoples were living or dying in the manner we have seen, it pleased our Lord God that from their midst there should appear a morning star to give them in the dense darkness in which they dwelt some glimmerings of natural law, of civilization, and of the respect men owe to one another. The descendants of this leader should thus tame those savages and convert them into men, made capable of reason and of receiving good doctrine, so that when God, who is the sun of justice, saw fit to send forth the light of His divine rays upon those idolators, it might find them no longer in their first savagery, but rendered more docile to receive the Catholic faith and the teaching and doctrine of our Holy Mother the Roman Church, as indeed they have received it—all of which will be seen in the course of this history."

The man who wrote these words, Garcilaso de la Vega ("El Inca"), in his person and his works combined two cultural traditions. His father was a Spanish aristocrat, his mother an Incan princess. His history of the Incan empire, the *Royal Commentaries*, mingled two intellectual traditions, for he intended to do more than correct the errors of Spanish historians and write a comprehensive and accurate history "about a state that was destroyed before it had been known." Rather, he shaped the history of the Incas with the template of Christian and humanist historiographic traditions. The quotation above is his interpretation of the origin of the Incan kings, and it makes clear his premises. For him, the Incan empire was the New World version of the Roman empire. Cuzco was its Rome, its rulers were "Caesars by their strength and just government," and the Incan empire performed an identical civilizing function as a preparation for the arrival of the one true religion, Christianity. Garcilaso thus enhances the stature of Incan culture and even has it surpass Old World civilizations in some respects. Here he describes an Incan fortress:

"To this extent this fortress surpasses the constructions known as the seven wonders of the world. For in the case of a long broad wall like that of Babylon, or the colossus of Rhodes, or the pyramids of Egypt, or the other monuments, one can see clearly how they were executed . . . But it is indeed beyond the power of imagination to understand how these Indians, unacquainted with devices, engines, and implements, could have cut, dressed, raised, and lowered great rocks, more like lumps of hills than building stones, and set them so exactly in their places. For this reason, and because the Indians were so familiar with demons, the work is attributed to enchantment."

In all this Garcilaso resembles European historians who sought to enhance the stature of their nations either by linking them directly with the Roman empire and thus making them a continuation thereof, or by arguing for the superiority or precedence of their national group.

Yet long before he published his account in 1604, some Europeans had already acknowledged that the sophistication of the Incan and Aztec civilizations challenged the assumed superiority of European culture. This is the question at the heart of the poignant essay "On Coaches" by Michel de Montaigne, which appeared in 1580. Here he mourns the destruction of New World civilizations and reduces the glory of the European conquest to a matter of technological superiority and deceitfulness:

"As for boldness and courage, as for firmness, constancy, resoluteness against pains and hunger and death, I would not fear to oppose the examples I could find among them [in the New World] to the most famous ancient examples that we have in the memories of our world on this side of the ocean. For as regards the men who subjugated them, take away the ruses and tricks that they used to deceive them, and the people's natural astonishment at seeing the unexpected arrival of bearded men, different in language, religion, shape, and countenance, from a part of the world so remote, where they have never imagined there was any sort of human habitation, mounted on great unknown monsters, opposed to men who have never seen not only a horse, but any sort of animal trained to carry and endure a man or any other burden; men equipped with a hard and shiny skin and a sharp and glittering weapon, against men who, for the miracle of a mirror or a knife, would exchange a great treasure in gold and pearls, and who had neither the knowledge nor the material by which, even in full leisure, they could pierce our steel; add to this the lightning and thunder of our cannon and harquebuses—capable of disturbing Caesar himself, if he had been surprised by them with as little experience and in his time—against people who were naked (except in some regions where the invention of some cotton fabric had reached them), without other arms at the most than bows, stones, sticks, and wooden bucklers; people taken by surprise, under color of friendship and good faith, by curiosity to see strange and unknown things: eliminate this disparity, I say, and you take from the conquerors the whole basis of so many victories."

Sources: Montaigne 1943; Garcilaso de la Vega 1966; Marichal 1976.

Figure 3.19 In this illustration in the sixth volume of Theodore de Bry's *America* (Frankfurt, 1596), the murder of the Incan emperor Atahualpa occurs in a thoroughly classical and European stage setting. The portrayal invests the event with the solemnity of a high Renaissance tragedy and enhances both the victim's heroism and Pizarro's treachery. The Incan empire is, by implication, a high civilization, and the Spanish, in effect, are barbarians.

explanations as irrelevant to a world that seemed to change so rapidly that no traditional form of knowledge could keep up with it, no classical text could match its uncompromising modernity. His essay clearly suggested, in the end, that the cannibals whose mores he described might have a civilization of their own, one as valid as any other, for all its radical violation of European norms. Cannibal society might even be more humane than the European world of religious war. [Montaigne made clear that the competing churches of his own day, whose authorities burned ignorant people for disagreeing with them on points of textual exegesis, seemed more cruel to him than cannibals, who merely ate their enemies.]

The authority of ancient texts—of books themselves—was clearly shaken. But their own proliferation and combat did more of the damage than their conflict with an extratextual world of inexplicable data. Cracks and contradictions within the canon—above all religious ones—brought on the most radical challenges to the authority of books. Scientists working within the classical traditions challenged them as sharply as explorers who had left the classical world behind them. The discoveries provided a clinching piece of evidence to those who wished to argue for a new vision of history, for the superiority of modern to ancient culture. But the substance of that vision, ironically enough, often came from the very ancient writers whose supremacy it denied.

Drugs and Diseases: New World Biology and Old World Learning

4

THE New World sent the Old more than gold and ideas. It also confronted Europeans with new animals, from bison to microorganisms, and new plants, from tobacco to potatoes. These proved both attractive and dangerous enough to change social life—sometimes, indeed, to cause what were perceived as social and cultural crises, like the rise of tobacco smoking and the spread of syphilis. Debates on new forms of debauchery and disease—unlike debates on refined points of early human history—moved rapidly from the study to the street. Participants ranged from highly trained academics to idiosyncratic amateurs. The forums in which they argued ranged from vast folios, thick with quotations, to one-page broadsides, the equivalent of modern supermarket media. These early modern arguments challenged traditional forms of biological and medical thought and accepted therapeutic practices. Yet a surprising number of the debaters still took their assumptions, arguments, and evidence from canonical texts.

The Herbal: Traditional Texts and the New Book of Nature

The medieval and Renaissance herbal was the medical practitioner's source for plant-derived cures. There he found each plant described,

CHRYSANTH. PERVNIANVM. 295

Figure 4.1 Throughout the sixteenth century, botanical illustration became increasingly precise. This illustration of a New World plant, the sunflower, appeared in the *Florum et coronariarum odoratarumque nonnullarum herbarum historia* (Antwerp, 1568) of Rembert Dodoens, who devised a classificatory scheme to cope with the explosion of botanical information resulting from the discovery of thousands of plants in Europe and abroad.

a list of its "virtues" or curative powers, recipes for concocting remedies, and directions for their application. Its pages enlivened with ever more detailed and sometimes beautifully hand-colored illustrations, the herbal makes an impressive monument to the efforts of scholars and physicians to restore and correct the texts of ancient authorities in light of the most advanced humanist philology. These men also sought to augment those texts by adding descriptions of every plant they could get their hands on. But however innovative the methodology, the underlying premise of their research was unchanged. The plant world was a God-given pharmacy, and the New World, with its hundreds, even thousands of unknown, sometimes strange plants, was a pharmaceutical supermarket. Indeed, Nicolas Monardes, the Spanish physician who authored *Joyfull Newes out of the Newe Founde Worlde* (1577), judged the discovery of America far more valuable for its plants than for its mineral wealth because health was ultimately more precious than riches.

The botanical section of the anonymous *Hortus sanitatis*, first published in 1491, describes more than five hundred plants, including the Tree of the Knowledge of Good and Evil and the Tree of Life, which could be found only in that divine horticultural prototype, the Garden of Eden. Published before the work of the great German Renaissance botanists Otto Brunfels, Jerome Bock, and Leonhart Fuchs, it represents a resurgence of the illustrated herbal. Such texts, which circulated in manuscript, were basic tools for physicians in the Middle Ages.[1] The *Hortus sanitatis* also contains basic features that would be refined as both botanical knowledge and knowledge of ancient texts expanded: an illustration of each plant, a description of its virtues, and a brief résumé of the ancients' knowledge of it. Its introduction provides a summary statement of the prevailing medical philosophy:

I have perused the marvelous and wondrous works of all nature created by the omnipotent and eternal God, and I have frequently meditated upon them: how, from the beginning of the world, God himself adorned heaven with stars. How he caused life and virtue to flow from these into all created things under heaven. By what means he also brought forth from nothingness the four elements . . . [I have contemplated] the manner in which, in addition to the plants, stones and all living things brought forth, he made and formed man to be the highest of all other creatures. And thus He arranged all things so that everything under heaven might possess life and movement. He assigned to the middle stars their nature and their abiding permanence. And he established in all things—plants and stones and also living things—their elemental nature from the four emerging elements: hot, cold, wet, dry and mixed. He also combined these things in the human body in a way measured and regulated so as best to maintain life and nature, and so that through the continued balance of this temperament, man might attain perfect health.

In the Galenic medical tradition, which survived well into the seventeenth century, all things had "temperaments" or "complexions" determined by the dominance of one quality over another: hot, moist, dry, and cold. Different organs had different complexions. Women were "moister" and "colder" than men, and complexions also differed according to age and ethnic group. Elemental theory even had a psychological component: the adjective "choleric" is the technical term for a temperament dominated by fire. Disease was caused by a disruption in the balance of the "humors"—four bodily fluids, each having its own complexion. What exactly caused a disruption was a matter of debate—bad air, domicile, God's wrath, even the stars could be culpable. But, whatever the cause, the problem of effecting a cure remained the same: the physician had to restore the balance by applying a remedy whose complexion opposed that of the symptoms. For example, an excess of heat required remedies whose dominant quality was cold.[2] Thus a herbal specified the qualities of a particular plant. For example, in the *Hortus sanitatis*, strawberries were described as cold and humid in the first degree.

John Gerarde's *Herball or Generall Historie of Plantes* (1597) gives a good sense of how the field of botany changed as its practitioners encountered New World flora. True, the work breaks no new ground, and its author was far more dependent on the work of others than he admitted. Of course, no herbalist started entirely from scratch; he was always dependent on other textual and illustrative sources. For example, the *Neuw Kreuterbuch*, published in Frankfurt in 1588–1591, contained illustrations that had previously appeared in the botanical writings of Leonhard Fuchs, Petrus Andreas Mattioli, Rembert Dodoens, and Charles l'Ecluse. The *Histoire des plantes* of Geofroy Linocier relied upon the works of Mattioli and Fuchs. Yet the apothecary-surgeon Gerarde transgressed even the very generous rules of Renaissance borrowing by presenting Dr. Priest's translation of Dodoens' *Pemptades* as his own. Gerarde's herbal was the definitive work in English for more than thirty years, however, and the 1633 version, amended by the far more reliable and intellectually responsible Thomas Johnson, is a substantial work indeed. It contains descriptions of thousands of plants and nearly three thousand illustrations drawn from the botanical works of one of the most important printers in Europe, the Belgian Christopher Plantin.

The herbal's title page prominently features the ancient authorities Theophrastus and Dioscorides, making explicit in images what Johnson proclaims in his lengthy historical introduction:

> From the Antients have sprung all or the greatest part of the knowledge that the middle or later times have had of Plants; and all the controversies of late time have so stuffed the books of such as have writ of this subject, had their beginning by reason that the carelessness

of the middle times was such, that they knew little but what they transcribed out of the Antients, never endeavoring to acquire any perfect knowledge of the things themselves.

Renaissance scientific knowledge, as we have seen, was also historical knowledge. An apothecary and botanist of humanist inclinations such as Johnson saw the history of the study of plants as central to the scientific enterprise itself. In his introduction, Johnson mentions Galen and Pliny, and he duly describes the fourth-century B.C. work of Theophrastus, pupil of Aristotle, a work completely unknown in Europe until it came to the West from Constantinople in the fifteenth century. Johnson's highest praise, however, is for Dioscorides: his *De materia medica* "attained to that perfection, that few or none since his time have attained to." Dioscorides, who lived during the first century, traveled widely and collected plants in the eastern parts of the Roman Empire. He also defined the format for a plant's entry name, description, provenance, and virtues. Restoring Dioscorides' text was a major preoccupation of humanist scholars interested in botanical and medical questions, and Dioscorides' greatest Renaissance commentator was the Italian Petrus Andreas Mattioli.

Mattioli's fastidious humanist scholarship resulted in plant descriptions encumbered with material seemingly irrelevant in a medical handbook.[3] The lengthy discussion of cinnamon, for example, is densely studded with the names of ancient authorities. We might ask, "Who cares whether Pliny knew about it—does it work?" But the Renaissance scientist appealed to authority as much as, sometimes more than, to results; his habitual question was, "Who knew about it, and do their opinions matter?" Given this criterion, it is not surprising that Johnson's harshest criticism of Gerarde was that he was "little conversant in the writings of the Antients."

The text of Gerarde's herbal differs greatly from that of the *Hortus*

Figure 4.2 The title page of John Gerarde's revised and expanded *Herball or Generall Historie of Plantes* (London, 1633) illustrates the continued prestige of the ancient authorities Theophrastus and Dioscorides, as well as the melding of classical mythology and Christian tradition. The goddesses Ceres and Pomona, both associated with fertility, flank the Garden of Eden and a citation from Genesis, "Behold, I have given you every plant yielding seed that is on the surface of the earth."

sanitatis. Entries are arranged not simply in alphabetical order, but according to Dodoens' classificatory scheme. This early attempt at organizing the tidal wave of botanical information from the New World categorized plants along roughly morphological lines, "putting things together as they have most resemblance one with another in external forme, beginning with Grasses, Cornes, etc." The illustrations are far more detailed and realistic than those in the *Hortus;* Gerarde's herbal, though hefty, could function as a true guide for the collector in the field. It was clearly intended to be a readily accessible medical reference work and contains many indices for old British plant names, common and obsolete names, Latin names, and plant virtues or symptoms. These last include, for example, no fewer than twenty-five entries for ulcers and ulcerations, as well as such entries "Good against Deafnesse," "For wind in the bowles," "To cure cattel of the cough of the lungs," and "To drive away Sadnesse." The book is even roughly cross-indexed—"To draw out Arrowheads, see Thornes and Splinters."

Tobacco: From Panacea to Plague

From the first, Europeans remarked the ceremonial and, to a lesser extent, the medical use of tobacco or "petun" among New World populations. Columbus and his men saw Indians smoking. Vespucci wrote contemptuously of the tobacco-chewing natives on Margarita Island, each with "his cheeks bulging with a certain green herb, which they chewed like cattle so that they could scarcely speak." André Thevet described cigarmaking and provided the first illustration of the medicinal uses of tobacco. Gradually interest in the properties of the plant overcame disgust at its strangeness, and it began to attract scientific interest.

Tobacco made a powerful impact on the quiet, busy world of the

Figure 4.3 A portrayal of tobacco use among native Americans in André Thevet's *La cosmographie universelle* (Paris, 1575).

Renaissance botanist. It dizzied those who, like Conrad Gesner, chewed it or smelled its smoke by way of experiment (Gesner promptly wrote to a friend to ask for a larger supply of this "intoxicating" new plant).[4] Yet it impressed many others, like the New World visitor Monardes, as a wonder drug. Gerarde's long section on tobacco relies heavily on Monardes, who wrote in his *Joyfull Newes* that "in any manner of griefe that is in the bodie or any part thereof it healpeth, beying of a cold cause, and applied therunto it taketh it awaie, not without great admiration."

Gerarde describes and illustrates three varieties of tobacco: *hyoscyamus Peruvianus*, or tobacco or henbane of Peru; *Sana Sancta Indorum*, or tobacco of Trinidado; and *Tabacum minimum*, or dwarf tobacco. His own experiments in cultivating the third variety remind us that the Renaissance botanical passion had its practical as well as scholarly side. The first botanical gardens were established at Pisa and Padua, in the 1540s, a northern counterpart at Leiden in 1577; trips to the field and the apothecary's shop became part of the medical student's training at many universities.

The temperament of tobacco, according to Gerarde, is hot and dry in the second degree. He also notes its psychotropic effects, comparing them to that of opium and remarking on the use of tobacco by "Indian priests and inchanters" to induce visions. Tobacco in a variety of preparations can cure or mitigate a truly dizzying list of ailments: migraine, "cold stomach," kidney pain, "fits of the mother," gout, toothache, worms, "agues," ulcers, scabies, nettles, burns, wounds from poisoned arrows, and wounds "made with gunnes or any other weapon." It is an antidote to poison (including wounds made by "venomous beasts"), a purgative, and a soporific. Its oil can be used to treat deafness. Gerarde retails his own remedy for "deep wounds and punctures made by some narrow sharpe pointed weapon." But he takes a dim view of tobacco smoking (or "drinking," as it was called), and he also appears vaguely aware of its addictive possibilities:

Figure 4.4 An early illustration of tobacco from the Spanish physician Nicholas Monardes' enthusiastic report on New World plants, soon translated into English as the *Joyfull Newes out of the Newe Founde Worlde* (London, 1577).

> The dry leaves are used to be taken in a pipe set on fire and suckt into the stomacke, and thrust forth againe at the nosthrils, against the paines in the head, rheumes, aches in any part of the bodie whereofsoever the originall proceed, whether from France, Italy, Spain, Indies, or from our familiar and best knowne diseases. These leaves do palliate or ease for a time, but never perform any cure absolutely: for although they empty the body of humors, yet the cause of the griefe cannot be so taken away . . . My selfe speake by proofe, who have cured of that infectious disease a great many divers of which had covered or kept under the sicknesse by the help of

Tobaco as they throught, yet in the end have bin constrained to have unto such an hard knot, a crabbed wedge, or else had utterly perished.

Some use to drink it (as it is termed) for wantonnesse or rather custome and cannot forbeare it no not in the midst of their dinner; which ende of taking is unwholsome and very dangerous: although to take it seldom, and that physically, is to be tolerated, and may do some good: but I commend the syrrup above this fume or smoky medicine.

Writing on tobacco was not solely the province of specialists, scholarly or otherwise. The 1595 pamphlet by Anthony Chute, *Tobaco*, exemplifies the popularizer's art. Chute's interests were more literary than scientific, and his pamphlet on tobacco depends heavily upon the work of others, including the French botanists Charles Estienne and Jean Liebault and, of course, Monardes. His breathless retelling of Nicot's nearly miraculous cures gives the work a sensationalist quality, apparent here when he describes the cure of a case of the King's evil or scrofula:

There was likewise a Captaine, whose sonne had that mortall and almost incurable disease which we call the Kinges evill, (because thought to be cured by none but the Princes themselves) he often resorted to the Embassador, bringing with him his sonne, to whome Monsieur Nicot ministred this hearbe (ordered as before) and it was not long ere he as the rest was made sound and well, without that ever any thing else was ministred unto him than Tabacco.

Chute views smoking more positively than Gerarde, but he, too, opposes casual tobacco use and counsels heavy fines to discourage it:

I could therefore wish it were a penal law, that whosoever should abuse it [tobacco] by unmeasurable and needlesse drinking, should

HYMNVS
TABACI
autore
Raphaele
Thorio

Figure 4.5 "Tobacco King of Plants I well may call; / Others have single vertues, this hath all," wrote the popular physician Raphael Thorius in his poem *Hymnus tabaci* (Leiden, 1625). Like the English poets Joshua Sylvester and John Beaumont, he gave it a pseudoclassical history in which Indians received the herb from the hands of Bacchus, god of wine and revelry, and Silenus, leader of the satyrs. Having discovered the salubrious effects of tobacco in a "courteous Vale" during a debauch, the deities awoke with enhanced courage and vigor. After defeating the Indians, they educated them in the use of tobacco as a gesture of peace; "Thus they with Smoke their inward Cares do smother, / And so by one Cloud do expel another."

sorfait at the pleasure of his Excelsitude, from three times upward, so much as he hath wasted toward the maintenance of Tabacco in the treasure, and by this means I fear not, but we should make that our singular profit, which we now turne to our disprofit and harme, and that wee should not remaine in that great want of good Tabacco which wee have done of a long time together, but that hoarding Apothicaries might be glad to abate their prises of their mingle mangle which forsooth they will not sell, under unreasonable rate, when there is scarse good to be got, although that which they have be as bad at the best, as the worst of but indifferent good, when good may be bought.

While tobacco attracted apothecaries and physicians on the basis of its curative powers, it appealed to a much wider public on the basis of that wonderful "species of intoxication" described by Gesner. Increasing recreational tobacco use gave rise to a lively debate, one framed by questions of the socially desirable and morally upright. Tobacco use, like the drunkenness with which it was identified, was viewed by most as a sin. Thus, though the anonymous author of the pamphlet *Work for Chimny-sweepers Or A warning to Tabacconists* also assails tobacco largely on medical grounds, he writes as well that, because tobacco was created by the devil, Christians who "detest and abhorre the divell, as a lyar and deciver of mankind" should eschew its use.

But the debate over recreational tobacco use was not conducted solely in prose. Tobacco made its appearance in plays and broadsides, in songs, in emblem books, and poems. The first full-length English poems on the substance, respectively pro- and anti-tobacco, provided rather convoluted and tongue-in-cheek accounts of its mythic origins and associations with classical pagan deities. They show just how decisively the debate about tobacco had shifted from medical to socioreligious grounds by the beginning of the seventeeth century.

Figure 4.6 Tobacco, or rather its smoke, rapidly became a symbol of the transience of life's pleasures and vanities. This illustration from the emblem book *Proteus ofte Minne-Beilden Verandert in Sinne-beelden* (Rotterdam, 1627), by Jacob Cats, is accompanied by a poem that tells of Cupid opening a tobacco shop as "[f]rom oldest time he ever dealt in Smoke; Thou Smoke, no other thing he sold, or made; Smoke all the substance of his stock in trade; His Capital all Smoke, Smoke all his store, 'Twas nothing else, but Lovers ask no more" (trans. Richard Pigot).

John Beaumont begins *The Metamorphosis of Tobacco* by evoking the powers of the plant to soothe even the most savage cannibal; tobacco "their cavell minds dost frame, / and after with a pleasing sleepe doth tame." Even the sun cannot resist the salubrious effects of the "sacred herb." The poem concludes with a description of tobacco's benefits that is worthy of any twentieth-century advertising copywriter. Not only does tobacco calm quarrels between the bitterest foes:

Figure 4.7 As the illustration from this 1641 London broadside, *The Sucklington Faction*, makes clear, tobacco use soon became identified with lifestyles deemed socially unacceptable and morally reprehensible. "These are the children of spirituall fornication," concludes the author after a lengthy description of the gallant's loose living. "These fall not onely from piety to impuritie, but also from Christian verities, to Antichristian vanities, fopperies, and trumperies."

The man that shall this smokie Magick prove,
Shall need no Philters to obtain his love,
But shall be deckt with farre more pleasing grace,
Then ere was Nireus or Narcissus face . . .
How a dull Cynick by the force of it
Hath got a pleasing gesture, and good wit . . .
How many Cowards base and recreant,
By one pipes draught were turned valiant.

In marked contrast, Joshua Sylvester's *Tobaco Batter'd: and the Pipes Shattered (About their Eares that idly Idolize so base and barbarous a Weed; or at least-wise over-love so loathsome Vanitie:) by a Volley of holy Shot Thundered from Mount Helicon* squarely identifies tobacco with the socially undesirable and morally reprehensible. Sylvester writes that the twin evils of tobacco and guns were foretold in the book of the Apocalypse, and he attacks tobacco on every available ground. Although tobacco is naturally associated with the devil, even the devil went reluctantly to his smoky hell, while the tobacco smoker gleefully creates his own. Tobacco causes melancholy, "Satan's fit saddle," not to mention sterility. Tobacco attacks not only the body but also the memory, the will, and, most terribly, the conscience:

Lastly, the Conscience (as it is the best)
This Indian Weed doth most of all molest;
Loading it dayly with such Weight of Sin,
Whereof the least shall at the last com-in
To strict Account, the Losse of precious houres,
Neglect of God, of Good, of Us, of Ours:
Our ill Example, prodigall Excess,
Vain Words, vain Oaths, Dice, Daring, Drunkeness,
Sloth, Jesting, Scoffing, turning Night to Day,
and Day to Night: Disorder, Disarray.

As if all this were not enough, Sylvester tars the tobacco smoker with the most damning labels an age that cast virtually every issue, social or political, in religious terms could apply—that of libertine and atheist.

Sylvester's effort is tedious, repetitive, and hysterical, yet not without insight. In a pithy couplet he grasps how, in tobacco's transportation from one cultural context to another, it passed from use to abuse, a pattern that would be repeated as other nonnative drugs came to Europe: "For, what to them [the native Americans] is Meat and Med'cinable, / Is turned to us a Plague intolerable." Nor was he alone when he rather poignantly voiced misgivings about the good fortune of the Old World in discovering the New. For Sylvester, the New World, the source of syphilis and tobacco, also occasioned an explosive indulgence in the sin of avarice. He saw the news from the New World as far from joyful:

> Should it be question'd (as right well it may)
> Whether Discovery of America,
> That New-found World, have yeelded to our Old
> More Hurt or Good: Till fuller Answer should
> Decide the Doubt, and quite determine it,
> This for the present might we answer fit:
> That, therby We have (rightly understood)
> Both giv'n and taken greater hurt then good:
> But that on both sides, both for Christians
> It had been better, and for Indians,
> That only good men to their Coast had com,
> Or that Evil had still staid at home.

Ancient Remedies and "New" Diseases

Some Europeans believed that new diseases appeared during the age of initial contact between Old World and New. This idea tested the limits of classical and medieval knowledge. But with few exceptions, ancient texts, long-standing scientific traditions, and established medical and legal practices shaped perceptions of current realities.

In the late fifteenth and early sixteenth centuries, three viewpoints about disease vied with one another. Some Europeans believed that they lived in an age of new diseases, without making any connections between these new diseases and the New World. Others refused to accept that there might be diseases that had been unknown to the ancients: any apparently new disease must be a manifestation in different form of something already described by ancient Greek medical writers. Still others held that each region produced both its own particular diseases and specific natural remedies for them; in this view the New World might be expected to have its own, hitherto unknown, diseases, just as it had hitherto unknown medicinal herbs.

One of the most notorious of the "new" diseases, widespread in sixteenth- and seventeenth-century Europe, was the affliction often popularly called *morbus gallicus*, or the French disease.[5] It first came to public attention and gained a name in Italy soon after 1494, when an epidemic there was associated with invading French troops. More than thirty years after Columbus' first voyage, a few writers began to claim that the disease had been imported from the New World by his sailors. This thesis was not universally accepted at the time and has remained controversial ever since.

The history of diseases in premodern Europe is a complex and difficult field of inquiry. Clinical and other contemporary accounts are scattered, incomplete, tradition-bound, and, from a modern perspective, highly unreliable evidence for the presence of specific microorganisms. For example, some medieval and Renaissance descriptions of leprosy include elements that could apply to syphilis. Even modern-day paleopathology and microbiology offer inconclusive evidence about the origins of venereal syphilis. The disease leaves lesions in bones, and such lesions have been found on bones from sites in the Americas said to predate contact with Europeans. But the other human diseases known as treponematoses (pinta, yaws, and nonvenereal syphilis) also leave such lesions. The only conclusion that seems tenable is that in one form or another treponematoses were present in human populations in various parts of the globe from an early stage of human evolution.

Until the advent of AIDS, venereal syphilis was the most serious sexually transmitted disease. Renaissance Europeans soon identified the primary and secondary stages, whose symptoms are manifest shortly after infection. But they did not relate the symptoms of the tertiary stage, which occurs only years later, and in some cases never, with *morbus gallicus*. (That relationship was not definitely established until the nineteenth century; the microorganism causing syphilis was not identified until 1905; and the Wasserman test, the first serological procedure for diagnoses of syphilis, dates from 1906. There was no fully effective treatment before the discovery of antibiotics.)

But the brief survey in the following pages demonstrates that biological factors are only one aspect of the history of human disease. In a double sense, that history is inseparable from social and historical circumstances. In the first place, the events of human history affect the transmission or prevalence of disease. Opportunities for infection by communicable diseases increase as a result of urbanization, increased trade and travel, war, migration, conquest, or changes in mores; transmission to new environments and different human populations may change the form in which diseases manifest themselves.

Clearly, the effects of contact on the health of the peoples of the Old World and the New were far more devastating for the latter, with uncounted deaths resulting from conquest, forced labor, and epidemics of diseases brought from Europe.

Second, but equally important, the recognition, naming, and definition of a disease—and the attitudes and perceptions it engenders—are themselves inevitably conditioned by the society and culture as well as by the scientific and medical theories of the age in which they occur.

In the twenty years after 1494 accounts of *morbus gallicus* pictured an epidemic of a highly contagious and frequently fatal disease. The role of sexual transmission was recognized almost immediately, although other means were also suggested. The first symptoms appeared on the genitals; some authors were careful to specify that the initial chancre was painless with hard edges. Subsequently, pustules appeared all over the rest of the body, accompanied by headache and severe pains in the joints and limbs. Later large swellings erupted, as well as ulcerations that could eat away features and reach the bone. Writers stressed the hideous sufferings and loathsome appearance of victims.

By the mid-sixteenth century the disease was no longer perceived as an epidemic, medical writers had ceased to describe it as fatal or incurable, and some claimed that the symptoms had modified. But the pox had become a permanent part of European life. Comparison with two diseases also widespread in the period, smallpox and plague, is instructive. Smallpox (so called to distinguish it from the "great," or venereal, pox), which seems to have become prevalent in Europe during the sixteenth century, was frequently fatal. But survivors of a childhood attack, though probably somewhat disfigured, stood in no danger of a recurrence. Plague occurred in the form of local epidemics, producing high mortality, chiefly among the poor. By contrast, *morbus gallicus* or pox struck people in all walks of life, and apparent cures were all too likely to be followed by continuing illness. Pox fitted easily into a universe of chronic ill health, which included a multitude of poorly distinguished conditions involving skin eruptions, ulceration, suppuration, and disfigurement.

Tradition shaped the numerous treatises on *morbus gallicus* written between the mid-1490s and about 1600. The fundamental ideas were ultimately derived from the medicine of ancient Greece. The chief model for specialized treatises on a contemporary epidemic was medieval: the genre of plague tracts stimulated by the Black Death in the fourteenth century and kept in existence by subsequent outbreaks of that plague. Similar works on *morbus gallicus* usually took the form of short, practical handbooks that described the disease, offered opinions as to its causes, and suggested treatments and remedies. Many of these treatises in effect endorsed—or advertised—the form of treatment that the author claimed to practice with success.

The contents of this literature were also traditional for the most part. Precedents for discussions of sexual transmission occurred in medieval medical accounts of *lepra*, a term that included the disease now called leprosy and other conditions as well. *Lepra*, actually rare in Europe after the thirteenth or fourteenth century, provided the classic example in medical literature and the Bible of a disease so loathsome and so readily communicable that those who suffered from it deserved to be shunned (in fact, leprosy is neither sexually transmitted or highly contagious). The occasional allegation that *morbus gallicus* among the French troops originated in sexual intercourse with lepers illustrates the lack of clear distinctions among diseases and the ease with which existing attitudes towards lepers could influence the lives and treatments of patients suffering from the new venereal disease.[6]

Some innovation took place, to be sure. Victims of the disease like Ulrich von Hutten enriched the medical literature with vivid personal accounts of what they had suffered. Humanistically educated physicians, as we will see, used new approaches in the controversies that raged over the nature of the disease. Some were cast in fashionable Latin literary forms that appealed to nonspecialists as well as specialists.

Probably the single most important feature of the works on *morbus gallicus* was that all of them were produced in the age of print. Many were small and evidently inexpensive books, and some were reprinted many times. As advice manuals, as contributions to scientific and medical debate, as publicity for particular forms of treatment, as records of personal experience, or as purported descriptions of exotic peoples, they may be assumed to have reached a wider audience than most of the earlier literature about any single disease.

God's will was universally recognized as the ultimate, though not necessarily the proximate, cause of all diseases. But certain diseases—notably epidemics and afflictions that disfigured the skin—were traditionally liable to be seen as special punishments sent by God. Medieval moralists regarded *lepra* in this light. According to the sixteenth-century French surgeon Ambroise Paré, as well as many preachers and moralists, the great pox, too, was a sign of the wrath of God, who had permitted it in order to rein in lasciviousness and concupiscence.

Renaissance Europeans also readily blamed disliked groups for disease. Current warfare and politics often determined the targets; thus Italian authors insisted on the role of French, and subsequently Spanish, troops in spreading *morbus gallicus*. A treatise published in 1564 and attributed to the anatomist Gabriele Falloppia accused the Spanish who fought against the French in the Naples campaign of 1494 of intentionally chasing beautiful infected prostitutes into the French camp, where they received an enthusiastic welcome. The variety of names given the disease—such as Spanish pox and Neapolitan evil—reflected popular belief in the various kingdoms of Europe that foreign enemies had disseminated it.

The idea that real or imagined enemies spread disease intentionally was embedded both in popular culture and in purportedly learned works. Such accusations had been leveled against persecuted minorities, most notably lepers and Jews, for centuries. Some medieval writers had asserted that lepers deliberately spread their disease by sexual contact. At the time of the Black Death, widespread rumors that Jews were spreading plague by poisoning wells led to extensive persecution. Similarly, transmission of *morbus gallicus* was blamed on lepers—and on leprous women in particular—and occasionally on Jews and marranos (converted Jews).

The poor, who tended to be regarded as a group rather than as individuals, were another natural target of suspicion and blame. Both actual social conditions and prevailing attitudes promoted belief that the poor were likely to be diseased, and they were usually perceived as spreading the disease rather than suffering from it. Thus physicians, moralists, and men of the world all warned that prostitutes were especially likely to be infected. The German knight, poet, and humanist Ulrich von Hutten exemplifies the attitude this perception engendered. He recounts his own sufferings at length but wastes no sympathy on the prostitutes who were his sexual partners, simply characterizing them as reservoirs of hidden (because internal) infection. Various authors' insistence that wetnurses were likely to infect the infants they were suckling for their employers also functioned to deflect blame onto lower-class women.

Although no one ever accused the inhabitants of the Americas of spreading disease deliberately, they inevitably joined these other groups, regarded for one reason or another as foreign, "other," as possible sources of *morbus gallicus*. Fernandez de Oviedo, who had spent several years in the Americas during the expeditions of con-

Figure 4.8 The title page from Ulrich von Hutten's popular and widely translated *Guaiacum* (Lyons, 1527). The biblical story of Job's boils, long emblematic of skin diseases, found new relevance as syphilis spread rapidly throughout Europe.

Ulrich von Hutten

ULRICH VON HUTTEN—humanist scholar, proponent of Lutheranism, and German patriot—wrote a brief treatise, *De morbo gallico*, in the 1520s. He discussed the history of syphilis and its arrival in Germany and advertised guaiacum as the most effective cure. Rapidly translated into many European languages, this pamphlet was one of the most influential works on the disease, its credibility perhaps enhanced by the fact that von Hutten's own experiences with syphilis and guaiacum are central to his account. The following excerpt from an English translation (spelling modernized) vividly illustrates the variety of cures for the pox, the sores that covered the syphilitic's body, applied by physicians and other medical professionals who based their treatment on what they believed were similar diseases.

"When the physicians were thus amazed, the surgeons came forward in the same error, and put to their brands, and first they began to burn the poxes with hot irons. But for as much as it was an infinite labour, to touch them all, they went about to anoint them by ointments, but diverse men used diverse ointments, and all in vain, except be added quicksilver [mercury] thereto . . . [a lengthy list of ingredients such as bayberries, coral, cinnabar, rust of iron, turpentine, swine's grease, and oil of roses] and with two or three of these foresaid things mingled together they anointed the sick man's joints, his arms, his thighs, his backbone, his neckbone, with other places of his body. Some anointed them once a day, some twice, some thrice, some four times. The patient was put in a stuff, kept with continual and fervent heat, some 20 and some 30 whole days: And some were laid in a Bed within the stew, and anointed, and covered with many clothes, and were compelled to sweat. Part of them at the second anointing began to faint marvelously. But yet the ointment was of such strength and effect, that what so ever disease was in the higher part of the Body, it drew into the stomach, and from thence up into the Brain, and thence the disease voided both by the nose and the mouth, that did put the patient to such pain, that except they took good heed, their teeth fell out, all their throats, their lungs, their roofs of the mouths, were full of sores, their jaws did swell, their teeth were loosed, and continually there voided the most stinking scum and matter, that could be, what so ever it ran upon, by and by it was polluted and infected . . . How be it scantly the hundredth person was eased, but mostly after set down again: so that this ease endured very few days. Whereby men may esteem, what I suffered in this disease, that proved this manner of curing 11 times, with great jeopardy and peril, wrestling with this evil 9 years."

Source: Hutten 1536.

quest, was one of the earliest to claim, in his *De la natural historia de las Indias* (1526), that the disease had originated in the New World. Inadvertently or otherwise, such writers incorporated the New World peoples into a traditional pattern, and thus helped to generate a hostile view of them.

The nature and transmission of disease were controversial topics in the late fifteenth and the sixteenth centuries. The medicine of the Renaissance, like that of the Middle Ages, continued to be based on medical ideas developed in ancient Greece. But Renaissance physicians attached new importance to intensive study of the original Greek sources. Their improved knowledge of ancient medical texts facilitated detailed comparison of current experience of disease with ancient descriptions, thus stimulating debate in which new ideas occasionally emerged.

Most physicians explained the immediate cause of illness in terms of an alteration in the balance of the patient's constituent humors (blood, bile, black bile, and phlegm). A rich vocabulary of names existed for individual diseases, but most of these were regarded merely as symptoms of internal imbalance, not as invasive entities. Epidemics were explained in terms of corruption or poisoning of the ambient air, which produced a similar imbalance of humors in many people at the same time. Some fourteenth- and fifteenth-century plague treatises had acknowledged a role for contagion in the form of poisonous vapors from a patient's breath or sweat capable of engendering disease in others. Belief in the corruption of the air could thus be reconciled with the observation that plague appeared to be transmitted from person to person (the actual transmission cycle of bubonic plague, involving fleas and their rat and human hosts, remained unknown until the late nineteenth century). Some theorists also alleged that corruption of the air was itself caused by astronomical events, usually planetary conjunctions. Thus in 1497 Niccolò Leoniceno of Ferrara explained the outbreak of *morbus gal-*

licus as the result of corruption of the air by an excess of heat and humidity. In a treatise first published in 1502 Juan Almenar, of the university of Valencia, offered the same type of explanation but blamed cold and dry humors caused by the entry of Saturn into Aries.

Leoniceno, a distinguished scholar of Greek, found discrepancies by exhaustively comparing the symptoms of *morbus gallicus* with ancient descriptions of diseases involving skin eruptions, sores on the genitals, and so on. However, he concluded that although diseases might manifest themselves in different forms or simply remain unnamed, there could be no such thing as an entirely new disease, since the same natural causes had always operated.

Morbus gallicus contributed to theories about disease transmission by providing powerful evidence of the role of contagion, since the fact of sexual transmission was hard to ignore. Medical practitioners and the general public alike readily accepted the idea that *morbus gallicus* was highly contagious, but most medical theories of contagion continued to be couched in terms of poisonous vapors or exhalations. These might either infect people directly or contaminate bedding, clothing, and household objects. Juan Almenar did sardonically acknowledge the role of contagion by noting that the disease "makes women and monks get the reputation of being unchaste." (He also made it clear that some victims would find it convenient to blame their infection solely on direct disturbance of the humors by corrupt air.)

The physician and natural philosopher Girolamo Fracastoro contributed to the debate about *morbus gallicus* in a unique way, not by his hypothesis that contagion was transmitted by invisible seeds of disease in the air—this notion had more to do with his reading of Lucretius' version of Epicurean atomic theory than with any anticipation of bacterial theory[7]—but by inventing the name by which the disease eventually became known. His Latin poem in dactylic hexameter, *Syphilis* (1530), describes the ravages of the disease in Italy, offers a versified regimen for sufferers, and concludes with two elaborate pseudoclassical myths about the origins of methods of treatment. One tells the story of the shepherd Syphilus, who was punished for blasphemy because he worshipped the king instead of the gods.

The extent to which *morbus gallicus* was regarded as blameworthy in individuals varied widely. Several early treatises express much sympathy for the patient, although descriptions seem to be most strikingly sympathetic when the victim is either a handsome young nobleman or the author himself. The characterization of *morbus gallicus* as a disease men caught from unchaste women was so frequently repeated as to become the norm. Yet women, too, might be perceived as innocent victims, if young, monogamous, and upper or middle class. In his colloquy *Coniugium impar* (Unequal Marriage) (1529) Erasmus attacked social-climbing parents who forced a daughter to marry a pox-stricken nobleman. Andrea Alciati took up the same theme in his popular emblem book, first published in 1550. Beneath the title "nupta contagioso," Alciati showed a picture of the ancient tyrant Mezentius of Caere, who supposedly punished a living man by having him bound to a corpse. The verse beneath the picture equates this cruelty with the act of a father who compels his daughter to marry a husband with *morbus gallicus*. A commentary by Claude Mignault in later editions of the *Emblemata* elaborates on the verse and refers the reader to Erasmus.[8]

Most depictions of *morbus gallicus* were far more graphic. Albrecht Dürer produced one of the earliest and most horrifying woodcuts. Lesser artists relied heavily on the old religious iconography of plague and leprosy, showing victims as simultaneously afflicted and protected by heaven. One early woodcut places a solitary sufferer in the position associated with the iconography of Job. In others

Figure 4.9 "Nupta contagioso," from Andrea Alciati's *Emblemata* (Lyons, 1550). In the accompanying poem, an ancient tyrant's punishment of a man by chaining him to a corpse is compared with the cruelty of a father who compels his daughter to marry a syphilitic.

groups of victims pray to the Virgin or Christ child to avert divine wrath and extend protection.[9]

Attempts to deal with *morbus gallicus* included public health measures, personal prophylactic advice, and remedies. Medieval and early Renaissance hospitals and sanitary regulations normally did not confine, categorize, or segregate the sick except in cases of leprosy or plague. In the twelfth and thirteenth centuries lepers were legally and socially isolated; in some cities they were confined in leper hospitals. Some southern European cities introduced quarantine regulations against plague in the late fourteenth century. But quarantine designed to deal with epidemics of limited duration and geographic range could not be effective against *morbus gallicus*, although cities occasionally attempted to expel or confine diseased prostitutes. Some hospitals continued to treat pox victims along with other patients; William Clowes claimed to have treated more than one thousand during five years as a surgeon at St. Bartholomew's Hospital in London. However, hospitals designed to segregate such patients were established.

Counsels of abstinence were of course proffered. The pragmatic Juan Almenar, recognizing the limited usefulness of such advice, added that if intercourse did occur both men and women should wash their genitals carefully afterward. He advised his readers, whom he assumed to be male, to bring their own clean towels and not to use those supplied by prostitutes. It is unclear what effect, if any, the association of prostitutes with *morbus gallicus* had on the complex social history of Renaissance prostitution. In the fifteenth and early sixteenth centuries prostitution was openly tolerated in many European cities. By the mid-sixteenth century a harsher and more punitive attitude developed, but the change apparently owed more to the moral rigor of the Reformation and Counter-Reformation than to fear of disease.[10]

Most treatment, however, took the form of medication after the fact. Since the long-delayed manifestations of tertiary syphilis were not recognized as such, *morbus gallicus* was viewed, in some cases at least, as a treatable disease. Throughout much of the sixteenth century two principal treatments competed. Mercury in one form or another, used throughout the Middle Ages to treat leprosy and other skin diseases, was employed against syphilis from soon after the first epidemic until the advent of salvarsan in the early twentieth century. This heroic therapy produced severe side effects. The patient was made to spend many days smeared with mercurial ointment heated as hot as possible. The resulting salivation and copious sweating were interpreted as the excretion of bad humors; loosened teeth and loss of hair were regarded as effects of the disease, not of the treatment.[11]

The second, less unpleasant form of treatment involved drinking a decoction of guaiacum, a tropical wood from the New World. Guaiacum was introduced some years after the first epidemic, when New World commerce had had some time to develop. Its merits were touted in a 1518 treatise by Dr. Leonard Schmaus and subsequently extolled by Hutten and others. Schmaus denied that *morbus gallicus* was a new disease, that it was sexually transmitted, and that it had been imported to Europe from the New World: it had always existed in the Old World but had simply not been known to Europeans until climatic conditions in 1494 had encouraged corruption of the air. But the peoples of the New World had done Europe the favor of showing European merchants the indigenous plant used as medicine for the disease—the marvelous guaiacum. Ironically, enthusiasm for the benefits of New World flora may have helped to foster the idea that the disease, too, had come from there.

The sharpest critic of guaiacum was the mystic and magus Paracelsus, who repudiated all orthodox medical theory and treatment, preferring a mixture of alchemical tradition and his own ideas. In

Figure 4.10 A seventeenth-century print from Theodor Galle's *Nova Reperta*, after Johannes Stradanus, details the preparation of a guaiac concoction (right), which is administered to a sufferer from syphilis (left). The print administers a moral as well: the painting on the syphilitic's bedroom wall depicts the lifestyle that resulted in the patient's infection.

1528–1530 Paracelsus maintained in a series of works on *morbus gallicus* both that the disease was an invasive entity and that other illnesses could turn into *morbus gallicus*. Regarding mercury as a fundamental principle of living beings that could both cause and cure disease, he substituted his own version of mercury treatment for current methods; his recognition of mercury's toxicity led him to advocate modification of its effects by alchemical means. Paracelsus also believed that nature had implanted signatures in certain plants and minerals showing them to be remedies for specific diseases, but he did not think guaiacum was one of them. He denounced it as a commercial scam, useful only to the Fugger of Augsburg, who held an import monopoly on the substance. As a result of Paracelsus' treatise on guaiacum in 1528, the Fugger exerted influence to suppress some of his other writings on *morbus gallicus*.[12]

In Renaissance Europe, the experience of sexually transmitted disease of unprecedented severity was yet another development that helped to break the mold of the medieval past. The prescriptive works in which contemporaries discussed, explained, debated, quarreled, and offered advice provide only incomplete glimpses of how the prevalence of serious venereal disease actually affected sexual life. The most striking feature of this literature is, indeed, the power of existing explanations, beliefs, and social attitudes, many of them traditional, to incorporate the experience.

The pox made profits for merchants and doctors, ruined lives, and sharpened medical debates. Its appearance around 1500 paradoxically made some Europeans, whose microbes had decimated the populations of the New World, regard the native inhabitants of the Americas as the sources of a loathsome disease. But its challenge did not and could not break the hold of established theories and therapies.

A New World of Learning

5

The Lord Chancellor Announces a Revolution

In 1620 Francis Bacon published a manifesto. He called for a *Great Instauration* of the temple of knowledge—an enterprise as vast, demanding, and central to human history as Solomon's Instauration of the original Temple of the Jews. Bacon argued that the adoption of new modes of study could bring about a revolution in natural philosophy—what we would call science. Philosophers had already spent far too long—had spent, in fact, almost all of human history—producing elegant arguments. Instead they should have done what Bacon's new natural philosopher would do in the future: produce knowledge that could affect the course of nature in useful ways, knowledge about how to ward off disease, improve crops, extend the span of life, and enhance the general welfare. The simple fact that such theories worked—their practical effectiveness and utility—would be the outward and visible sign of their correctness: "Fruits and works are as it were sponsors and sureties for the truth of philosophies."

Such theories should not rest on citation of ancient authorities, any more than claims to personal virtue should rest on lists of distant noble ancestors. And they should not take the elaborate forms of presentation typical of earlier scientific writing. In each case, the facts of the matter—not the ancestry or elegance of the theory—required testing. Straightforward collection of the facts, direct inference of scientific laws plainly stated, application of these in practice—these simple processes would yield what thousands of years of philosophical argument had not.

Both the New World and ancient texts played key roles in Bacon's dramas of scientific discovery, but their parts contrasted as radically as those of Horatio and Iago. From the start, he took the discovery of the New World by Europeans as the model for all intelligent efforts to obtain new knowledge. The title page of the *Great Instauration* shows a ship sailing past classical columns that represent the Pillars of Hercules, the ancient limits of navigation and knowledge. The scene deliberately reuses—and subverts—traditional images and values. The emperor Charles V had taken the pillars as his symbol, glossing them with the cautious humanist motto *Ne plus ultra*, "Do not go too far." Bacon kept the pillars but sent his ship past them and lopped a vital word from the accompanying Latin tag. *Plus ultra*, he urged his readers: "Too far is not enough." Discovery, not reading, has become the central mode of obtaining important knowledge. And the knowledge that awaits discovery does not lie within the existing resources of Western culture, between the covers of the books that weigh down library shelves, but outside it, just as the New World had lain outside what men knew. The fact of geographical discovery licensed men—indeed, required them—to undertake intellectual voyages of equal bravura, undeterred by the fact that they could not know where they would land: "Surely it would be disgraceful if, while the regions of the material globe—that is, of the earth, of the sea, and of the stars—have been in our times laid widely open and revealed, the intellectual globe should remain shut up within the narrow limit of old discoveries."

Scholars and books served as the foil to Columbus and his ship.

Figure 5.1 The title page of Francis Bacon's *Instauratio magna* (*Great Instauration*) (London, 1620).

To be sure, Bacon insisted on the need to study the textual traditions. But he looked back at them in anger and expected his readers to do the same. One should study past thought not as authority but as history, in order to see how it had gone wrong. Bacon described the study of the canon not as an exercise in meditation, a survey of the cultivated, elegant landscape of European thought, but as a Herculean effort to clean a structure that had been filthy for centuries, to clear an enormous clogged drain. Anyone who inspected the history of thought carefully had to find the prospect deeply depressing: "For out of the five and twenty centuries over which the memory and learning of men extends, you can hardly pick out six that were fertile in sciences or favorable to their development." And anyone who carried out the inspection, as Bacon did, with open eyes, knew exactly at whose doors to lay the blame for the human race's general failure to think for itself.

The Greeks stood at the beginning of the story, already infected with two sorts of original sin. They had theorized too much and they had known too little. The character of their thought had been fixed in advance by the larger nature of their society. Working competitively in large cities, sophists taught for pay and philosophers for reputation. Both sorts of thinker had naturally tried less to find the truth than to win debates. Their philosophy, accordingly, concentrated less on the workings of nature than on the tricks of argument: "The wisdom of the Greeks was professorial and much given to disputations, a kind of wisdom most adverse to the disquisition of truth."

On the other hand, the character "of the time and age" had done as much harm as that of Greek society. The Greeks had possessed "but a narrow and meager knowledge either of time or place." Their knowledge of the past was short and confused, "only fables and rumors of antiquity." Their geography and ethnography were even more pathetic:

Of the regions and districts of the world they knew but a small portion, giving indiscriminately the name of Scythians to all in the North, of Celts to all in the West; knowing nothing of Africa beyond the hither side of Ethiopia, of Asia beyond the Ganges. Much less were they acquainted with the provinces of the New World, even by hearsay or any well-founded rumor; nay, a multitude of climates and zones, wherein innumerable nations breathe and live, were pronounced by them to be uninhabitable; and the travels of Democritus, Plato, and Pythagoras, which were rather suburban excursions, were talked of as something great.

Even those ancient philosophers who had had some inkling of the need to study nature directly, like Aristotle, had framed their hypotheses first and only then looked for data that confirmed them. Most of them had ignored the need to find data—and many had not investigated nature at all, but ethical and political problems that could not yield sharp positive answers.

Ancient ignorance, however, was only part of the problem that confronted modern philosophy. Later thinkers had exacerbated the mistakes of Greeks and Romans, because they tried not to alter or extend but only to verify their authoritative systems. They had done so in different ways, to be sure: the scholastics by spinning still subtler webs of hypotheses, the humanists by gilding still more gaudily the lilies of rhetoric. But all modern thinkers shared the same delusion. They agreed that the ancients had known far more and thought far more profoundly than they could, and all took the agreement of their own views with those of the old sages as a sign of their validity. Yet this whole enterprise of looking for truths in texts was miscast. It rested on a misplaced "reverence for antiquity" and for "the authority of men accounted great in philosophy." Its proponents failed to see that thanks to their greater opportunities to gather real knowledge, those who came later were actually older, not younger, than the so-called ancients: "the old age of the world is to be accounted the true antiquity, and this is the attribute of our own times, not of that earlier age in which the ancients lived, and which, though in respect of us it was the elder, yet in respect of the world it was the younger." The habit of taking one's terms and theories from books was a basic methodological error, one of the "idols" that had occupied the temple of wisdom and confused the minds and senses and mankind. Bacon smashed these with the double zeal of an Old Testament prophet cleansing the Temple and a Platonic philosopher exposing the phantasms of the cave.

The true philosopher must learn not to let the books he read "break and corrupt" the nature he could know purely. The rich leather folios and quartos, the dizzying Himalayas of printed matter that had challenged, terrified, inspired, and baffled a Bodin or a Montaigne, revealed not progress but stagnation, not inquiry directed to a clearly defined goal but arguments without end:

> And again, if a man turn from the workshop to the library, and wonder at the immense variety of books he sees there, let him but examine and diligently inspect their contents, and his wonder will assuredly be turned the other way. For after observing their endless repetitions, and how men are ever saying and doing what has been said and done before, he will pass from admiration of the variety to astonishment at the poverty and scantiness of the subjects which till now have occupied and possessed the minds of men.

Not only Ptolemy or Galen, then, but a whole canon's worth of ancients lay prostrate, and their legions of interpreters with them.

Bacon's theories did not all win assent, and his detailed prophecies about the growth of science were not all borne out. He had little grasp of classical mathematics or astronomy, much less of the advances made in both fields in the sixteenth century. His own scientific practice often contradicted his sapient precepts. When he

Figure 5.2   Columbus' and Vespucci's opening up of the New World forms a focus of Theodore Galle's *Nova Reperta* (after Johannes Stradanus). This is a celebration of discoveries both geographical and technological. The latter include gunpowder, the compass, the clock, printing, silk weaving, distillation, and the saddle with stirrups. Such devices and the discoveries were considered by many as evidence of progress and the superiority of contemporary European civilization to that of the ancients.

charmed off his warts, using the sympathetic influence of the rotting lard he had nailed up above his door, he revealed his considerable debt to an older tradition of writers of natural magic. Other scientific prophets—above all René Descartes—elaborated rival programs of inquiry into nature that proved at least as influential as his, and that contributed more to the actual development of new scientific methods. Thomas Hobbes, who worked as Bacon's secretary for a time, was not the only one who felt that as a philosopher, Bacon was a good lord chancellor.

Nonetheless, Bacon makes an appropriate as well as a powerful spokesman for the new mood of many innovative intellectuals. Educated at Cambridge and Gray's Inn in London, he knew the most up-to-date humanist scholarship and savored its challenges to the supremacy of Aristotelian logic and Roman law. Growing up in the second half of the sixteenth century, he knew from childhood what Bodin and others had had to discover by reflection: that the moderns had surpassed the ancients in vital areas of technology and philosophy. He also lived through a period of scientific discoveries, not all of which he appreciated, which shattered beyond restoration the scientific authority of the ancients.

In the forty years after 1572, the balance of scientific authority had gradually tilted. The discovery that comets and new stars appeared in the heavens finally destroyed the notion, basic to Aristotle and Ptolemy, that the heavens differed fundamentally from the Earth because they never changed. The discovery that blood passed from arteries to veins not through the septum in the heart, which had no holes after all, but through capillaries, did away with one foundation of the cardiovascular physiology that medical schools had taught for hundreds of years. Tycho Brahe's huge, magnificent instruments, erected at vast expense on his observatory island in Denmark, enabled him to attain a level of precision previously unimaginable in observing the skies. Galileo's telescope revealed irregularities on the theoretically perfect surface of the moon and new moons, unheard-of in theory but undeniable in practice, orbiting around Jupiter. William Gilbert—one scientist whom Bacon did appreciate—carried out a dazzling course of planned experiments on the magnet. Simple allegiance to classical authority came to seem less and less reasonable. And even in areas—like the study of politics and history—where the ancients still held sway, they did so not because their general authority was unchallenged but because they had described a world of absolute rulers and corrupt courts strikingly similar to the world of the late sixteenth century. Analogy, not antiquity, secured their authority.

In fact the most distinguished students of the ancient world now agreed with Bacon that the moderns had discovered much that no ancient could have known. By 1600 no scholar would have pronounced as hesitantly as Mercator had thirty years before that Ptolemy's *Geography* now had only a historical interest. A general belief in the pastness of the past was common ground. Accordingly, even Bacon's diatribes—like many other manifestos, before and since—were less iconoclastic paradoxes then pregnant statements of ideas widely shared, though not always articulated with so much edge and vigor. Others—like John Wilkins—would apply them to new fields, asserting that modern astronomy, for example, had radically outstripped that of the ancients.

Bacon drew his spatial images of discovery, his polemical evocation of a new continent or globe of knowledge, from the most recent literature on the New World. In the decades just before and after 1600, the New World continued to provoke detailed historical treatments, scriptural exegeses, and polemical tracts. The same insoluble questions arose again and again, intractable and unavoidable as the criers of new faiths at Hyde Park Corner: Where did the Indians

Figure 5.3 This title page makes a strong polemical point. Johannes Kepler had begun his *Rudolphine Tables* with a frontispiece depicting the progress of astronomy from ancient Babylon to Tycho Brahe. John Wilkins, however, asserts his independence by depicting only modern authorities—Copernicus, Kepler himself, and Galileo—on the title page of his *A Discourse concerning A New World & Another Planet In 2 Bookes* (London, 1640).

come from? Were they connected to the other high civilizations and nomadic tribes of the previously known world? Did the canonical writings of the ancients include references to their habitats, their origins, and their customs? The same passages that had always stimulated discussion—pseudo-Aristotle on the Carthaginians, Plato on Atlantis, the passages of the Bible and Apocrypha on the wanderings of the Jews—were canvassed again and again. But the results of these dialogues between moderns and ancients had no clear precedent in the century of previous debates and discussions.

To be sure, historians and polemicists still accepted certain textual ground rules as absolute. Catholics like the Jesuit José de Acosta, author of the most original and influential of all histories of the New World, and Protestants like Sir Walter Raleigh, author of one of the grandest histories of the Old World, took the Bible as the only fully valid account of the past. All men, Indians as well as Europeans, must descend somehow from Adam via one of the three sons of Noah who had survived the Flood. The existence of the New World must not undercut the authority of the Old Testament. And the truths of Christian theology must still explain the origin and nature of basic New World customs and beliefs. If Indians cherished myths of a great flood or worshipped a single God, for example, they did so for a reason as evident as it was orthodox: the devil, that brilliant dissimulator, had brought them within his spell by teaching them a parodic Black Sacred History, one modeled on the real thing but inverted, like the magicians' Black Mass.

Within that common scaffolding of assumptions, however, intellectuals now found it possible to erect wildly different structures. When Acosta reviewed the ancient texts that might refer to the Americas, he did so *de haut en bas*. They showed, he concluded, at the very most that the ancients had had a confused and indirect knowledge of the other continents. None of their myths or histories applied in detail to the New World peoples. Those peoples had reached their habitat by ways traceable not through texts, but only through rational conjectures: by land migration from Asia. Their story, accordingly, though still confined chronologically within the biblical history of man, was basically new. It must be excavated from the evidence of continental shores and tribal customs rather than read about in authoritative texts. And it must match, at least roughly, the story of European pagans' progress from wretched isolation to civilized society, as told by Cicero in his account of the socializing force of oratory.

Raleigh's great book appeared in 1614, a decade after the English translation of Acosta. An explorer himself, Raleigh took the opening up of the New World as one of the great events of history. On his frontispiece history, the "witness of time" holds up a globe showing the site of Paradise with Adam and Eve about to commit their sin. But the globe shows North and South America as well as the Old World, with modern ships at war in the north Atlantic and a lone explorer's galleon in the south. Later chapters and maps laid out Noachian genealogies for every imaginable people. And ancient authorities still bulked large. Raleigh still admired the magical prowess of ancient Near Eastern sages like Zoroaster; he was shocked by Isaac Casaubon's powerful argument that the supposed revelations of the Egyptian sage Hermes Trismegistus were in fact late Greek forgeries. When he discussed the nature of the Tree of Knowledge of Good and Evil in Paradise, he used his own experience only to refute the notion of an earlier writer, Goropius Becanus, that it must have been a *ficus Indica*; Raleigh, who had seen such trees in the New World, knew that they were not so large as his bookish opponent thought. But he took his own solution to the problem from another ancient text—the writings of the Jewish philosopher Philo. Yet Raleigh, too, offered conjectures in place of texts when

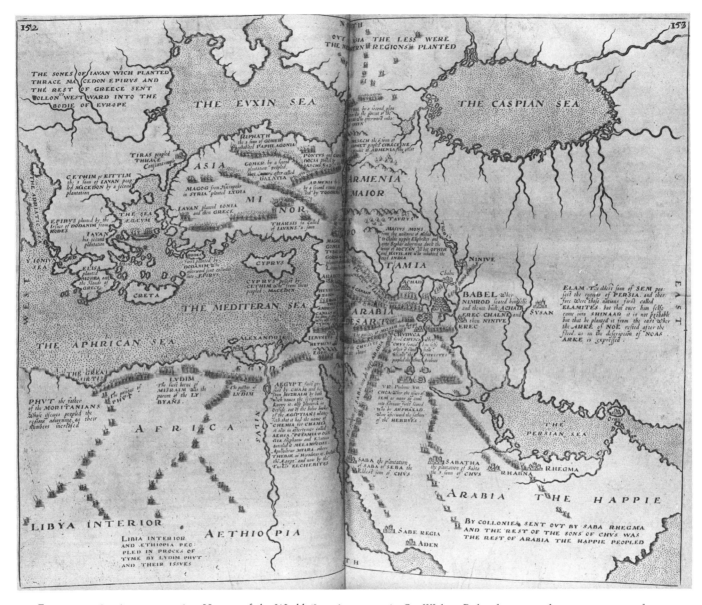

Figure 5.4   In this map in his *Historie of the World* (London, 1634), Sir Walter Raleigh traces the movements of Noah's descendants through Asia, parts of Europe, North Africa, and the Middle East.

Hugo Grotius and Isaac La Peyrère

THE celebrated Dutch humanist scholar Hugo Grotius is best known for his pioneering works on international law such as the *De jure belli ac pacis*. But he also wrote *De origine gentium Americanarum* (1625), a short treatise in which he presented a complicated theory of the origins of New World peoples based on etymological evidence and comparison of customs and religion. Although his conclusions were novel, his premise was the same as others writing on the subject: "From the start it must be maintained that the race of mankind was diffused into all parts of the world either from the time of Noah or from the time of the erection of the Tower of Babel."

As the T–O map of Isidore of Seville shows (Figure 2.3), Europeans had long believed that each of the three known races—European, Asian, and African—had descended from one of the three sons of Noah, respectively Japheth, Shem, and Ham. A race not accounted for by this tidy tripartite scheme was one of those inconvenient facts that had potentially disastrous consequences for biblical authority.

Yet the theory would be saved if, by some means, the New World inhabitants could be said to have descended from some people of the Old World. A variety of opinions about the origins of New World peoples were offered and refuted: Marc Lescarbot held that Noah had personally settled in Brazil, Manasseh Ben Israel argued that they were the lost tribes of Israel, Edward Brerewood believed them Tartars, Georgius Hornius adopted a theory as elaborate as Grotius (that is, that New World peoples derived from more than one Old World stock), and pet theories were advanced in maps as well as in prose.

Grotius argued that the northern peoples were descended from the "Germans," or, more specifically, Scandinavians who island-hopped across the North Atlantic from Iceland to Greenland to North America. He argued this on the basis of such etymological "evidence" as the similarity of place-name endings: Is*land* and Groen*lant* in Germanic languages, Quaxit*lan* and Ocot*lan* in America. Another argument came from Tacitus; because, for Grotius, Indian marriage customs were similar to those of the ancient Germans, there had to be a connection between the two groups. Comparisons of customs led Grotius to believe that the peoples of the Yucatan peninsula came from Ethiopia and those of South America from southeast Asia—except for the Peruvians, whose sun worship and high civilization suggested that they hailed from China.

Grotius' work reflects his anxiety about the New World's challenge to biblical authority. In the sixteenth century, both Paracelsus and Giordano Bruno had argued that New World peoples were unrelated to those of the Old. In the seventeenth, the idea of polygenesis received impetus when Isaac La Peyrère took up the thesis in two books published in midcentury. Grotius, in writing his treatise, clearly had La Peyrère's ideas in mind:

"[If it is argued that] these peoples are not Germans on the grounds that many of their words reveal them not to be so, then they will not be descended from any people because their words are not like those of any other people; then we must believe, with Aristotle, that they have been present throughout all eternity, or that they sprung from the Earth, as the legend has it about Sparta, or from the ocean, as Homer would have it, or before Adam there were other unknown men, as has recently been imagined by some in France. If these things are believed, I see a great danger to piety; if my theses are believed, I see no danger at all."

La Peyrère, however, was no more eager to destroy biblical authority than was Grotius. Far from it: he argued that Adam was not literally the first man, but only first father of all men in an allegorical sense because first father of all sinners. He thought he had thus reconciled faith and reason and reconciled biblical chronology with those of other civilizations:

" the History of Genesis appears much clearer and agrees with itself. And it is wonderfully reconciled with all prophane Records whether ancient or new, to wit, those of the Caldeans [sic], Egyptians, Scythians, and Chinensians; that most ancient Creation on which is set down in the first of Genesis is reconciled to those of Mexico, not long ago discovered by Columbus; It is likewise reconciled to those Northern and Southern nations which are not known, All whom, as likewise those of the first and most ancient creation were, it is probable, created with the Earth itself in all parts thereof, and not propagated from Adam."

La Peyrère's *Praeadamitae* (1655) attests widespread speculation about life in the state of nature and natural law, and he evidently did not realize that, by comparing a sacred history with profane histories, he considerably demoted the former. His fresh if rather naive excursion into biblical exegesis was seemingly motivated by the best of intentions: by making Genesis a more reasonable text, he would make it more convincing, and thus the heathen would be more receptive to it and would more willingly convert to the true religion, Christianity.

Sources: Allen 1949; Hodgen 1964; Rubiés 1991.

it came to the New World, using physical science to create a story of the people of this area because he had no written sources—so he thought—to go on.

The debates of the seventeenth century on American origins would be no more disinterested—and would shed no more light—than those of the late sixteenth. When Hugo Grotius attacked the question, using etymology and the evidence of customs to establish the descent of some Indians from the Lapps, he no doubt did so at least in part with an eye on the interests of the Swedish monarchy he served. His thesis provided a historical basis for a claim to New World colonies as well as a genealogy for the native peoples there. His attacker Jan de Laet, though far more knowledgeable—he sent Grotius a copy of Acosta, with his compliments—was no more open-minded. Both men proved far more critical and discriminating when they attacked the theories of others, brilliantly exposing their opponents' arbitrary use of single etymologies or isolated parallels in customs, than when they defended their own.

Almost all the North European controversialists, however, agreed on the vital point: the classical stories no longer offered lasts to which New World origins could be bent. Only the Bible remained, and even that provided only limits to the range of hypotheses one could frame, not precise guidance in framing them. The New World had become a preeminently new thing, the clearest evidence not only of the limits of the ancients' travels but also of the limits of their knowledge. Bacon—who read Bodin, Acosta, and Raleigh—only annexed the most up-to-date views of the new continents when he refused to explain how their peoples had arrived and insisted on their novelty so far as Europeans were concerned. In a sense he followed Acosta even when he situated his own unfinished utopia, the New Atlantis, firmly within a conjectural history of the movements of ancient peoples. Like Acosta's history of the Indians, Bacon's fantasy fitted within the cradle of biblical time but lacked any connection with the details of biblical history. Clearly the most up-to-date theories about the New World did much to shape Bacon's view of history.

Yet Bacon relied more on ancient texts than he admitted in his polemical statements. He looked for anticipations of his views in texts—not, to be sure, in the elaborate sand-castles of ancient theory that he trampled on, but in the fragmentary views of pre-Socratics concealed under them. When arguing that the perpetual debates of the Greek thinkers had been sterile, he significantly quoted Heraclitus, who had said much the same some two thousand years before. Bacon also hoped to find profound ideas about nature in the Greek myths. He retold and analyzed these allegorically, drawing heavily on Renaissance writers about the ancient gods; though he wriggled uncomfortably as he found these treasures of ancient wisdom, which suggested that Greek thought had had profound elements after all. Bacon never fully resolved this dilemma, but he adumbrated a way out. He argued that the Greeks, in their ignorance of history and nature, were not primitive but forgetful: as the Egyptian priests had told Solon and Hecataeus, the Greeks had failed to keep records and so lost track of an older, wider wisdom, bits of which survived fragmentarily in the myths which their poets had retold without understanding them. The *Great Instauration*, for all its bashing of tradition, offered a program for the recovery of a lost wisdom.

Even when Bacon made his most strident and iconoclastic efforts to reframe the whole course of cultural history, in fact, the most canonical of texts guided him. Both his history of ideas and his program for science centered on his assertion of the possibility of progress, his belief in the reality of the new. Far more radically than Bodin or Leroy, Bacon insisted that the discoveries had made a different world. The moderns not only knew more than the ancients

Cyrano de Bergerac and the Men in the Moon

JOHN WILKINS in his 1640 *Discourse concerning a New World and Another Planet* wrote that the experience of discovering continents and peoples previously unknown ought to lead one to believe life on other worlds possible. Savinien de Cyrano de Bergerac did him one better: he claimed to have visited just such another inhabited world—the moon.

Cyrano de Bergerac was without doubt the most original of French freethinkers, and his *Comical History of the States and Empires of the Worlds of the Moon and Sun* is a sophisticated satire of the contemporary European world of learning and travel literature in general. Among other things, he pokes fun at the Aristotelians, "proves" via his flight the rotation of the earth and the gravitational pull of the moon, and argues most logically that the life of a cabbage is infinitely more precious than that of a man. When Cyrano describes moon dwellers who subsist solely on the fumes of food, we are reminded of Pliny's apple smellers. Odd modes of locomotion, as well as peculiar dietary habits, had always been hallmarks of the monstrous races—hence, the moon dwellers walk on all fours rather than upright and, like good Renaissance earth dwellers, make their posture a claim to quasi-divine human status.

Cyrano's account is significant for the story of cultural contact as well. Cyrano, it appears, was one of the few Europeans who could imagine himself as the outsider, the intruder whose presence provokes debate about fundamental issues such as what defines a human being. Imprisoned with a Spaniard who had also made his way to the moon, Cyrano learns the aristocratic moon language based on musical tones and, as language is the hallmark of humanity and civilization, inadvertently creates real conceptual problems for his keepers:

"[I]t was decreed, That at best, I should only pass for a Parrot without Feathers, for they confirmed those, who were already perswaded, in that I had but two Legs no more than a Bird, which was the cause I was put into a Cage, by express orders from the Privy Council.

"There the Queen's Bird-keeper, taking the pains daily to teach me to Whistle, as they do Stares or Singing-Birds here, I was really happy in that I wanted not Food: In the mean while, with the Sonnets the Spectators stunned me, I learnt to speak as they did; so that when I was got to be so much Master of the Idiom, as to express most of my thoughts, I told them the finest of my Conceits. The Quainteness of my Sayings, was already the entertainment of all Societies, and my Wit was so much esteemed, that the Council was obliged to Publish an Edict forbidding all People to believe, that I was endowed with Reason; with express Commands to all Persons, of what Quality or Condition soever, not to imagine, but that whatever I did, though never so wittily, proceeded only from instinct."

Source. Cyrano de Bergerac 1687.

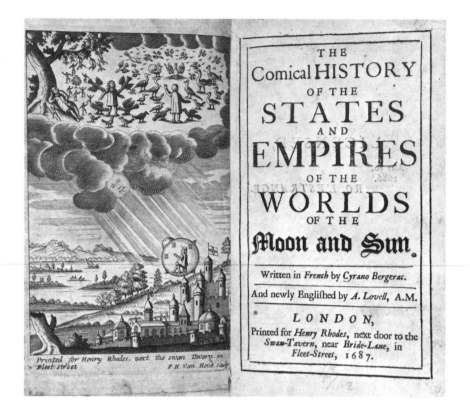

Figure 5.5 The frontispiece and title page of Savinien de Cyrano de Bergerac's fantastic voyage of discovery, one more ambitious than that of Columbus but perhaps inconceivable before him; from his *Comical History of the States and Empires of the Worlds of the Moon and Sun* (London, 1687).

about certain things; their knowledge of the world had increased exponentially, irreversibly. Bacon's own reform of science was meant to have similarly shattering effects on the knowledge of natural processes.

The title page of the *Great Instauration* makes clear the origin and basis of Bacon's confidence that the intellectual globe would soon be turned upside down. He relied on a text. At the bottom of the design appears a quotation from the biblical book of Daniel—a description of the consequences of the end of human time in terms that gave that terrifying moment a glow of hope: "Many," said Daniel, "shall pass to and fro, and knowledge shall be increased."

Bacon saw the discoveries as fulfilling the first half of this prophecy; his new science would bear out the second. The most traditional of sanctions underpinned his command to throw off all tradition. And it seems evident throughout Bacon's work—with its prophetic analogies, its attack on "idols," its passionate sense that history could really change—that he, like Columbus, understood the future in the terms of prophecy because the one text he considered unchallengeable guided him in that direction. Bacon could imagine a new world, in short, not only because he knew new facts, but because he had inherited the most vivid of visions of novelty from what he thought the oldest of books. Textual authority still catalyzed the interaction among data even when the data no longer came from texts. Parts of the temple of canonical books would remain in place even after Bacon had torn down its Aristotelian textual pillars.[1]

Bacon stands not as the spokesman of an idiosyncratic program but as the *portavoce* for two generations of Europeans. In his hesitancies as much as in his assertions, his continued recourse to the textual authorities he disliked, his experience reveals something profound about the European mind of his time.

Where the Facts Are: Museums, Academies, and Universities

Across Europe, intellectuals moved into new habitats. In courts and cities from Prague to Copenhagen, monarchs, scientists, and amateurs were studying in an environment as remarkable for its lack of books as the traditional scholar's study had been defined by their presence. Variously called the museum, the cabinet of curiosities, the *Kunst- und Wunderkammer*, the new locale was furnished not with texts but with exactly the sort of natural objects that Bacon had demanded that scholars study.

One of the most famous of these—Ole Worm's Musaeum Wormianum in Copenhagen—is recorded in detail in a printed catalogue.

Figure 5.6 The opening up of the world of learning, portrayed in the frontispiece of Joseph François Lafitau's *Moeurs des sauvages amériquains comparées aux moeurs des premiers temps* (Paris, 1724) contrasts powerfully with the title page of Reisch's *Margarita philosophica* (Figure 1.1). The student, seated at right, is encouraged to pursue knowledge not just through ancient texts, but also in objects such as sculpture, medallions, and New World accounts, maps, and curiosities. The disordered assemblage of objects in the foreground suggests the ever-popular cabinet of curiosities, in contrast to the neat and symmetrical world of closed disciplines two centuries before.

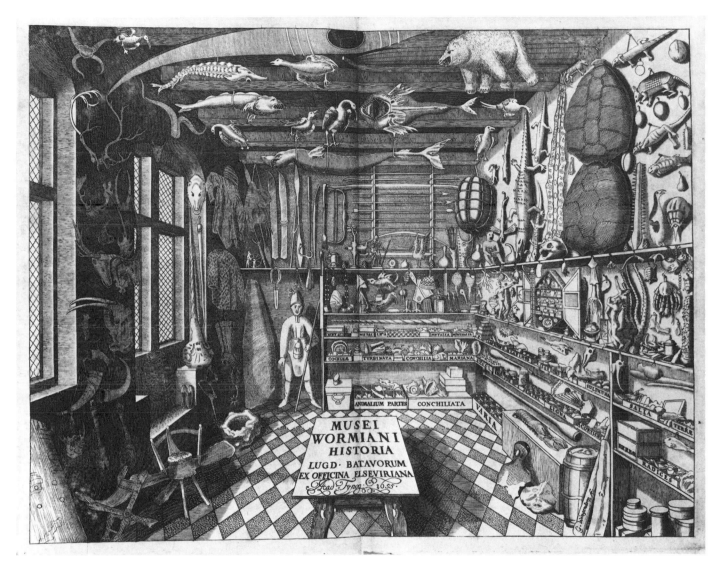

Figure 5.7 The title page of Ole Worm's *Musei Wormiani historia* (Leiden, 1655).

It confronted the visitor with a spectacular range of solid, material objects—the concrete evidence that made scholarly and scientific progress possible. The room it filled, as depicted on the title page of Worm's book, calls to mind many earlier portrayals of scholars' studies—the sort of orderly space, lit by large leaded windows, paved with neat tiles, where St. Jerome and his lion or Erasmus might have felt perfectly at home. But the furniture would certainly have alarmed them. The shelves swarm not with books but with specimens: minerals, seashells, roots, and parts of animals. Canoes, birds, and fish hang from the rafters; the shells of seagoing turtles and the skulls of horned animals decorate the walls. A massive display of artifacts and weapons reveals Worm's specific interest in the early history of man—an interest that led him to study and decipher runes, master the primitive calendars of pre-Christian Scandinavia, and excavate the megalithic tomb sites where, he thought, the ancestors of modern Danes had shed the blood of animals to honor their own ancestors. Worm pursued this study not in books but across the countryside, bringing draftsmen to make careful records of the sites he investigated and working with a technique so meticulous that Bacon would certainly have been impressed. He slowly brushed the dirt and plant life from the monuments, carefully distinguished between letters and cracks, and refused to interpret until he had described with care. Bacon would have appreciated the narwhal's skull and horn which Worm used to refute the traditional belief that such horns came from unicorns.

To be sure, Worm's principles of classification are not modern ones. His scheme led him to put all stones together, those that had been formed by nature and those, like the ax-heads called thunderstones, that had been shaped into tools by men, rather than to distinguish between natural phenomena and artifacts. But the environment in which he deliberately immured himself—the three-dimensional display of the new world of natural fact, with its concrete details of the life of primitive men—clearly reflects the new imperative. Like Bacon, Worm believed that one should obey nature, by collecting thousands of instances of natural processes in action, before trying to command her, by stating theories about natural laws. Similar rooms, equally profuse in things displayed and loved for their own sake, decorated the imperial *Kunst- und Wunderkammer* in Prague, the electoral one in Dresden, Athanasius Kircher's museum in Rome, and Elias Ashmole's museum in Oxford.[2]

In each case natural objects, carefully arrayed in rational order but allowed to speak for themselves rather than through texts, display the new sense of nature and the new rhetoric of the specialized laboratory to which Bacon gave voice. The learned traveler like the young English virtuoso John Evelyn, who explored Europe in the 1640s, found Catholics and Protestants, priests and laymen equally disposed to show off "perpetual motions, Catoptrics, Magnetical experiments, Modells, and a thousand other crotchets & devises." "Rattling bones to cast dyes in use among the Romans . . . the true Remora . . . about the bigness of an Hering and not much unlike it in length of Shape . . . and supplied with a Sucker like a Leach . . . the knee Bone of a Gyant 23 Inchees in compass all Anotamist(s) concluding it to have been of a man"—these were only some of the exciting natural and human antiquities that Roman virtuosi allowed Evelyn to inspect. The thing had joined the book as a prime object of study; and nothing had done more to encourage men to make this change than the discovery of that greatest and most unexpected thing to the West.

Study itself, moreover, had begun to be transformed. In 1480 the European scholar read and thought alone, in retirement, and passed on his knowledge in company, in the university or the printer's shop. In Bacon's time and after, by contrast, the scholar tended more and more to work with others. Reformed institutions of learning had sprung up—the Academy of the Lincei in Rome, Gresham's College in London, the Athenaeum Illustre in Amsterdam, courts from Prague to London—where men of the book and men of the lens and the lathe met and argued over nature's secrets. A new ideal of learning, collective rather than solitary, based on a common effort to identify and understand the new rather than a solitary dedication to understanding and preserving the old, had taken root. Before the end of the century it would flower in the Paris Academy of Sciences and the Royal Society of London, those great organizations dedicated to new visions of truth and argument that owed much to Bacon and Descartes. [3]

Like Bacon's own books, the new institutions of seventeenth-century learning often leavened their new habits of mind and action with substantial helpings of tradition. Even the members of the Royal Society expressed their claim to intellectual independence with a motto quoted from the Roman poet Horace. The best way to taste the mixture is to move from the stimulating but baffling wonders of Worm's museum and similar places to an institution equally radical in many ways, but far longer-lasting and much larger: the newest university in Bacon's Europe, that of Leiden, near The Hague in the Low Countries province of Holland. Radical from the start, the university was founded in 1575 to celebrate the city's successful resistance to a Spanish siege—one of the most dramatic events of the dramatic revolt that transformed Holland and the other northern provinces into Europe's newest state. Even its charter had to be forged, since the supposed monarch of the Low Countries, Philip II of Spain, would hardly have given royal sanction to his own worst enemies. Tiny at the outset, Leiden soon became the largest university in Europe, drawing many students from Germany and England—including Sir Thomas Browne. By 1625—when the ancient historian Johannes Meursius celebrated its first jubilee by publishing a detailed description of its facilities and faculties, significantly titled *Athenae Batavae* (The Dutch Athens)—it had also become a center of intellectual innovation.

The university, as Meursius carefully showed, was anything but a retired place of calm and contemplation. Its medical students learned about the properties of plants not only in their books but in the botanical garden, founded by the brilliant naturalist Charles de l'Escluse, where formal lectures took place in the summer and experiments went on all year round. "Here," Meursius commented, "experts in botany find many gifts of our climate to admire." They learned about anatomy in an elaborate theater dedicated to the subject, founded in 1597, where Petrus Pauw, who combined extraordinary dexterity as an anatomist with great wit and learning, had "dissected in the space of 22 years both animals of various kinds and sixty human bodies of both sexes." Engineers could master their craft—vital to Holland, which depended on dikes and windmills, trade and craft—in a special school directed by Simon Stevin, where lectures were held in Dutch rather than the usual Latin.

In Leiden even lectures on classical subjects—like Roman history—had a keen modern edge. They dealt less with abstract virtues than with concrete tactics—the details of camp-building and fortification, maneuvers, and chains of command by which the Romans had defeated all comers. Maurice of Nassau, the brilliant Dutch general who defeated the Spanish, learned much of what he put into practice on the battlefield in the Leiden classroom, where he was taken through Polybius' description of the Roman armies by the charismatic historian Justus Lipsius. Leiden scholars pursued languages rarely studied in the West, like Arabic and Persian, and introduced new subjects to the curriculum, like geography.

Leiden, then, though it called itself by the traditional name of

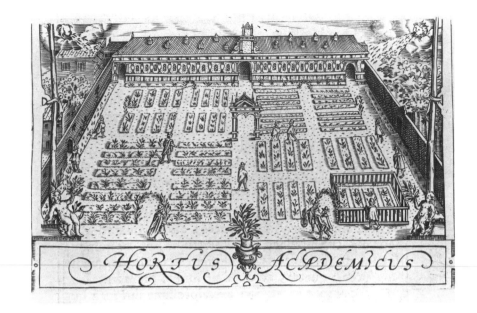

Figure 5.8 The University of Leiden's botanical garden, in Johannes Meursius' *Athenae Batavae* (Leiden, 1625).

university, was in fact as modern as any site of learning in the world. Meursius' description dramatized the novelties that students and visitors would encounter in Leiden. The anatomy theater, for example, was not merely an auditorium with a table for cutting up bodies. Arranged in meticulous order on its walls and between its circular rows of seats appeared the same sorts of natural and human objects that so delighted Ole Worm:

> dried human intestines, stomach and skin; all the bones of a man and a woman, artfully connected; also those of many animals, a horse, a cow, a stag, a wolf, a bear, a goat, a monkey, a dog, a fox, a cat . . . the bones and teeth of a whale; and finally human bodies, preserved with spices and dried, and other bodies, brought here from Egypt and donated by the merchant Peter Guilelmus. Moreover anatomical diagrams, and a cupboard stocked with all the instruments needed for dissection.

The cabinet of curiosities had joined the university.

Evelyn, that connoisseur of the new science, was unimpressed by the university's professors. But he took considerable interest and pleasure in his

> sight of their anatomy-school, theatre and repository adjoining, which is well furnished with natural curiosities, from the whale and elephant to the fly and spider, which last is a very delicate piece of art, to see how the bones—if I may so call them of so tender an insect—could be separated from the mucilaginous parts of that minute animal. Amongst a great variety of other things, I was shown the knife newly taken out of a drunken Dutchman's guts . . . The pictures of the chirurgeon and his patient, both living, were there.

In this environment Bacon's program seems at once realized and qualified. The world of the book and the book of the world, the traditions of learning and the traditions of the craftsmen, have already been united. The Dutch culture of observation—which in the seventeenth century expressed itself so vividly in both the vividness of oil painting and the precision of microscopy—had wedded itself to the culture of academic tradition.

Yet the university's fabric, even more than that of Bacon's books, retained a strongly classical weave and texture. Most lectures continued to address specific ancient texts rather than subjects or problems in the modern vein. The university devoted its resources as lavishly to its famous, splendid library as to its sites of direct study of nature. Meursius took great pleasure in displaying the rich provision of "dead teachers" who appeared on the shelves of the library's neatly classified benches: "These original authors," he explained, "set out in a public place, promote the studies of the young through reading as [the live professors do] through lectures." The library as well as the anatomy theater bore the decorations that showed how highly the university curators esteemed it: a huge drawing of Constanti-

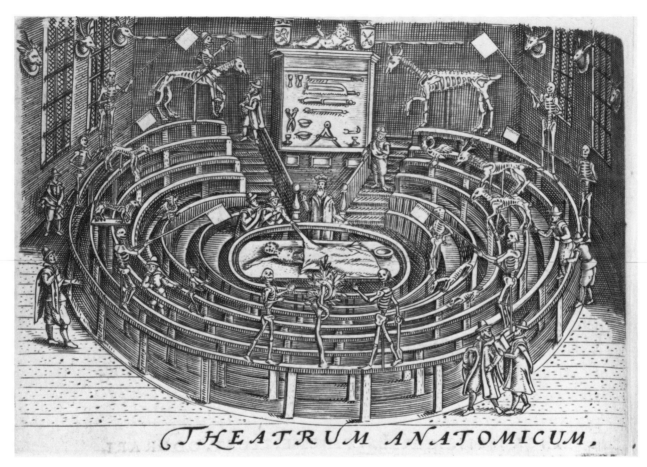

THEATRUM ANATOMICUM.

Figure 5.9 The University of
Leiden's anatomy theater, in
Johannes Meursius' *Athenae
Batavae* (Leiden, 1625).

nople and the portraits of those professors whose publications had
won them reputations. Even the skeletons in the anatomy theater
were laid out to teach traditional moral lessons about the fragility
of human life as well as novel scientific ones about the structure of
the human frame.

Books still counted. The massed sages of the faculties of philosophy and theology, when asked their opinion on the licitness of

BIBLIOTHECA PUBLICA.

Figure 5.10 The University of Leiden's library, in Johannes Meursius' *Athenae Batavae* (Leiden, 1625).

trials for witchcraft, responded firmly that the traditional water test did not in fact provide a valid diagnostic tool. But their reasoning was as steeped in traditions—in this case, those of Galen's physiology—as their conclusions were iconoclastic. The old women normally accused of witchcraft, they pointed out, often suffered from melancholy, an excess of black bile over the other three humors. This condition made them flatulent, and the gases they produced—

rather than the water's virtuous refusal to admit a witch—made them float. An updated form of scholasticism ruled in the theological faculty, where students learned to build, sand, and polish an up-to-date structure of Calvinist dogma as they read the New Testament. An updated form of humanism remained the center of the faculty of philosophy, where students continued to write elegant speeches and poems in Latin. The most prestigious scholars in the university— Joseph Scaliger and Claude Saumaise, both of whom received appointments that did not require them to teach at all—won them for their ability as classical scholars.[4]

In this encyclopedic culture, where at every turn books pressed on objects, the new world of unpredicted, unaccommodating fact rubbed against the old one of traditional, canonical texts. Yet Leiden's scholars went in for negotiation, not confrontation. Less radical than Bacon—and more self-consciously aware than he that the canonical texts could not be jettisoned as a whole—they integrated new information and new civilizations into their traditional studies. Leiden scholars sought to deal with the New World and the newly precise reports of Jesuits about China and Japan, while still offering a coherent introduction to the development of human civilization.

Scaliger, for example, arrived in Leiden as a famous man, the greatest expert in the world in what was then the fashionable subject of chronology: the study that sought to establish the dates of ancient and medieval history and reconstruct the calendars used by ancient civilizations. As a young man, he had insisted that the peoples of the ancient Mediterranean were not the only ones whose intelligence and knowledge of the world had taken permanent form in a sophisticated system of reckoning days and weeks. The ancient Saxons and Gauls, for example, had also devised an accurate lunar year, one far less plagued by systematic error than the calendar of their conquerors, the Romans. "Not all wisdom," Scaliger concluded, "was

Figure 5.11   In the inaugural procession at the University of Leiden, shown in Johannes Meursius' *Athenae Batavae* (Leiden, 1625), the disciplines are represented by the classical authorities. The procession must have been like an animated version of the title page of Reisch's *Margarita philosophica* (Figure 1.1).

possessed by Chaldaeans and Orientals. The men of the west and north were also reasoning beings." *Oh, shut it.*

On his arrival in Leiden in 1593, Scaliger gained access to a wider and wider array of information. The Dutch merchants who ranged the seas of the world for profit brought back letters in Arabic for him to translate, and rewarded him by showing or giving him Chinese books and maps of the Great Wall (not to mention a bird of paradise without a head). The ever-growing literature of travel,

Joseph Lafitau

THE ethnographic information that poured into early modern Europe, though hardly impartial, spurred the development of what we today call comparative anthropology. But when the Jesuit Joseph Lafitau, who spent five years in a Canadian mission, compared American Indian customs to those of ancient Old World civilizations, his concern was to combat atheism. His comparisons, he believed, proved the argument for the existence of God by virtue of universal consent, an argument derived from *De natura deorum* by the Roman orator and philosopher Cicero. For Lafitau, then, the religious stakes would be perilously high should it be proved that there were peoples utterly without religious awareness:

"But this argument [from universal consent] falls, if it is true that there is a multitude of diverse nations brutish to such an extent that they have no idea of a god, nor any established customs to render the cult that is due him; for on that basis the atheist seems to be correct in concluding that if there is nearly a whole world of nations who have no religion, the religion found among others is a work of human prudence and an artifice of rulers who invented it to lead peoples by the fear born of superstition."

The basis of Lafitau's comparisons is the emerging concept that civilizations, rather than declining from some Golden Age in the distant past, develop and progress over time, passing through roughly the same stages. Lafitau believed himself justified in comparing early stages of European civilizations with New World cultures:

"I compared these customs [those of the Indians with those written about by the ancients], and I admit that, if the ancient authorities gave me insights to support some successful conjectures with respect to the savages, the customs of the savages gave me insights to understand more easily and to explain many things found in the ancient authors."

When Lafitau writes of the religious custom of maintaining a sacred fire in America, he ranges freely over time and geography:

"Fire has something sacred in all eras and among all the nations of America which use it; but the wandering tribes, and the majority of sedentary ones, did not have a perpetual fire, nor a temple to conserve it. I do not know if the Iroquois or the Hurons ever had temples. No remains of them appear today, nor [are they discussed] in the oldest accounts. But their hearth fires, which the ancients made their domestic gods, took the place of an altar for them, their council huts served as temples as they did among the ancient Persians, and they [the Indians] differed not at all from the Prytanies of the Greeks or the Roman curias."

Sources: Hodgen 1949; Kors 1990.

Figure 5.12 In *Moeurs des sauvages* (Paris, 1724), Joseph François Lafitau compares the ancient Persian and Roman cultures with the native American culture of Louisiana. The sacred fire, he writes, was common to all these people, and thus, for him, helped to prove universal belief in God.

mercantile and missionary, brought him tidings of the Far East and West. By 1598, when Scaliger brought out a second edition of his great work on chronology, the *De emendatione temporum*, he discussed problems of early Chinese history along with those of the Chaldeans and Egyptians—even though he insisted that all of these peoples were wrong to think their histories extended before the biblical Flood. And he inserted in his treatment of the solar year a detailed account of the Meso-American calendar.

Scaliger drew all the information he could from the accounts of Peter Martyr, Lopez de Gómara, and Acosta. He included a depiction of the Aztecs' calendar stone and carefully described their fifty-two-year cycle. He compared their year with that of the Egyptians and Persians and argued that they carefully inserted days to keep their 365-day year synchronized with the actual movement of the sun. True, he did insist, like so many other European scholars, that the similarities between this New World calendar and Old World ones proved the descent of the former from the latter, since the "barbarous" inhabitants of the New World could not have devised it on their own. But he also described, lucidly and without comment, the Indians' belief that the world might end at the end of each period of fifty-two of their years. And he made no effort to trace the exact paths by which the New World people or their calendar might have passed westward. He made brilliant fun, moreover, of Montano's effort to identify Peru with Ophir, arguing that the former had been completely unknown to the ancients and that the latter was completely unknown to moderns. Both Scaliger's attention to New World materials and his reticence at the many points where the sources gave out reveal his kinship to Acosta and Bacon.[5]

Two generations later, another Leiden historian, Georgius Hornius, made students as well as the smaller public of the erudite for whom Scaliger wrote confront the real complexities of world history.

Hornius, a German who settled in Holland because he liked its cosmopolitan society, taught at the small provincial university in Harderwijk before he came to Leiden. Even there he innovated. The theses that he drew up for his students to debate in their public disputations included collections of classical tags about the virtues of the three forms of Western government defined by Aristotle, monarchy, aristocracy, and democracy. But they also included elaborate lessons on the more modern history of the West and the East. Hornius taught the history of the Huns as happily as that of the Romans, arguing that Attila himself had really been a humane ruler, whose character had been blackened by the propaganda of Roman historians. He used the experience of the Aztecs as readily as that of the Greeks as a basis for political reflection, showing that their institutions and decisions could provide Westerners with salutary lessons.

Once in Leiden, Hornius set out to provide students with a world history that embodied these new materials and morals. The field was dominated by old books, like Johannes Sleidanus' *De quatuor summis monarchiis libri tres* (Three Books on the Four Great Monarchies), which still ignored all Far Eastern, modern European, and New World history and forced even the events they did cover into the straitjacket of Daniel's vision. Hornius' book bore a traditional title: *Arca Noae* (Noah's Ark). Its content, however, was as radical as its appearance was modest. He told a comprehensive story—one in which the Chinese and the inhabitants of the New World made early bows, at the points where he thought traces of them appeared in the canonical texts. They received far more detailed treatment in his account of modern history, which began, for him, with the European voyages. He made clear to readers that he offered them the first really comprehensive history of the world, and divided modern history into innovative and revealing categories: Eastern

(European, Asian, African); Western (American); and Southern (a triumph of optimism about the actual extent of the inhabited world).

Hornius assumed that biblical chronology provided a frame beyond the borders of which history could not go. He still believed that the New World peoples derived from identifiable Old World peoples: he canvassed both the wild Tartars, or Scyths, and the civilized Chinese, the former as the ancestors of the nomadic Indian tribes and the latter as those of the Aztecs and Incas. The connection between New World barbarians and Near Eastern sages became ever closer.

The schemes of classical ethnography remained adequate for most of Hornius' intellectual and rhetorical needs. Herodotus' account of the Scyths taking their victims' scalps, he commented, "depicts for us precisely the Florida or Huron Scyth, cutting into the head of his dead enemy so that he can take the skin away with the hair." But his account clearly followed ordering principles, included peoples, and traced morals that no ancient text or texts could fully support. Occasionally, too, Hornius showed his sensitivity to the real novelties in the accounts he drew on—as when he followed Acosta in making no effort to provide a detailed time-line for early Indian history. "To fill this chronological hiatus," he remarked, he would describe not names and dates but *mores*, customs. Ethnography took the place of chronology; a summary of eyewitness description, based on contemporary reports, filled the gaps left by supposedly more authoritative books.

Still writing in Latin, still living in biblical time, still believing that a single human race had spread throughout the world in the last few millennia, still reposing confidence in the intellectual tools of the ancients, Hornius tacitly abandoned many positions that even Scaliger would have defended strongly. He made no effort to show that Providence had directed the peoples in their movements, or

Figure 5.13   The title page of
Georgius Hornius' *Arca Noae*
(Lyons and Rotterdam, 1666).

that the devil had provided the Indians with a false account of their past and a parodic liturgy and code of conduct. He did not insist on the superior civilization of the West. History as well as natural science had undergone a great instauration, one no less radical for the modesty with which it was carried out, more as a matter of tacit practice than one of polemical pronouncements.

The title page of Hornius' book—like that of Bacon's—mirrors his situation. It shows the Ark tossing on the water. But the four animals that leer at it cannot literally represent the old four empires. More likely they embody the world of myth and fabulous animals that existed before the Flood. The new learning of Leiden could accommodate the New World—but only at the cost of abandoning the complete, coherent genealogies that the old learning had confidently constructed.[6]

The Book at Melting Point

Equilibrium was not to be reached. The cracks in the canon, never satisfactorily filled, had now gaped into frightening crevasses. The authoritative texts, more accessible and more widely read than ever before, threatened one another with mutual assured destruction. Meanwhile the flood of new information continued, and even the most ingenious efforts to channel and control it confirmed the thesis that the old ways could not survive. Two books, one tiny and one huge, one published secretly and condemned, one published luxuriously and sought after, reveal in complementary ways the tremors of what would finally become an intellectual earthquake.

The tiny book appeared in Holland in 1655. The work of a Protestant traveler and writer, perhaps of marrano origins, named Isaac La Peyrère, it advanced an argument that now seems simple, but that brought down on its author a fantastic storm of abuse and refutation—twelve full-scale rebuttals in the first year alone. No professional scholar, but a dedicated reader, La Peyrère despised those who simply skimmed their texts without thinking and failed to detect the historical and literary land-mines that lurked under their smooth surfaces. He read his Bible over and over again. He browsed the classics and modern scholarly treatments of them and encountered all the old claims for the antiquity of Chaldea, Egypt, and Atlantis that scholars had known for almost two centuries. An explorer himself, the author of charming accounts of Scandinavia, he knew all about the North American natives, who clearly existed even though they had no firm footing in the biblical family tree of nations. He had also heard something of the Chinese, who told the Jesuit missionaries that their Inner Kingdom had existed for hundreds of thousands of years. La Peyrère found himself inextricably trapped between the assumption that the Bible told the complete story of mankind and the assertions of the pagans; between the coherence old Christians were told to find in the biblical histories and the chilly, contradictory new facts.

Unlike the trained theologians, La Peyrère refused to allegorize away the apparent repetitions and contradictions of the Bible. If Genesis 1 told one story of the Creation and Genesis 2 told a second one, they must refer to different Creations: the first that of mankind as a whole, the second that of the Jews. If the Pentateuch spoke of Moses' death and later events, Moses must not have written it. And if the Bible referred to parallel books no longer in existence, gave inconsistent and incomplete accounts of events, and contradicted the more accurate records of the most civilized Near Eastern nations, it must be not the literally inspired Word of God but the faulty work of men, produced by ordinary writers who had botched the job of copying and excerpting the original accounts. Close study of the Bible did not buttress but destroyed the text.

La Peyrère trusted the ancients implicitly. He refused to shrink their chronologies by such traditional expedients as reducing the nine thousand years of Plato's Egyptians to lunar months. Close study of the pagan histories, in fact, strongly supported his attack on the Bible. It showed that one needed a long chronology to account for the movement of non-Jews to the New World and the long duration of the astronomical records of Babylon and the ancient kingdoms of Egypt and China. Theology must be rebuilt on new foundations. a proper attitude of irreverence toward holy scripture and a proper attitude of respect for pagan history. Otherwise man must remain in darkness.

La Peyrère's book received no good reviews. Even his friends made fun of him for reading the ancients so credulously, for explicating the Bible without knowing Greek or Hebrew, for treading so boldly where a Scaliger or Hornius showed reticence and reserve. His enemies denounced him point by point, at length—forgetting that by doing so they only gave wider currency to his theses. La Peyrère was not burned, as Bruno had been when he put the canonical pieces together in a similarly radical way half a century before; the mildness of the reaction is significant. But he was discredited, and finished his life in a sort of honorable house arrest with the Oratorian Fathers, the object of one of the first great intellectual smear campaigns in modern history.[7]

Yet La Peyrère expressed dilemmas widely shared. Within a generation, far deeper thinkers—who normally denied that they owed him any debts—would stand beside him in the moat, using far more powerful engines to besiege the castle of biblical authority. The Jew Benedict Spinoza would reduce the Old Testament to a work of limited scope and authority, designed to speak to the primitive Jews of olden times, not to modern man. The Catholic Richard Simon would use the most up-to-date Near Eastern scholarship to prove

Louis Armand de Lahontan

I N AN AGE when unorthodox opinions could prompt persecution, many European social or religious critics adopted the literary convention of presenting their views as those of an outsider. The burgeoning of utopian literature no doubt owes much to the caution of freethinkers, and the genre, whether circulated in published books or in clandestine manuscripts, had for many the appeal of the intellectually forbidden. Louis Armand de Lom d'Arce, baron de Lahontan, put his critique of Christianity in the mouth of a Huron Indian utterly unimpressed by the teachings of the Jesuits. Much in Lahontan's *Dialogues de Monsieur le baron de Lahontan et d'un sauvage dans l'Amerique* (1704) is daring in tone. Adario rejects celibacy and the monastic life as worthless, indicates contradictions in Christian doctrine, demotes Christianity from true religion to social custom, and espouses natural religion instead. He also rejects so-called Christian truths because they cannot be proved in the light of pure reason.

At one point Lahontan urges Adario to cast off his prejudices and weigh the scriptural message seriously. Adario's response reveals how two centuries of biblical criticism and research undertaken as a support to faith had undermined biblical authority:

"These are the stories which the Jesuits have already told me more than a hundred times. They would have it that for five or six thousand years, all that has happened has been written down without modification. They begin by speaking of the manner in which the earth and the heavens were created; that man was made from earth and woman from one of his ribs, as if God could not have made her from the same matter; that a serpent tempted this woman in a garden of fruit-bearing trees to make her eat an apple, which is the reason why the Great Spirit killed his son expressly to save all men

. . . now, according to what you told me one day, writing was invented only three thousand years ago, printing only four or five centuries ago. How, then, can you be so confident of so many diverse events occurring through so many centuries? Surely, it would be very credulous to adhere to all the daydreams contained in that big book which the Christians want us to believe. Books written by Jesuits about our country have been read to me. Those who read them have explained them to me in my language, but I recognized twenty lies one after another. Now if we see with our own eyes printed falsehoods and things different from those written down on paper, how can you want me to believe in the truthfulness of these Bibles written so many centuries ago, translated from several languages by igno-ramuses who could not conceive the true sense of the text or by liars who would change, increase and decrease the words that one finds there today "

Source: Lahontan 1701.

beyond reasonable doubt that the Pentateuch was a mosaic of lost earlier texts. And the Protestant Isaac Vossius—like La Peyrère an admirer of ancient Egypt and modern China—would influentially insist that one must follow the Greek text of the Old Testament, which gave a longer chronology than the Hebrew, in order to resolve the problems La Peyrère had brought to light. Even the original text of the Bible was no longer easy to identify: was it Hebrew or Greek, the lost sources or the existing Pentateuch? "Strong wits" across Europe gossiped enjoyably about the origins of Cain's wife and the authorship of the report of Moses' death in Deuteronomy. The most powerful of texts had tumbled down.[8]

America and the Americans played a part in La Peyrère's construction of a new, long world history—but only that of subsidiary evidence. The problems within the texts bulked far larger than those outside them. La Peyrère was driven to interpretative extremes by the contradictions natural in a canon of texts diverse in nature, origin, and context. Once translated, edited, printed, made available to incautious and stubborn amateurs, the canon tore itself apart. La Peyrère and many of his contemporaries would have reached a newfound historical land even if no one had reached America.

The big book, Joan Blaeu's *Great Atlas,* also appeared in Holland, in 1662. But it was completely respectable in authorship and content and shatteringly spectacular in form. The cartographer and printer Blaeu was the son of a mapmaker and a product of the University of Leiden. His twelve-volume compendium drew on a universe of sources, old and new, to describe the universe of nature. It was precise, detailed, and catholic; the Protestant Blaeu happily drew his account and maps of China from the Jesuit Martino Martini. The finished book stood out even in an age of great printers. A noble Rolls-Royce among the humble results of mass production, the *Atlas* could come, if a customer so desired, with magnificent hand-colored maps, special bindings done to order, even custom-built cases to house it. Copies sailed throughout the world, to Barbary pirates and Turkish potentates as well as European princes; such was the unprecedented demand created by its price (the highest ever demanded for a printed book), its beauty, and its vast range of information neatly assembled.

Unlike La Peyrère, Blaeu certainly did not set out to be a revolutionary. His preface emphasized the age and nobility of the geographer's art, paying due tribute to Marinus and Ptolemy as well as Ortelius and Mercator. His title pages inserted even the most novel of his material into traditional settings. The America volume, for example, begins with a full-page spread of familiar images. A grinning European strikes down a naked, winged figure whose hands terminate in long, sharp claws. Both hover in the air above an armed Indian woman or Amazon, who dominates the landscape. In the background native labor converts the ores—no doubt of Ophir—into bars of precious metal, while strange flora and a large, growling lizard identify the landscape as exotic. Blaeu's grand map of Africa is surrounded, like Mercator's long before, by swimming monsters to indicate strangeness and European ships to show that the foreign became real only when Western explorers found it. The border—like that of the list of races in the *Nuremberg Chronicle*—swarms with peoples that, though not monstrous, are certainly primitive and exotic.

Yet Blaeu's atlas clearly embodies a new ideal of knowledge. The one institution of learning described at length, with several illustrations, is Tycho Brahe's laboratory at Hveen—that monument to direct study of nature, which alone could replace ingrained error with new truth. To be sure, the texts in Blaeu sometimes hint at a belief in ancient wisdom—as when Martini, describing China, remarks with pleasure that his time there had taught him the truth of Aristotle's view that Asians were especially fit for despotic gov-

Figure 5.14 America personified on the title page of the America volume of Joan Blaeu's *Geographia*, vol. 11 (Amsterdam, 1662).

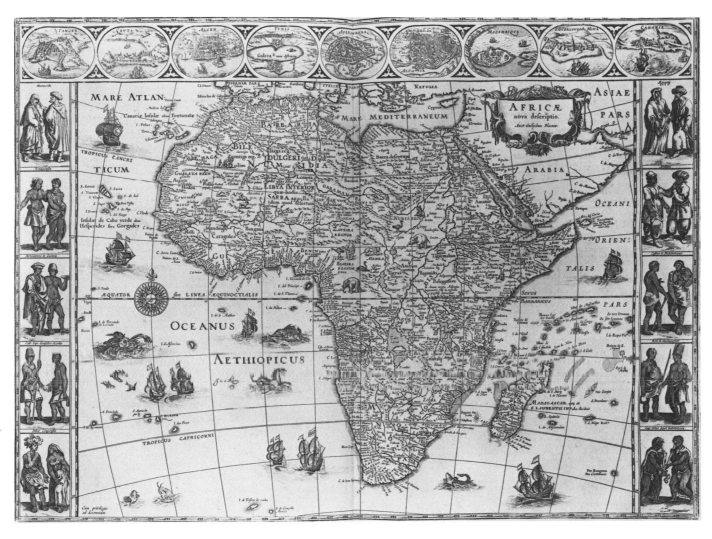

Figure 5.15 Joan Blaeu's map of Africa, from the *Grooten Atlas*, vol. 2 (Amsterdam, 1648–1664). Like Hartmann Schedel in the *Nuremberg Chronicle* (Figure 1.9), Blaeu inserts in marginal strips the races that inhabit the far parts of the world. His images are certainly conventional but hardly monstrous.

Figure 5.16 The new authority of science is made plain in Joan Blaeu's *Geographia*, vol. 1 (Amsterdam, 1662), by this magnificent image of Tycho Brahe's Hveen observatory in Denmark. Brahe's instruments, though they did not include the telescope, enabled him to make by far the most accurate celestial observations ever compiled, and his data provided the foundation for Johannes Kepler's new astronomy. By making Tycho's observatory the one institution of learning depicted in detail, Bleau makes a powerful statement about the empirical foundation of scientific knowledge.

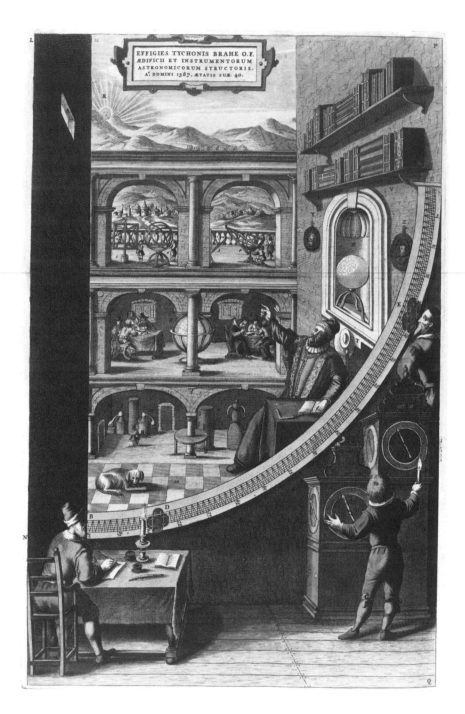

ernment. But for the most part ancient writers and the ancient past do not appear. Blaeu and his sources rarely quote authorities. And they make no effort to trace the origins of the varied peoples of the world. Like Hornius, Blaeu preferred describing customs that could be known in detail to constructing genealogies by conjecture.

Like Hartmann Schedel in the 1480s, in other words, Blaeu produced an encyclopedic survey, a book that almost lived up in range and artistry to its universal ambitions. But he organized it by completely different principles. Schedel had seen time as the axis on which one could most comfortably arrange the facts of human culture. After all, time was fully known; history followed a divine plan, fell into neat stages, had a clear beginning and would probably come to a rapid end. Space, by contrast, posed many problems; the coherent organizing system laid out by Ptolemy had no room for the new information of the Portuguese.

Blaeu, by contrast, had clearly lost any confidence that he could survey all of time. Space, however, he could plot in full. Cartography, not chronology, rested on principles in which all could trust. But the clarity was bought at a high price. Cartography, after all, yielded facts, not morals. Blaeu's maps presented the most accurate picture of the world obtainable at the time, but they could not show that the information they purveyed resulted from a neat, predictable divine plan, of the sort that Schedel and Reisch had once rejoiced in. Their strange peoples and monsters, ships and cartouches were merely window-dressing. The old encyclopedia, to be sure, had admitted awkward questions and contradictions, had given its reader occasional small shocks of recognition that history was complex. But the new one had a far looser structure, one that—like Ptolemy's *Geography* before it—invited the reader not to sit back and contemplate but to add new materials as they became available. For all its stately appearance, the *Great Atlas*, too, gives testimony to the intellectual whirlwinds that were shaking Europe by the middle of the seventeenth century.[9]

In the State of Nature: The New World Triumphant

The afterlife of the ancients certainly did not end in the mid-seventeenth century. The education of European aristocrats and state officials continued to be classical for centuries to come. The ancient texts continued to be read, translated, and admired, to provide the model genres for ambitious modern writers: epic, history, tragedy. And belief in progress would not become universal in the West for a very long time; not even in the Enlightenment would it find universal assent. In the years around 1700, indeed, serious intellectuals in England would mount what came to be known as the Battle of the Books—an intellectual encounter, one side in which maintained that the ancients were still unsurpassed, that they had written the best books that could be written. The Bible, of course, remained the core of Judaism and most forms of Christianity. But the ground had shifted. Those who knew the ancient world best—the professional scholars—took the side of the Moderns in the Battle, arguing that the ancients had in fact known far less than moderns about nature, the surface of the world, and much else. New standards of argument—based, supposedly, on "facts" rather than mere texts—played a larger and larger role in many fields.[10]

In political and social thought, for example, the seventeenth century saw the rise of what seemed a whole new form of argument. To many philosophers, the ancients seemed a bank with no deposits; their wealth exhausted, they could not guide the political thinker in dealing with the absolute monarchs and fundamentalist revolutionaries of the time, much less with the strange states and half-states of the non-European world. Traditional disciplines creaked and stretched; a Leiden-trained historian and lawyer, Hermann Conring, proved once and for all that the Holy Roman Empire of modern Germany was not a continuation of the original Roman one—thus throwing the study of public law into some confusion. Comparison, Bodin's great tool, had lost some of its promise. It seemed to show, the great German lawyer Samuel Pufendorf remarked, that no custom or law was so bizarre that some people had not accepted it—exactly the point that Herodotus had used ethnographic comparisons to prove. All efforts to define the laws of nature, then, were doomed to parochialism, since all of them stemmed from the prejudices of the nation doing the defining. These would seem as perfectly barbarous to others as the "barbarians" of the New World did to German scholars.

At lower levels, to be sure, the ancients still seemed powerful; but they were less fruitful than dangerous. Thomas Hobbes, who lived through the great English and European revolutions of the mid-seventeenth century, described these years as the most dramatic period the world had ever seen—a sort of "high place" in the otherwise smooth surface of time. But he also deplored these events as destructive, and knew exactly what had given rise to them. Reading old texts had caused modern revolutions. Theologians had misread the Bible, turning it from a source of clear doctrine to a grab-bag of technical puzzles, around each of which quarrels broke out. Humanists and their young pupils had read the classics too credulously, learning from them to despise monarchies and admire only republics. And ordinary people, once the Bible had become available in the vernacular, had found it a fruitful source for discontent and disobedience. It had given them what they wrongly saw as grounds for criticizing and tearing down what should have been the unchallengeable authority of the state. Books still posed a danger to the peace and quiet of the West, and offered no solutions to the problems they called into being.

Accordingly, Hobbes redirected political studies. In his *Leviathan*

(1655) he asked not what ancient texts asserted about what states should be, but rather how states had come into being in the first place. He argued that men, in their original existence, had been possessed by an unquenchable desire for power and possessions. Each naturally warred on his neighbor, since he had no central authority to restrain him, and failing that he could have no moral sense. The natural state of mankind, accordingly, was one of warfare—a "war of all against all," limited only by the fact that no single person could overcome all the rest. Natural human life was necessarily wretched: "solitary, poor, nasty, brutish and short."

Men devised the state, Hobbes argued, to force themselves not to behave as they wished. By creating it and endowing it with absolute authority, they built a framework within which they could write the laws and create the institutions that made civilized life possible. The state, endowed with vast powers and unhampered by fundamental restraints, was terrifying—as Hobbes indicated when he called it a Leviathan, the biblical term for a whale, and portrayed it as a vast artificial being made up of tiny men. But only it stood between men and human nature, between man and man.

Some philosophers denounced Hobbes's impiety, his cynicism, his critical attitude toward the Bible. Others—above all John Locke—refuted him in terms closer to his own, by taking a more optimistic view of the operations of human nature. But more and more thinkers accepted his view that politics must explain the origins of society and the state, deriving these not from biblical or classical authority but from the nature of men as they had lived before states had formed. Appeal to a basic sociological argument—one that traced human life from primitive origins to sophisticated modernity, stage by stage—replaced the appeal to a basic set of texts.

Even these most innovative of thinkers knew their ancient writers. Hobbes's view of man owed much to the histories of Thucydides, which he translated from the Greek. Locke's more optimistic evocation of life in the earliest states owed something to Ovid, whom he quoted, and much to the modern ethnographers whose books he bought and scanned. When these men came to ground their arguments in authority, modernity—and the New World—played a powerful rhetorical part. Hobbes, anticipating the objection that the state of nature he described had never existed on earth, located it squarely in the West: "For the savage people in many places of America, except the government of small families, the concord whereof dependeth on natural lust, have no government at all; and live at this day in that brutish manner." Locke, wanting to subvert the traditional arguments in favor of the divine virtue and original creation of monarchy, used the example of the "West Indies"—whose inhabitants, he thought, did not live in the state of nature described by Hobbes even though they did not have rulers. He argued that the first societies chose monarchs only because they needed supreme commanders in wartime; in peacetime neither the war-leader nor anyone else had any authority over the other members of the society.

Naturally, neither Hobbes nor Locke nor the many later writers who developed their theses in the Enlightenment described the New World "as it really was"—or even as the travel writers of the time, ever more inclined to contrast New World virtues with Old World vices, described them. It had long been known that the Aztecs and Incas lived in organized states, and the more detailed accounts of the late sixteenth and seventeenth centuries made clear that the tribes of Canada and Virginia also had recognizable laws, magistrates, and institutions.

But Hobbes and Locke attributed a new status to the misinformation they deployed at such strategic points. Locke insisted that the experience of a wider world underpinned his psychology and politics alike. To prove that no truth found universal acceptance, he appealed directly to "any who have been but moderately conversant in the history of mankind and looked abroad beyond the smoke of their own chimneys." His critic the Earl of Shaftesbury was on the mark when he denounced his opponent, "the credulous Mr. Locke, with his Indian, barbarous stories of wild nations," which he preferred to "learned authors" and "ancient philosophy." But Locke, not Shaftesbury, carried conviction.

Rhetorically, the New World had replaced the ancient texts. It had become the prime metaphor for the right way to discover new facts about the world and the prime source for new theories about human society. If the essential question about society and the state was how they had begun—a question no ancient text could answer—then the primitive life of the peoples newly known offered the only relevant firsthand evidence.

Or did it? Sociological comparisons, analogies between the original state of Western society and the primitive societies that still survived outside it, belonged to the same classical tradition that Hobbes and Locke claimed to abandon. The authority of the ancients lay in ruins; but the ancient authorities remained, still providing essential assumptions and tools. Like Bacon, Locke and Hobbes relied more on the substance of classical texts than their style allowed them to suggest. Even at this late date it took classical tools to make the New World, suitably transformed, part of a nascent, modern canon of texts and ideas—one as riven with fruitful contradictions as the older canon it replaced.[11]

Epilogue

WE HAVE watched a rich set of intellectual traditions change, flourish and decline. What conclusions should we draw from the spectacle? Many possible interpretations invite discussion and stimulate thought. Karl Marx, for example, began his *Eighteenth Brumaire of Napoleon Bonaparte* with a brilliant, blazing denunciation of the durability of classical ideas and rhetoric:

> The tradition of all the dead generations weighs like a nightmare on the brain of the living. And just when they seem engaged in revolutionizing themselves and things, in creating something that has never yet existed, precisely in such periods of revolutionary crisis they anxiously conjure up the spirits of the past to their service and borrow from them names, battle cries and costumes, in order to present the new scene of world history in this time-honoured disguise and this borrowed language.

This conveys something of the experience of European intellectuals between 1450 and 1700. Ancient texts did rise like revenants around them, paradoxically providing the language and images that enabled them to explain away a fact unknown to the classical writers they revered. A potentially revolutionary discovery was given a noble name, a biblical pedigree, a place in existing geographies and ethnographies; much of its sting was thus removed.

Yet Marx's brilliant rhetoric—here as elsewhere—conceals as much as it reveals. Ancient texts provided Renaissance intellectuals with vital facts and objective methods of description as well as with stereotypes about other races on the periphery of the world. More important still, the ancient texts provided not only the intellectual foundations of European hegemony, but also the sharpest challenges to it. Bodin and Las Casas drew as heavily on books as Columbus or Vespucci, and to far more radical effect. Nor are we likely, in this age of renewed religious belief, to imitate Marx and interpret appeals to scriptures, religious or secular, as merely the disguises in which intellectuals wrapped their perceptions of "the real world." Hobbes knew his own world better than Marx could. The ancient texts formed as solid a presence in early modern European culture as the continent to the distant west.

Joseph Levenson, the great historian of Confucian China, suggests a different approach. Classic texts, he argues, begin as a culture's vital organs but wind up, after long centuries of internal social change and outside challenge, as its superficial ornaments. In time, history shows that the factual content of any canon is incomplete. In time, moreover, the world changes even the staunchest traditionalists. Even those whose power rests on their command of texts will finally have to admit that they have ceased to live by the values that their books teach. Like fine clothing worn too long, the texts cease to keep out the cold drafts of history. They can be preserved only by being taken out of daily use. Even though they retain their position in education and their claim to supreme age and beauty, their period of real cultural authority has passed. What began as weapons in an arsenal wind up as exhibits in a museum; what had been articles to be used with deadly seriousness become things of beauty to be visited on holidays.

Levenson's history of China also captures something of the Western experience we have examined. Ancient natural philosophy, in 1500 the basis of all serious study of the natural world, lost its hold over scientific theory and practice. Ancient history lost its claim to universal validity, ancient geography lost its claim to comprehensive coverage, and old providential schemes lost their power to impose order and direction on the chaos of world history. The Bible retained its place in almost all organized religions, and the classics retained their hold over elite education. But most scholars, scientists, and political theorists in seventeenth-century Europe, from Giovanni Battista Vico's Naples to Pierre Bayle's Holland, knew that they could no longer inhabit the close-fitting mental library that had satisfied their fifteenth-century forebears. In this new intellectual world, rude facts contradicted venerable books, and debate and research might challenge any inherited verity. Surely the authoritative texts had been transformed from organs to ornaments, from function to decoration.

Levenson's schema is richer and more flexible than Marx's, and many European scholars have seen it as applicable to the Western case. But it, too, conveys only part of the experience we have surveyed here. It brilliantly evokes the experience of a few intellectuals who walked the perilous leading edge of European thought. But it fails to convey the continued power of texts, their remarkable ability to remain sharp enough to threaten and to cut, their durable power to inspire challenges to intellectual and political authority. And it does not bring out the extraordinary rifts and crevasses already present in the Western canon at what seemed the zenith of its cultural eminence.

Perhaps no causal scheme or image can convey the richness, the complexity, and the frequent self-contradiction of the Western canon. Less like an orderly library than like Ole Worm's fantastic museum, it contained many bizarre juxtapositions, many odd couplings of the exotic and the normal, the natural and the human, the historical and the mythic. Its fate was correspondingly complex.

And yet, one point seems eminently worth statement and reflection. The classical texts and concepts have been, for the west, above all a set of tools. Like any other tools, they perform different—and sometimes contradictory—tasks. Some of them are primitive and some sophisticated; some are simple and solid, others complex and brittle. Some of them have proved to be as irreplaceable as they are ancient, and others have proved adaptable to jobs that their inventors could not have imagined. In the fifteenth and sixteenth centuries they were filed and sanded, organized in new ways, and some were superseded by newer and more powerful implements. Yet many of them retained their gleaming appeal, and some retain it even now.

Herodotus drew from the experience of cultural difference the lesson that societies could differ absolutely, that in some ways each would seem strange and unintelligible to every other. Absolute difference, he concluded, challenged absolutism; the experience of what seemed bizarre beliefs and practices imposed tolerance on intelligent observers. Like Archimedes' distant point to stand on, the distant point of foreignness enabled the intellectual who occupied it to move the world.

Westerners did not often apply this lesson as they conquered the rest of the inhabited world. Those few who did, like Las Casas and Montaigne, were spirits as rare as they were precious. Yet it seems clear that we have little improvement to make on Herodotus' simple statement that men and women can live and believe in many different ways, none of which must or can claim universal adherence. The discovery of the New World did not inculcate humanity and tolerance; but those values were waiting to be rediscovered. The tool awaited use, at the bottom of a crowded basket of more destructive implements.

Notes

Introduction

1. See Elliott 1970; Gliozzi 1977; Ryan 1981.
2. See Schafer 1967.
3. Said 1978; Bernal 1987.

1. A Bound World

1. For an informative survey of this literature see Heninger 1977. Wilson 1976 treats a far wider range of subjects than its title suggests. The Old World picture has often been surveyed; two excellent recent accounts are Sears 1986 and Burrow 1986.
2. See in general the *Cambridge History of Renaissance Philosophy* 1988. Earlier developments—and the manifold debates of late medieval philosophy, mentioned below—are surveyed in the *Cambridge History of Later Medieval Philosophy* 1982.
3. For authoritative surveys done from a variety of points of view see the *Cambridge History of Renaissance Philosophy* 1988; Kristeller 1979; Garin 1958.
4. On humanist biblical scholarship see Bentley 1983; for a more comprehensive introduction to the history of humanist scholarship, see Reynolds and Wilson 1991. A fine case study is D'Amico 1988. For the more general issue of the transformation of Christendom see the challenging survey in Bossy 1985.

5. Grafton 1991, chap. 3.
6. See Hankins 1990.
7. Hodgen 1964 surveys—and exaggerates—the influence of the classical encyclopedic tradition at the start of her vastly informative book.
8. See in general Momigliano 1966, 127–142; Momigliano 1990, chap. 2; Kaiser 1969; Nippel 1990, chap. 1.
9. Wittkower 1942; Friedman 1981; Romm 1992. On the solid core of fact in Greek descriptions of India see, e.g., Thapar 1961.
10. Dodds 1973; Nippel 1990.
11. Goldschmidt 1938.
12. Mandowsky and Mitchell 1963; Momigliano 1966, 1–39; Weiss 1969; Gaston 1988; McCuaig 1989; Momigliano 1990, chap. 3.
13. Edgerton 1987, 12–15.
14. See in general Dilke 1985. For the development of Ptolemaic cartography see Nordenskiöld 1889 and Campbell 1987. On medieval cartography see Kimble 1938. The new *History of Cartography*, edited by D. Woodward and in course of publication, will provide the first authoritative survey of the whole field.
15. See the classic study of Rowe 1964.
16. See in general Goldschmidt 1938.

2. *Navigators and Conquerors*

1. On Dati see Brucker 1967; Green 1972, chap. 4; *Dizionario biografico degli italiani* s.v. Dati, Goro.
2. See *Portugal-Brazil: The Age of Atlantic Discoveries* 1990.
3. See Campbell 1987, which surveys learned and less learned, Latinate and vernacular traditions, providing a rich bibliography.
4. See Friedman 1981, chap. 7; Ginzburg 1989, 41–49.
5. Friedman 1981.
6. For contrasting accounts of Columbus see Todorov 1982; Flint 1992.
7. See in general Brading 1991; on Vespucci Romeo 1954.
8. Cortés 1986; Brading 1991, chap. 2; Clendinnen 1991.

3. *All Coherence Gone*

1. For Münster's upbringing see Wolkenhauer 1909. For his life see esp. his letters (Münster 1964); for his use of earlier ethnographers see Hodgen

1964. And for the tradition of compendia of curious lore to which his work belongs—one in which Münster's method of reprocessing old materials and letting them bounce off new information was normal—see Céard 1977 and Blair forthcoming.

2. See Schmitt 1981, 1983; Siraisi 1987; Ruderman 1988; Schmitt et al. 1988; Lestringant 1991.
3. See Popkin 1979; Schmitt et al. 1988; Morford 1991.
4. Klempt 1960; Franklin 1963; Burke 1969; Kelley 1970; Hassinger 1978.
5. Kendrick 1950.
6. Pagden 1991.
7. On these debates see Hanke 1959; Pagden 1982; Nippel 1990, chap. 2.
8. See Robertson 1966.
9. For contrasting accounts of this process of inquiry see Edmonson 1974; Gruzinski 1988; Brading 1991; MacCormack 1991. On the methodological problems involved see esp. Ginzburg 1989, 156–164.
10. By far the fullest study of the politicized histories of the New World called forth by French and English, as well as Portuguese and Spanish, colonial enterprises is Gliozzi 1977. For the English case see also Williams 1979.
11. See Allen 1949, Huddleston 1967, Gliozzi 1977.

4. Drugs and Diseases

1. Sources for the historical development of the herbal and Renaissance botany include Stannard 1969b, 1974; Debus 1978; Reeds 1979; Arber 1986.
2. For more on Galenic medical tradition, see Debus 1978; Siraisi 1990.
3. For more on Mattioli, see Stannard 1969a.
4. This translation and other historical information on tobacco in this chapter is based on *Tobacco—Its History Illustrated by the Books, Manuscripts and Engravings in the Library of George Arents, Jr.* 1937, which constitutes the catalogue of the New York Public Library's Arents Collection.
5. This general account owes much to Quetel 1991, chaps. 1–3; Arrizabalaga forthcoming. Also useful are Grmek 1989, 133–151 and B. J. Baker and G. J. Armelagos, "The origin and antiquity of syphilis . . . ," *Current Anthropology* 29 (1988), 703–737.
6. This and other beliefs about syphilis are well analyzed in Foa 1990; on medieval treatment of and attitudes toward lepers see also Moore 1987, 45–60.

7. On Fracastoro's theories, their reception, and the general debate about contagion, see Nutton 1991.
8. Erasmus 1965, 403–412 ("Coniugium impar"); Alciato 1583, emblem 197, 629–632 (the numbering varies from edition to edition).
9. On the early iconography of syphilis from the standpoints, respectively, of cultural history, history of medicine, and history of art, see Gilman 1988, 248–257; Foa 1990, 38; Sudhoff 1928, xxiii–xxiv; Panofsky 1961, 1–33.
10. Rossiaud 1988, 49–51, 161–166; of the numerous Venetian regulations on prostitution from 1514 to 1774 published in Barzaghi 1980, very few mention the disease.
11. Temkin 1955, 309–316.
12. Pagel 1958, 24–31, 138–139, 166–167, 200–201.

5. A New World of Learning

1. Of the rich literature on Bacon, see esp. Rossi 1968; Whitney 1986.
2. Klindt-Jensen 1975.
3. The fullest survey remains Hodgen 1964. See also Park and Daston 1981; Impey and MacGregor 1985; Schapin and Schaffer 1985.
4. Lunsingh Scheurleer et al. 1975; Grafton 1988.
5. See Grafton 1991, chaps. 4 and 7.
6. Klempt 1960 gives the best account of Hornius and other Dutch scholars and thinkers who enlarged the compass of Latin learning. For an important but perhaps overstated critique see Hassinger 1978.
7. The fullest study is Popkin 1987; for La Peyrère's reading of Plato see esp. Vidal-Naquet 1990, chap. 6.
8. See in general Allen 1949; Popkin 1979; Grafton 1991, chaps. 8–9.
9. Koeman 1970.
10. For a wide-ranging study see Levine 1991. On the continued existence of beliefs in the superiority of much of ancient culture and the decline of the modern world, see also Spadafora 1990; Vyverberg 1958.
11. The richest study of the state of nature is Landucci 1972.

Bibliography

Acosta, J. de. N.d. *The Natural and Moral History of the Indies*, trans. E. Grimston. New York.

Agnese, Battista. 1540. *Portolan*.

Ailly. *See* d'Ailly.

Alciato, A. 1550. *Emblemata*. Lyon

———— 1583. *Omnia . . . emblemata cum commentariis . . . per Claudium Minoem*. Paris.

Allen, D. C. 1949. *The Legend of Noah*. Urbana.

———— 1970. *Mysteriously Meant*. Baltimore.

Amadis de Gaule. 1544. *Le quatriesme livre d'Amadis de Gaule*. Paris.

Arber, A. 1978. *Herbals, their Origin and Evolution*. Reprint. Cambridge.

Arens, W. 1979. *The Man-Eating Myth: Anthropology and Anthropophagy*. Oxford.

Arias Montano, B. 1593. *Antiquitatum iudaicarum libri ix*. Leiden.

Arrizabalaga, J. Forthcoming. "Syphilis." In *The Cambridge History and Geography of Human Disease*, ed. K. F. Kiple. Cambridge.

Bacon, F. 1620. *Instauratio magna*. London.

———— 1879. *Works*. London.

———— 1960. *The New Organon and Related Writings*, ed. F. H. Anderson. Indianapolis.

Barzaghi, A. 1980. *Donne o cortigiane? La prostituzione a Venezia, documenti di costume dal xvi al xvii secolo*. Verona.

Beda Venerabilis. 1537. *Opuscula cumplura*. Basel.

Bentley, J. H. 1983. *Humanists and Holy Writ*. Princeton.

Bernal, M. 1987. *Black Athena*. Vol. 1. New Brunswick, N.J.

Bible [*Textus biblie cum glossa ordinaria, Nicolai de Lyra postilla, moralitatibus eiusdem*]. 1506–1508. Basel.

Biblia [*Complutensian Polyglot*]. 1514–1517. Alcala.

Blaeu, J. 1662. *Atlas maior.* Amsterdam.

Blair, A. Forthcoming. *Restaging Jean Bodin.* Princeton.

Blundell, S. 1986. *The Origin of Civilization in Greek and Roman Thought.* London.

Bodin, J. 1945. *Method for the Easy Comprehension of History,* trans. B. Reynolds. New York.

Boemus, J. 1611. *The Manners, lawes and customes of all nations,* trans. E. Aston. London.

Bossy, J. 1985. *Christianity in the West, 1400–1700.* Oxford.

Brading, D. A. 1991. *The First America.* Cambridge.

Brucker, G., ed. 1967. *Two Memoirs of Renaissance Florence,* trans. J. Martines. New York.

Bry, Theodore de. 1590–1634. *America.* 13 vols. Frankfurt am Main.

———— 1987. *L'Amérique de Théodore de Bry,* ed. M. Duchet. Paris.

Buchet, B. 1977. *La sauvage aux seins pendants.* Paris.

Burke, P. 1969. *The Renaissance Sense of the Past.* New York.

Burrow, J. A. 1986. *The Ages of Man.* Oxford.

Bury, J. B. 1932. *The Idea of Progress.* 1932.

Campbell, T. 1987. *The Earliest Printed Maps, 1492–1500.* Berkeley.

Cats, J. 1627. *Proteus.* Rotterdam.

Céard, J. 1977. *La nature et les prodiges.* Geneva.

Chiapelli, F., ed. 1976. *First Images of America.* Berkeley.

Clendinnen, I. 1991. "'Fierce and Unnatural Cruelty': Cortes and the Conquest of Mexico." *Representations* 33, 65–100.

Columbus, C. 1493. *Epistola de insulis noviter repertis.* Basel.

La conquista del Peru. 1534. Seville.

Copernicus, N. 1543. *De revolutionibus orbium coelestium libri sex.* Nuremberg.

Cortes, H. 1524. *Praeclara Ferdinandi Cortesii de nova maris oceani Hispania narratio.* Nuremberg.

———— 1986. *Letters from Mexico,* trans. and ed. A. Pagden. New Haven.

———— N.d. *Five Letters, 1519–1526,* trans. F. Bayard Morris. New York.

Crosby, A. W., Jr. 1972. *The Columbian Exchange.* Westport, Conn.

Cuningham, W. 1559. *The Cosmographical Glasse.* London.

Cyrano de Bergerac, S. de. 1687. *The Comical History of the States and Empires of the Worlds of the Moon and Sun.* London.

d'Ailly, P. 1483. *Imago mundi.* London.

——— 1490. *Concordantia astronomiae cum theologia.* Augsburg.

D'Amico, J. 1988. *Theory and Practice in Renaissance Textual Criticism.* Berkely.

Dati, G. N.d. *La sfera.* Two manuscripts, held in Rare Book and Manuscript Division, New York Public Library.

de Bry. *See* Bry.

Debus, A. 1978. *Man and Nature in the Renaissance.* Cambridge.

Dee, J. 1577. *General and rare memorials pertaining to the perfect arte of navigation.* London.

Diaz de Isla, R. 1542. *Tractado llamado fructo de todos los santos: contra el mal serpentino.* Seville.

Dilke, O. A. W. 1985. *Greek and Roman Maps.* London.

Doctrina christiana. 1554. Mexico City.

Dodds, E. R. 1973. *The Ancient Concept of Progress and Other Essays on Greek Literature and Belief.* Oxford.

Dodoens, R. 1568. *Florum et coronariarum odoratarumque nonnullarum herbarum historia.* Antwerp.

Durán, D. 1971. *Book of the Gods and Rites and Ancient Calendar,* trans. and ed. F. Horcasitas and D. Heyden. Norman, Okla.

Edgerton, S. Y., Jr. 1987. "From Mental Matrix to *Mappamundi* to Christian Empire: The Heritage of Christian Cartography in the Renaissance." In *Art and Cartography,* ed. D. Woodward. Chicago.

Edmonson, M. S. 1974. *Sixteenth-Century Mexico.* Albuquerque, N.M.

Elliott, J. H. 1970. *The Old World and the New.* Cambridge.

Erasmus, D. 1965. *The Colloquies of Erasmus,* trans. C. R. Thompson. Chicago.

Evelyn, J. 1955. *The Diary of John Evelyn,* ed. E. S. de Beer. Oxford.

Fabris, A. de. N.d. *Diversarum nationum habitus.* Padua?

Flint, V. 1992. *The Imaginative Landscape of Christopher Columbus.* Princeton.

Foa, A. 1990. "The New and the Old: The Spread of Syphilis (1494–1530)." In *Sex and Gender in Historical Perspective,* ed. E. Muir and G. Ruggiero. Baltimore.

Franklin, J. H. 1963. *Jean Bodin and the Sixteenth-Century Revolution in the Methodology of Law and History.* New York.

Friedman, J. B. 1981. *The Monstrous Races in Medieval Art and Thought.* Cambridge, Mass.

Froschauer, J. 1505. *Dise figur anzaigt uns das volck und insel die gefunden ist durch den christenlichen Künig zu Portigal oder von seinen underthonen.* Augsburg.

Garcilaso de la Vega, P. 1966. *Royal Commentaries of the Incas and General History of Peru*, trans. H. V. Livermore. Austin.

Garin, E. 1958. *L'umanesimo italiano*. Bari.

Gaston, R., ed. 1988. *Pirro Ligorio, Artist and Antiquarian*. Florence.

Gerarde, J. 1633. *The Herball or Generall Historie of Plantes*. London.

Gilman, S. L. 1988. *Disease and Representation*. Ithaca.

Ginzburg, C. 1980. *The Cheese and the Worms*, trans. J. Tedeschi and A. Tedeschi. Baltimore.

—— 1989. *Clues, Myths, and the Historical Method*, trans. J. Tedeschi and A. Tedeschi. Baltimore.

Gliozzi, G. 1977. *Adamo e il nuovo mondo*. Florence.

Goldschmidt, E. P. 1938. *Hieronymus Münzer und seine Bibliothek*. London.

Grafton, A. 1988. "Civic Humanism and Scientific Scholarship at Leiden." In *The University and the City*, ed. T. Bender. Oxford.

—— 1991. *Defenders of the Text*. Cambridge, Mass.

Green, 1972. *Chronicle into History*. Cambridge.

Grmek, M. D. 1989. *Diseases in the Ancient Greek World*. Baltimore.

Grotius, H. 1643. *De origine gentium americanarum dissertatio altera adversus obtrectatorem, opaca quem bonum facit barba*. Paris.

Gruzinski, S. 1988. *La colonisation de l'imaginaire*. Paris.

Hale, J. R. 1968. *Renaissance Exploration*. New York.

Hanke, L. 1949. *The Spanish Struggle for Justice in the Conquest of America*. Philadelphia.

—— 1959. *Aristotle and the American Indians*. Bloomington.

Hankins, J. 1990. *Plato in the Italian Renaissance*. Leiden.

Hassinger, E. 1978. *Empirisch-rationaler Historismus*. Bern.

Heninger, S. K., Jr. 1977. *The Cosmographical Glass*. San Marino, Calif.

Herodotus. 1862. *History*, trans. G. Rawlinson. London.

Hobbes, T. 1651. *Leviathan*. London.

Hodgen, M. T. 1964. *Early Anthropology in the Sixteenth and Seventeenth Centuries*. Philadelphia.

Hornius, G. 1666. *Arca Noae*. Leiden.

Huddleston, L. E. 1967. *Origins of the American Indian*. Austin.

Huppert, G. 1970. *The Idea of Perfect History*. Urbana.

Hutten, U. von. 1527. *Guaiacum*. Lyon.

—— 1536. *Of the Wood Called Guaiacum*. London.

Impey, O., and A. MacGregor. 1985. *The Origins of Museums*. Oxford.

Isidore of Seville. 1473. *Etymologiae*. Strasbourg.

James I. 1609. *A Counterblaste against Tobacco*. London.

Kaiser, M. "Herodots Begegnung mit Aegypten." In Morenz 1969, 243–304.

Kelley, D. R. 1970. *Foundations of Modern Historical Scholarship*. New York.

———— 1990. *The Human Measure*. Cambridge, Mass.

Kendrick, T. D. 1950. *British Antiquity*. London.

Kimble, G. H. T. 1938. *Geography in the Middle Ages*. London.

Klempt, A. 1960. *Die Säkularisierung der universalhistorischen Auffassung*. Göttingen.

Klindt-Jensen, O. 1975. *A History of Scandinavian Archaeology*. London.

Koeman, C. 1970. *Joan Blaeu and His Grand Atlas*. Amsterdam.

Kors, A. C. 1990. *Atheism in France, 1650–1729*. Vol. 1. Princeton.

Kramer, H., and J. Sprenger. 1971. *Malleus maleficarum*. Ed. and trans. M. Summers. New York.

Kretzmann, N., et al., eds. 1982. *Cambridge History of Later Medieval Philosophy*. Cambridge.

Kristeller, P. O. 1979. *Renaissance Thought and Its Sources*, ed. M. Mooney. New York.

Lafitau, J. F. 1724. *Moeurs des sauvages ameriquains comparées aux moeurs des premiers temps*. Paris.

Lahontan, L. A. de Lom de l'Acre. 1704. *Dialogues de Monsieur le Baron de Lahontan et d'un sauvage dans l'Amerique*. Amsterdam.

Lancre, P. de. 1613. *Tableau de l'inconstance*. Paris.

Landucci, L. 1972. *I filosofi e i selvaggi 1580–1780*. Bari.

La Peyrère, I. 1655. *Praeadamitae. Systema theologicum, ex Praeadamitarum hypothesi*. N. p.

Las Casas, B. de. 1614. *Narratio regionum Indicarum*. Oppenheim.

———— 1822. *Oeuvres*, ed. J.-A. Llorente. Brussels.

———— 1974. *In Defense of the Indians*, trans. S. Poole. De Kalb, Ill.

Leon Pinelo, A. de. 1636. *Question moral si el chocolate quebranta el ayuno ecclesiastico*. Madrid.

Léry, J. de. 1586. *Historia navigationis in Brasiliam, quae et America dicitur*. N. p.

———— 1927. *Le voyage au Brésil*. Paris.

Lestringant, F. 1991. *L'atelier du cosmographe*. Paris.

Levenson, J. 1958–1965. *Confucian China and Its Modern Fate*. Berkeley.

Levine, J. 1991. *The Battle of the Books*. Ithaca.

Lunsingh Scheurleer, T. H., et al., eds. 1975. *Leiden University in the Seventeenth Century*. Leiden.

Lycosthenes, C. 1557. *Prodigiorum ac ostentorum chronicon*. Basel.

MacCormack, S. 1984. "From the Sun of the Incas to the Virgin of Copacabana." *Representations* 8.

———— 1991. "Demons, Imagination, and the Incas." *Representations* 33, 121–146.

Mandeville, Sir J. 1483. *Reysen und Wanderschafften durch das Gelobte Land*. Strasbourg.

———— 1508. *Monteuille compose par Messire Jehan de Monteuille*. Lyon.

———— 1968. *Mandeville's Travels*, ed. M. C. Seymour. London.

Mandowsky, E., and C. Mitchell. 1963. *Pirro Ligorio's Roman Antiquities*. London.

Marichal, J. 1976. "The New World from Within: The Inca Garcilaso." In Chiapelli 1976.

Marx, K. 1963. *The Eighteenth Brumaire of Louis Bonaparte*. New York.

McCuaig, W. 1989. *Carlo Sigonio*. Princeton.

Meisner, M., and R. Murphey. 1976. *The Mozartian Historian: Essays on the Works of Joseph R. Levenson*. Berkeley.

Mercator, G. 1538. *Orbis imago*. Louvain.

Meursius, J. 1625. *Athenae Batavae*. Leiden.

Momigliano, A. 1966. "The Place of Herodotus in the History of Historiography." In *Studies in Historiography*. New York.

———— 1990. *The Classical Foundations of Modern Historiography*. Berkeley.

Monardes, N. 1577. *Joyfull newes out of the newe founde world*. London.

Montaigne, Michel de. 1943. *Complete Works*, trans. D. Frame. Stanford.

Moore, R. I. 1987. *The Birth of a Persecuting Society*. Oxford.

More, T. 1516. *Utopia*. Louvain.

Morenz, S. 1969. *Die Begegnung Europas mit Aegypten*. Zurich and Stuttgart.

Morford, M. 1991. *Stoics and Neostoics*. Princeton.

Münster, S. 1550. *Cosmographia universalis*. Basel.

———— 1964. *Briefe*, ed. K. H. Burmeister. Ingelheim am Rhein.

Nanni, G. 1498. *Commentaria*. Rome.

Nicholas of Lyra. *See Bible*.

Nippel, W. 1990. *Griechen, Barbaren und "Wilde."* Frankfurt am Main.

Nordenskiöld, A. E. 1889. *Facsimile-Atlas to the Early History of Cartography*. Stockholm.

Nutton, V. 1991. "The Reception of Fracastoro's Theory of Contagion: The Seed That Fell Among Thorns?" *Osiris* 6, 196–234.

Ortelius, A. 1570. *Theatrum orbis terrarum.* Antwerp.

Ortus sanitatis. 1496. Strasbourg.

Pagden, A. 1982. *The Fall of Natural Man.* Cambridge.

———— 1991. "*Ius et factum:* Text and Experience in the Writings of Bartolomé de Las Casas." *Representations* 33, 147–162.

Pagel, W. 1958. *Paracelsus.* Basel.

Panofsky, E. 1961. "Homage to Fracastoro in a Germano-Flemish Composition of about 1590?" *Nederlands Kunsthistorisch Jaarboek* 12, 1–33.

Park, K., and L. Daston. 1981. "Unnatural Conceptions: The Study of Monsters in France and England." *Past & Present* 92, 20–54.

Piggott, S. 1976. *Ruins in a Landscape.* Edinburgh.

Popkin, R. H. 1979. *The History of Scepticism from Erasmus to Spinoza.* Berkeley.

———— 1987. *Isaac La Peyrère (1596–1676).* Leiden.

Portugal-Brazil: The Age of Atlantic Discoveries. 1990. Lisbon.

Ptolemy. 1482. *Geography.* Ulm.

———— 1513. *Geography.* Strasbourg.

———— 1525. *Geography,* ed. W. Pirckheimer. Nuremberg.

———— 1542. *Geography,* ed. S. Münster. Basel.

Quetel, C. 1991. *The History of Syphilis.* Baltimore.

Raleigh, Sir W. 1634. *History of the World.* London.

Ramelli, A. 1558. *Le diverse et artificiose machine.* Paris.

Reeds, K. M. 1979. "Renaissance Humanism and Botany." *Annals of Science* 34, 519–542.

Reisch, G. 1503. *Margarita philosophica.* Freiburg.

Reynolds, L. D., and N. G. Wilson. 1991. *Scribes and Scholars.* 3d ed. Oxford.

Robertson, D. 1966. "The Sixteenth-century Mexican Encyclopedia of Fray Bernardino de Sahagún." *Journal of World History* 9, 617–627.

Rolewinck, W. 1474. *Fasciculus temporum.* Cologne.

Romeo, R. 1954. *Le scoperte americane nella coscienza italiana del Cinquecento.* Milan.

Romm, J. 1992. *The Edges of the Earth in Ancient Thought.* Princeton.

Rossi, P. 1968. *Francis Bacon,* trans. S. Rabinovitch. Chicago.

Rossiaud, J. 1988. *Medieval Prostitution.* Oxford.

Rowe, J. H. 1964. "Ethnography and Ethnology in the Sixteenth Century." *Kroeber Anthropological Society Papers* 30, 1–19.

Rubiés, J.-P. 1991. "Hugo Grotius's Dissertation on the Origin of the American Peoples and the Use of Comparative Methods." *Journal of the History of Ideas,* 52, 221–244.

Ruderman, D. 1988. *Kabbalah, Magic, and Science*. Cambridge, Mass.

Ryan, M. T. 1981. "Assimilating New Worlds in the Sixteenth and Seventeenth Centuries." *Comparative Studies in Society and History* 23, 519–538.

Sacks, K. 1990. *Diodorus Siculus and the First Century*. Princeton.

Said, E. 1978. *Orientalism*. New York.

Scaglione, A. 1976. "A Note on Montaigne's 'Des Cannibales' and the Humanist Tradition." In Chiapelli 1976.

Scaliger, J. J. 1629. *Opus novum de emendatione temporum*. Geneva.

Schafer, E. 1967. *The Vermilion Bird*. Berkeley.

Schapin, S. and S. Schaffer. 1985. *Leviathan and the Air-Pump*. Princeton.

Schedel, H., et al. 1493. *Liber chronicarum*. Nuremberg.

Schmitt, C. B. 1981. *Studies in Renaissance Philosophy and Science*. London.

———— 1983. *Aristotle and the Renaissance*. Cambridge, Mass.

Schmitt, C. B., et al., eds. 1988. *The Cambridge History of Renaissance Philosophy*. Cambridge.

Sears, E. 1986. *The Ages of Man*. Princeton.

Siraisi, N. 1987. *The Canon of Avicenna in Fifteenth-Century Italy*. Princeton.

———— 1990. *Medieval and Early Renaissance Medicine*. Chicago.

Spadafora, D. 1990. *The Idea of Progress in Eighteenth-Century Britain*. New Haven.

Staden, H. 1557a. *Warhafftige historia*. Frankfurt.

———— 1557b. *The True History of His Captivity*. Reprint 1928. London.

Stannard, J. 1969a. "P. A. Mattioli: Sixteenth-Century Commentator on Dioscorides." *University of Kansas Bibliographical Contributions* 1, 59–81.

———— 1969b. "The Herbal as a Medical Document." *Bulletin of the History of Medicine* 43, 212–226.

———— 1974. "Medieval Herbals and Their Development." *Clio Medica* 9, 23–33.

The Sucklington Faction. 1641. London.

Sudhoff, K. 1928. *The Earliest Printed Literature on Syphilis: Being the Tracts from the Years 1495–1498*, ed. C. Singer. Florence.

Tacitus. 1962. *Complete Works*, trans. A. J. Church and W. J. Brodribb. New York.

Temkin, O. 1955. "Therapeutic Trends and the Treatment of Syphilis before 1900." *Bulletin of the History of Medicine* 29, 00–00.

Thapar, R. 1961. *Asoka and the Decline of the Mauryas*. Oxford.

Thevet, A. 1557. *Les singularitez de la France Antartique*. Paris.

———— 1575. *La cosmographie universelle*. Paris.

Thorius, R. 1625. *Hymnus tabaci*. Leiden.

Tobacco—Its History Illustrated by the Books, Manuscripts and Engravings in the Library of George Arents, Jr. 1937. New York.

Todorov, T. 1982. *The Conquest of America*, trans. R. Howard. New York.

Vesalius, A. 1555. *De humani corporis fabrica libri septem*. Basel.

Vespucci, A. 1503. *Albericus Vespuccius Laurentio Petri Francisci de Medicis . . . salutem plurimam dicit*. Paris.

Vidal-Naquet, P. 1990. *La démocratie grecque vue d'ailleurs*. Paris.

Vigneras, L.-A. 1977. "Saint Thomas, Apostle of America." *Hispanic American Historical Review* 57, 82–90.

Vyverberg, H. 1958. *Historical Pessimism in the French Enlightenment*. Cambridge, Mass.

Weber, E. 1894. *Virorum clarorum saeculi xvi et xvii epistolae selectae*. Leipzig.

Weiss, R. 1969. *The Renaissance Discovery of Classical Antiquity*. Oxford.

White, H. 1976. "The Noble Savage Theme as Fetish." In Chiapelli 1976.

Whitney, C. 1986. *Francis Bacon and Modernity*. New Haven.

Wilkins, J. 1640. *A discourse concerning a new world & another planet*. London.

Williams, G. A. 1979. *Madoc*. Oxford.

Wilson, A. 1976. *The Nuremberg Chronicle*. Amsterdam.

Wittkower, R. 1942. "Marvels of the East. A Study in the History of Monsters." *Journal of the Warburg and Courtauld Institutes* 5, 159–197.

Wolkenhauer, A. 1909. "Sebastian Münsters handschriftliches Kollegienbuch aus den Jahren 1515–1518 und seine Karten." *Abhandlungen der königlichen Gesellschaft der Wissenschaften zu Göttingen*, n.s. 11.

Worm, O. 1655. *Musaei Wormiani historia*. Leiden.

Yves, d'Evreux, P. 1615. *Suite de l'histoire des choses plus memorables advenues en Maragnan*. Paris.

Illustration Sources

All illustrations in this book reproduce materials held in the research collections of The New York Public Library. Bibliographical details for each object appear in the relevant caption; the following list identifies the specific collections to which they belong:

Arents Tobacco Collection: 3.13; 3.14; 4.2; 4.3; 4.5; 4.6; 4.7

Berg Collection of English and American Literature: 1.12; 3.7; 5.1

Map Division: 5.15

Print Collection, The Miriam and Ira D. Wallach Division of Art, Prints and Photographs: 2.2; 2.7; 4.10; 5.2

Rare Books and Manuscripts Division: 1.1; 1.1; 1.2; 1.3; 1.4; 1.5; 1.6; 1.7; 1.8; 1.9; 1.10; 1.11; 1.13; 2.3; 2.8; 2.9; 2.10; 2.11; 2.12; 3.1; 3.2; 3.3; 3.4; 3.5; 3.6; 3.8; 3.9; 3.10; 3.11; 3.12; 3.15; 3.16; 3.17; 3.18; 3.19; 4.4; 4.8; 4.9; 5.3; 5.4; 5.5; 5.6; 5.7; 5.8; 5.9; 5.10; 5.11; 5.12; 5.13

Spencer Collection: 2.1; 2.4; 2.5; 2.6; 4.1; 5.14; 5.16

Acknowledgments

I N 1989 Vartan Gregorian summoned me, gently but irresistibly, to undertake a voyage of discovery. He asked me to explore the resources of The New York Public Library, to see if they would support an exhibition on the cultural effects of the great meeting of states, peoples, and cultures that began in 1492. This book and the exhibition it describes stem from his invitation. Both are the products of collaboration, and it is a pleasure and a privilege for me to thank all those whose collective work and generous help made them possible.

In the first instance, I owe thanks to the generous dead: to those public-spirited New Yorkers and others whose private collections have come together under one splendid public roof at Fifth Avenue and Forty-second Street. Some of them—like James Lenox, a pioneering student of Americana whose collections form the nucleus of the Library's rare book room, and Obadiah Rich—wished above all to illustrate the history of the Americas after 1492. Others, like William Augustus Spencer, collected lovely books in less relevant fields but left the Library the funds that made possible vital purchases. Assembled in the Library, their collections and the acquisitions they supported have fused into a single, inexhaustible archive of widely varied contents, where physically beautiful books and manuscripts, associated artifacts, and hundreds of externally unimpressive but historically fascinating texts and images shed light on Europe's wrenching effort to understand the great new fact of the Americas. Their wide interests and intelligent philanthropy have resulted in a research collection of spectacular interest—one which enables the scholar to view the problem studied here from dozens of complementary points of view. We hope that this book may draw still more attention to this matchless deposit of documents, so much of which remains to be mined.

The staff of the Library have done everything imaginable to facilitate the preparation of this show. Dr. Gregorian's successor as President of the Library, Dr. Timothy Healy, has provided warm encouragement and complete intellectual freedom. Susan F. Saidenberg, Manager of the Exhibitions Program, and Jeanne Bornstein, Research Coordinator, *sine quibus non*, provided guidance through the mazes of the Library's collections, continual research support, and constant practical help. They also coordinated the successful grant applications without which no show could have been mounted and arranged for Dante Gnudi—to whom our warmest thanks are owed—to design a book wheel, which serves as the centerpiece of the exhibition. Lou Storey, Installation Specialist, designed both the main exhibition and the traveling panel show with a sympathy and flair that inspired awe; he also oversaw the details of their construction and installation, in collaboration with Chief Preparator Tracy Edling and assisted by Doug Long and Lawrence Ardin. Jean Mihich, Registrar, assisted by Caryn Gedell, Sandra Spurgeon, and Russell Drisch, coordinated the inventorying and conditioning of all objects for the exhibition. Myriam de Arteni, Exhibitions Conservation Specialist, handled the conservation of material requiring preservation and restoration, assisted by Maria Vivar. Susan Rabbiner, Education Specialist, created interpretive educational materials and school programs based on the exhibition.

Miles Wortman, acting as a consultant, produced a fascinating and useful overview of relevant materials in the Library's collections. Finally, the overworked but always genial keepers of the keys to the Library's kingdoms lavished their unique knowledge of books and manuscripts, texts, and images on outsiders who would have been lost without their help. For the good spirits and accurate information with which they responded to repeated queries, we thank Bernard McTigue, formerly Curator of the Arents Collections and Keeper of Rare Books; Lisa Browar, Brooke Russell Astor Librarian for Rare Books and Manuscripts; Mimi Bowling, Manuscripts Collection; Beth Diefendorf, General Research Division; Leonard Gold, Jewish Division; Alice Hudson, Map Division; Francis O. Mattson, Berg Collection of English and American Literature; Robert Rainwater, Spencer Collection; and Roberta Waddell, Print Collection, Miriam and Ira D. Wallach Division of Art, Prints and Photographs. Virtually the entire staff of the Library's Special Collections also deserve warm thanks for their good humor and patient attention to detail while bringing my colleagues and me the far too many books, manuscripts, and prints that we asked to see.

For help with the exhibition, I thank Paul Fasana, Andrew J. Mellon Director of The Research Libraries; Rodney Phillips, Associate Director for the Center for Humanities, Social Sciences and Special Collections; Elizabeth Kirkland Cahill, Director of External Affairs; David Cronin and the staff of the Public Education Program Office; Judith Hudson and William Leo Coakley of the Graphics Office; Myrna Martin, Volunteer Office; Tara M. Phethean, Kimberlee Krasko, and Donna Fields of the Public Relations Office; Bonnie Rosenblum and the staff of the Development Office; and Kay Cassell, Associate Director for Programs and Services, The Branch Libraries.

Several scholars kindly gave advice and help. I thank the members of the exhibition's advisory committee—especially James Hankins,

David Ruderman, and Noel Swerdlow, who visited the Library, examined some of the proposed exhibits, and offered a thorough, constructive critique of the original plan. Two anonymous referees helpfully criticized the text of this volume. And many colleagues have helped us to formulate some of the arguments offered here. Members of Anthony Grafton's Folger Library Seminar in the Spring of 1991 will recognize ideas that they heard there and suggestions and criticisms that they offered; special thanks are owed to Robin Barnes, James Grubb, Mack Holt, and Monique Hulvey, all of whom are drawn on here. The Program on the Ancient World at Princeton University invited Noel Swerdlow and Anthony Grafton to lead a discussion on "Orientalism before Orientalism" in the spring of 1991; this provided an ideal forum for trying out a presentation of the argument as a whole. Ted Champlin, who both organized the seminar and challenged the arguments offered there, contributed greatly to this exercise in modern history.

Robert D. Rubic photographed most of the materials illustrated in this book; a few photographs, from the Special Collections Archives, were made by the Library's Reprographic Services staff. Lindsay Waters, Alison Kent, Jennifer Snodgrass, Donna Bouvier, Gwen Frankfeldt, and the lynx-eyed Ann Hawthorne of Harvard University Press made possible the rapid and efficient transformation of typescript into book. And the Department of History at Princeton University provided technical facilities and a matchless working environment.

Nancy Siraisi and April Shelford took part in every phase of the work. Professor Siraisi advised on every section of the exhibit and wrote a section of this volume. Ms. Shelford served as Research Curator for the exhibition as a whole, examined and selected many of the exhibits, and wrote the vignettes as well as a section of the book. My warmest thanks to both; their erudition, support, and criticism have been essential.

Anthony Grafton
Guest Curator

Index